WILLIAMS-SONOMA

Baking

The Best of Williams-Sonoma Kitchen Library

Baking

GENERAL EDITOR
CHUCK WILLIAMS

RECIPE PHOTOGRAPHY
ALLAN ROSENBERG

OxmoorHouse®

Contents

Introduction

So many of life's happy memories are tied to good things from the oven. The sweet aroma of apple pie wafting through the kitchen; quiet conversation over coffee and muffins; traditional holiday cookies; that last lick of frosting in the mixing bowl: Each such moment enriches the lives of those who share it. No other recipe category offers such delightful variety. That is truly the power and delight of baking.

The following pages reveal the wondrous diversity of baked goods: easy muffins and quick breads; lovingly kneaded yeast breads; artful flat breads and pizzas; cookies, bars, and brownies for the child in everyone; and cakes, pies, tarts, and fruit desserts to rival the finest bakeshop. There are many treats to end a meal, still more to complement other courses, and baked goods for every time of day and every occasion.

As varied as the 205 recipes in this book are, they share strong common traits. All begin with very basic ingredients: flour and other grains; leavening agents; sweeteners or savory seasonings; milk, butter, and other dairy products or fats to moisten and enrich. All use fairly simple equipment and techniques, as discussed on the following pages. And each recipe will help you create wonderful new memories.

MIXED AND BAKED IN MINUTES

In the eighteenth century, cooks noticed that when wood ash from the fire mixed with flour, water, and heat, the mixture bubbled (the carbonate-rich ash was acting to release carbon dioxide gas). They began to add these precursors of baking powder and baking soda to thick batters or thicker doughs to make them rise, resulting in the earliest muffins and quick breads.

Muffins are the easiest of the rapid baked goods. They are baked in pans specially designed to shape them, and are made from either simple batters wherein the ingredients are quickly combined for tender results, or cakelike batters made by creaming together butter and sugar, then alternately adding wet and dry ingredients. These methods lead to many variations, from sweet treats such as Banana-Bran Muffins or Poppy Seed Muffins to those that can accompany savory dishes, like Buttermilk-Bacon Muffins or Chili-Corn Muffins.

Most quick breads differ from muffins only in that they are baked in a loaf pan that creates a rectangular shape easily cut into serving slices of sweet recipes such as Lemon Bread or savory ones like Pistachio-Olive Bread. (See the basics section at the end of the book for jams and butters to spread on the slices.) Try other traditional forms like Currant Scones and Irish Soda Bread to taste classics from three centuries ago.

TRADITIONAL YEAST BREADS

Around 3600 BC, the ancient Egyptians discovered that dough would ferment and rise if left in the open air. A millennium and a half passed before the airborne micro-organism called yeast was identified as the cause and particular strains were developed—the first sourdough cultures—for highly precise results.

Mix store-bought dry yeast with lukewarm liquid and flour; thoroughly knead the dough to develop its microscopic three-dimensional network of gluten, the elastic fibers in wheat flour; and leave the dough in a warm, draft-free place. For an hour or more, the yeast eats the sugars in the flour, giving off carbon dioxide gas that is trapped by the gluten, which stretches, causing the dough to rise. The oven's heat makes both the gas and the bread expand further, resulting in a loaf with a soft, chewy crumb and crunchy crust.

You will find traditional yeast breads from several cultures featured here. Recipes ranging from Scottish Floury Baps, Swedish Cardamom Twist, and German Pumpernickel to French Baguettes and San Francisco Sourdough bring multicultural flair to any table.

For the best results, be sure to gauge temperatures and measure ingredients accurately. Also take care to knead the dough and let it rise precisely as described.

WHEN BREAD IS DELIBERATELY FLAT

So much attention is paid to ensuring well-risen bread that the notion of flat bread might seem contradictory. But thrifty bakers learned centuries ago that leftover dough scraps could be rolled out and embellished with savory or sweet toppings. As a bonus, flat breads bake quickly, turning crisp underneath while still rising slightly. The result is an easy treat with great appeal: Witness the world's most popular flat bread, the pizza.

The five pizza recipes in this book suggest the endless possibilities for elaborating flat breads. Their toppings range from tomato and cheese, to onions, peppers, and olives, to smoked gouda, chile peppers, and cilantro. A simple lesson emerges: If a topping sounds appetizing and can be cooked in a matter of minutes, chances are that it will make a delicious pizza topping.

The same is true for other flat breads. Several examples of focaccia, Italian flat bread made by spreading soft yeast dough in a rimmed pan and dimpling it with toppings, represent more creative options, from Crusty Corn Focaccia to Focaccia with Pancetta (Italian bacon) to Sweet Focaccia with Grapes. But Italy is not the only nation represented. Earthy Scottish Oatcakes and tangy Swedish Limpa demonstrate how the inventiveness of bakers knows no boundaries.

TREATS FROM THE COOKIE JAR

For some, baking begins and ends with cookies, bars, and brownies. And why not? Nearly all are easy to prepare, and the endless variety of recipes means a lifetime could be spent sampling them all.

In this book, you will find drop cookies, such as Old-Fashioned Oatmeal Cookies, formed by spooning batter onto a baking sheet; cookies sliced from rolls of refrigerated dough, such as Cinnamon–Chocolate Chip Refrigerator Cookies; cookies cut from rolled-out dough, like Walnut, Chocolate, and Ginger Shortbread Fans; and those formed with a press that forces pliable dough through a design plate for elaborate shapes, as with the Chocolate-Peppermint Cookie-Press Cookies.

Bars and brownies further expand the repertoire. Pressed flat in a pan, then baked and cut into small portions, such recipes as Lemon Squares, Granola Bars, and Chocolate-Mint Brownies have undeniable homespun appeal. Hazelnut Biscotti, a version of the popular Italian cookie, defines yet another easy cookie-making concept. *Biscotti* means "twice-cooked," referring to the fact that they are first baked in flat loaves, then sliced and baked again until crisp. Cookies, bars, and brownies are so easy to make, they are perfect to wrap up as festive gifts.

TREATS THAT TAKE THE CAKE

The word "cake" covers a very broad category of baked goods, with specialties suited to every time of day and year. This book features morning-time treats such as Buttermilk–Berry Crumble Coffee Cake and afternoon specialties like Lemon Clove Tea Cake. Reine de Saba makes a perfectly elegant dessert in the evening.

Some are simple one-layer cakes baked in a pan and cut into squares, such as Applesauce Spice Cake and Gingerbread with Crystallized Ginger. Still other cakes gain special-occasion appeal by being layered, filled, and frosted: The Carrot Cake and Orange Layer Cake are two classic examples. Beaten egg whites contribute ethereal lightness to cakes baked in tube pans, such as Chocolate Angel Food Cake.

Cupcakes, like Raspberry Surprise Cupcakes and Chocolate Chip–Banana Cupcakes, are the perfect individual-sized treats for adults and children alike to enjoy. And rich, dense cheesecakes—with flavors like lemon, espresso, eggnog, and chocolate mint—are just a few of the many great ways to end a meal.

Nothing compares to the impact of beautiful cakes, cupcakes, and cheesecakes. Fresh Strawberry–Vanilla Layer Cake makes a delicious addition to an early-summer wedding party, and Pumpkin-Hazelnut Cheesecake can liven up any holiday table.

PIES, TARTS, AND FRUIT DESSERTS

Crisp apples, succulent peaches, plump cherries, zesty oranges: Fruits, like no other single category of fresh ingredients, provide a wide variety of satisfying desserts when on their own. There is a cornucopia of choices for every occasion, no matter what the season.

Add the magic of baking, however, and the end-of-meal appeal of fruit grows even greater. Enclosed between two layers of buttery, flaky pastry as with the Rhubarb-Raspberry or Apple-Pear Pie, fruits produce desserts that are crispy and golden on the outside and filled with tantalizing juices on the inside. Nestle them inside a pastry shell to showcase the beauty of fresh fruit, as in Blue Plum Tart, or cooked fruit, such as Pear Clafouti or the classic French Tart Tatin.

Some fruit desserts do not demand even rudimentary pastry-making skills. Several recipes in this book require only tossing together a simple topping or batter to complement the featured ingredient, as in Three-Berry Cobbler, Apple Crumble, or Pear Clafouti.

The broad categories of pies and tarts both embrace more than fruit alone, however. Such recipes as Maple-Pecan Pie, Ginger-Carrot Pie, Sugar Tart, and Banbury Tart testify to the fact that many sweet ingredients reach a kind of perfection when married with golden brown pastry.

BACK TO BASICS

Every one of the many and varied recipes in this book has been kitchen-tested and then carefully written to provide you with all the information you need to get great results. Some recipes rely on basic elements that you may want or need to refer to again and again. You will find these in the final chapter, including basic and flavored glazes for muffins and quick breads, a Pie Pastry, Tart Pastry, Vanilla Buttercream for cakes, and Whipped Cream to top pies and tarts. In addition, that chapter also features other embellishments for baked goods, including Strawberry Jam, Pear-Ginger Jam, and two different Savory Butters.

You will also find a useful section explaining in detail some of the techniques used in this book. From creating a classic lattice-top pie crust to learning how to shape loaves of bread for creative presentations, these skills are part of what makes the art of baking such an wonderful tradition. Not only are the final products delicious, but learning how to get successful and beautiful results can lead to an enjoyable and lifelong pastime.

The many pleasures of baking have endured as long as cooks have pulled muffins, quick breads, yeast breads, cakes, cookies, pies, and tarts from their ovens for all to enjoy. Using the wide variety of skills and recipes inside this book, anyone who enjoys eating baked goods can learn how to bake them, and enjoy baking them, as well.

Muffins

Orange-Yogurt Muffins

A generous measure of grated orange zest (page 329) gives these muffins an extraordinary taste, and cooking the zest briefly with sugar extracts more flavor. Squeeze the juice from one of the oranges to make the Orange Glaze, if desired.

3 large oranges

1/2 cup (4 oz/125 g) sugar

2 tablespoons water

5 tablespoons (2 1/2 oz/75 g) unsalted butter, plus extra for greasing

2 cups (10 oz/315 g) all-purpose (plain) flour

1 1/4 teaspoons baking powder

1 teaspoon baking soda (bicarbonate of soda)

1/2 teaspoon salt

2 eggs

3/4 cup (6 oz/185 g) plain yogurt

3/4 cup (6 fl oz/180 ml) milk

Orange Glaze (page 317) for drizzling (optional)

Preheat the oven to 375°F (190°C). Grease standard muffin pans to make 18 muffins, filling any empty cups with water to prevent warping.

For an optional garnish, using a vegetable peeler, remove 2 strips of zest about 1 inch (2.5 cm) wide and 3 inches (7.5 cm) long from 1 of the oranges, removing only the bright orange portion of the peel (page 329). Cut into fine julienne, set aside, and finely grate the remaining zest from the oranges. Otherwise, grate all the zest; you should have about 1/4 cup (1 oz/30 g) of grated zest.

Combine the grated zest, 1/4 cup (2 oz/60 g) of the sugar, and the water in a small saucepan. Stir over medium heat for about 2 minutes, just until the sugar dissolves. Add the butter and stir until melted, about 1 minute longer. Set aside.

In a bowl, stir together the flour, baking powder, baking soda, salt, and the remaining 1/4 cup sugar. Set aside. In another bowl, whisk together the eggs, yogurt, milk, and reserved orange mixture until smooth. Add the combined dry ingredients and stir just until blended.

Spoon the batter into the prepared muffin pans, filling each cup about three-fourths full. Bake until a toothpick inserted into the center of a muffin comes out clean, 15–20 minutes. Let cool in the pans for 3–5 minutes, then remove. Drizzle with glaze and sprinkle with the julienned zest, if desired.

Makes 18 muffins

Lemon Slice Muffins

Serve these muffins warm, with the bottoms upturned so the glazed lemon slice is visible. If you like, cut a slice from the top of each muffin so that it will sit flat on the plate. Garnish with fresh mint and a bit of lemon zest.

Preheat the oven to 400°F (200°C). Grease a 12-cup muffin pan.

Finely grate the zest from the lemons (page 329), removing only the bright yellow portion of the peel. Set the lemons aside. Combine the zest, the water, and ¼ cup (2 oz/60 g) of the sugar in a small saucepan. Stir over medium heat for 2 minutes, just until the sugar dissolves. Add the butter and stir until melted, about 1 minute longer. Set aside.

With a sharp knife, remove and discard all the remaining peel from the lemons. Cut the lemons crosswise into slices about ¼ inch (6 mm) thick; discard any seeds. You will need 12 nicely shaped slices. Put about 1 teaspoon of the remaining sugar in the bottom of each prepared muffin cup and place a lemon slice on top.

In a bowl, stir together the flour, baking powder, baking soda, and salt. Set aside. In another bowl, whisk together the eggs, milk, and the reserved lemon mixture until smooth. Add the combined dry ingredients and stir just until blended.

Spoon the batter into the prepared muffin pans, filling each cup about three-fourths full. Bake until a toothpick inserted into the center of a muffin comes out clean, 15–20 minutes. Immediately invert the pans onto wire racks. Let cool in the pans for 3–5 minutes, then lift away the pans; the muffins should fall out. If they resist, nudge them with a knife.

Makes 12 muffins

3 lemons

1 tablespoon water

About ½ cup (4 oz/125 g) sugar

6 tablespoons (3 oz/90 g) unsalted butter, plus extra for greasing

2 cups (10 oz/315 g) all-purpose (plain) flour

2 teaspoons baking powder

½ teaspoon baking soda (bicarbonate of soda)

½ teaspoon salt

2 eggs

1 cup (8 fl oz/250 ml) milk

Strawberry-Orange Muffins

Slice the berries very thinly — about ⅛ inch (3 mm) if possible — then pat the slices dry on paper towels to keep their juices from coloring the batter. These muffins have a dab of strawberry jam hidden in the center.

Unsalted butter for greasing

2¼ cups (11½ oz/360 g) all-purpose (plain) flour

2 teaspoons baking powder

1 teaspoon baking soda (bicarbonate of soda)

½ teaspoon salt

¾ cup (6 oz/185 g) sugar

½ cup (4 fl oz/125 ml) milk

½ cup (4 fl oz/125 ml) sour cream

⅓ cup (3 fl oz/80 ml) canola oil

1 egg

1 tablespoon finely grated orange zest (page 329)

1 cup (6 oz/185 g) thinly sliced fresh strawberries

About ⅓ cup (4 oz/125 g) Strawberry Jam (page 315)

Preheat the oven to 400°F (200°C). Grease standard muffin pans to make 16 muffins, filling any unused cups with water to prevent warping.

In a bowl, stir together the flour, baking powder, baking soda, and salt. Set aside. In another bowl, whisk together the sugar, milk, sour cream, oil, egg, and orange zest until smooth; stir in the strawberries. Add to the combined dry ingredients and stir just until blended.

Place a spoonful of batter into each prepared muffin cup. Add a scant teaspoon of strawberry jam to each, then spoon the remaining batter on top, filling each cup about two-thirds full. Bake until a toothpick inserted into the center of a muffin comes out clean, 15–18 minutes. Let cool in the pans for 3–5 minutes, then remove.

Makes 16 muffins

Cherry Muffins

Dried cherries look like big raisins, and they pack a lot of tart, sweet cherry flavor. You may substitute dried cranberries, if you wish. Soaking the dried fruits in hot water helps to plump them a little.

Preheat the oven to 375°F (190°C). Grease a 12-cup standard muffin pan.

In a bowl, pour the boiling water over the cherries. Let stand for about 5 minutes.

In another bowl, stir together the flour, baking powder, baking soda, and salt. Set aside. To the cherries and water, add the sugar, melted butter, eggs, lemon zest, and almond extract and stir to combine. Add the combined dry ingredients and stir just until blended.

Spoon the batter into the prepared muffin pan, filling each cup about two-thirds full. Bake until a toothpick inserted into the center of a muffin comes out clean, about 20 minutes. Let cool in the pan for 3–5 minutes, then remove.

Makes 12 muffins

1/2 cup (4 fl oz/125 ml) boiling water

1 cup (5 oz/155 g) pitted, dried cherries, coarsely chopped

2 cups (10 oz/315 g) all-purpose (plain) flour

2 teaspoons baking powder

1 teaspoon baking soda (bicarbonate of soda)

1/2 teaspoon salt

2/3 cup (5 oz/155 g) sugar

1/3 cup (3 oz/90 g) unsalted butter, melted, plus extra for greasing

2 eggs, beaten

1 teaspoon finely grated lemon zest (page 329)

1/2 teaspoon almond extract (essence)

Blueberry Muffins

These muffins are sweet, buttery, and delicately spiced, with a cakelike texture. Fresh blueberries are best used here, but if you only have frozen berries, stir them into the batter without thawing, or their dark juice will turn the muffins purple.

2 cups (10 oz/315 g) all-purpose (plain) flour

2/3 cup (5 oz/155 g) sugar

2½ teaspoons baking powder

¼ teaspoon baking soda (bicarbonate of soda)

½ teaspoon salt

1 teaspoon ground cinnamon

1 cup (8 fl oz/250 ml) milk

½ cup (4 oz/125 g) unsalted butter, melted, plus extra for greasing

2 eggs

1 cup (4 oz/125 g) blueberries

Preheat the oven to 400°F (200°C). Grease standard muffin pans to make 16 muffins, filling any unused cups with water to prevent warping.

In a bowl, stir together the flour, sugar, baking powder, baking soda, salt, and cinnamon. Set aside. In another bowl, whisk together the milk, melted butter, and eggs until smooth. Add the combined dry ingredients and stir just until blended. Add the blueberries and stir just until evenly incorporated.

Spoon the batter into the prepared muffin pans, filling each cup about three-fourths full. Bake until a toothpick inserted into the center of a muffin comes out clean, 15–20 minutes. Let cool in the pans for 3–5 minutes, then remove.

Makes 16 muffins

Pear-Pecan Muffins

These muffins are studded with bits of pear, pecan, and candied ginger. Use 6 large muffin cups for delectable giant-sized treats. For dessert, split the muffins and top with Whipped Cream (page 316) and fruit.

1¹/₂ cups (12 fl oz/375 ml) boiling water

¹/₂ cup (4 oz/125 g) dried pears

2 cups (10 oz/315 g) all-purpose (plain) flour

2 teaspoons baking powder

¹/₂ teaspoon baking soda (bicarbonate of soda)

¹/₂ teaspoon salt

2 eggs

³/₄ cup (6 oz/185 g) sugar

¹/₃ cup (3 oz/90 g) unsalted butter, melted, plus extra for greasing

¹/₂ cup (2 oz/60 g) pecans, toasted (page 326) and chopped

¹/₂ cup (3 oz/90 g) chopped candied ginger

In a bowl, pour the boiling water over the pears. Let stand for 15 minutes. Drain, reserving ¹/₂ cup (4 fl oz/125 ml) of the liquid. Let the liquid cool. Using a pair of kitchen scissors or a sharp knife, cut the pears into ¹/₂-inch (12-mm) bits; set aside.

Preheat the oven to 400°F (200°C). Grease a 12-cup standard muffin pan.

In a bowl, stir together the flour, baking powder, baking soda, and salt. Set aside. In another bowl, whisk together the reserved pear-soaking liquid, the eggs, the sugar, and the melted butter until smooth. Stir in the pears, pecans, and candied ginger. Add the combined dry ingredients and stir just until blended.

Spoon the batter into the prepared muffin pan, filling each cup about three-fourths full. Bake until a toothpick inserted into the center of a muffin comes out clean, about 20 minutes. Let cool in the pan for 3–5 minutes, then remove.

Makes 12 muffins

Date-Nut Muffins

Though it adds to the total preparation time, the extra step of soaking the dates yields incredibly moist, tender muffins. Leave out the nuts, if you prefer, or substitute chopped walnuts or hazelnuts (filberts).

Preheat the oven to 375°F (190°C). Grease a 12-cup standard muffin pan.

In a small saucepan over medium-high heat, bring the water to a boil. Stir in the dates, sugar, and butter, remove from the heat, and let stand until the dates have absorbed most or all of the liquid and have cooled to lukewarm, about 15 minutes.

Transfer the dates and any remaining liquid in the pan to a bowl. Add the vanilla. One at a time, add the eggs, beating well after each addition until thoroughly incorporated. In another bowl, stir together the flour, baking powder, baking soda, and salt. Add the date mixture and the nuts and stir just until well combined.

Spoon the batter into the prepared muffin pan, filling each cup about three-fourths full. Bake until a toothpick inserted into the center of a muffin comes out clean, about 20 minutes. Let cool in the pan for 3–5 minutes, then remove.

Makes 12 muffins

1 cup (8 fl oz/250 ml) water

1 cup (6 oz/185 g) date nuggets or chopped pitted dates

1/2 cup (4 oz/125 g) sugar

1/2 cup (4 oz/125 g) unsalted butter, plus extra for greasing

1/2 teaspoon vanilla extract (essence)

2 eggs

2 cups (10 oz/315 g) all-purpose (plain) flour

2 teaspoons baking powder

1/4 teaspoon baking soda (bicarbonate of soda)

1/4 teaspoon salt

1/3 cup (1 1/2 oz/45 g) chopped pecans

Currant Muffins

Currants taste wonderful, full of flavor and sweetness. Even a small amount of them in a batter can seem like an abundance. These muffins also have a simple cinnamon-sugar topping, giving them a taste and texture akin to coffee cake.

Preheat the oven to 375°F (190°C). Grease a 12-cup standard muffin pan.

To make the topping, in a small cup, combine the sugar and cinnamon.

To make the batter, in a bowl, stir together the flour, sugar, baking soda, baking powder, and salt. Set aside. In another bowl, whisk together the buttermilk, melted butter, egg, marmalade, and currants until smooth. Add to the combined dry ingredients and stir just until blended.

Spoon the batter into the prepared muffin pan, filling each cup about three-fourths full. Sprinkle each muffin with about 1 teaspoon of the topping. Bake until a toothpick inserted into the center of a muffin comes out clean, about 15 minutes. Let cool in the pan for 3–5 minutes, then remove.

Makes 12 muffins

Unsalted butter for greasing

FOR THE TOPPING:

¼ cup (2 oz/60 g) sugar

1 teaspoon ground cinnamon

FOR THE BATTER:

1½ cups (7½ oz/235 g) all-purpose (plain) flour

¼ cup (2 oz/60 g) sugar

1 teaspoon baking soda (bicarbonate of soda)

½ teaspoon baking powder

½ teaspoon salt

¾ cup (6 fl oz/180 ml) buttermilk

6 tablespoons (3 oz/90 g) unsalted butter, melted

1 egg

¼ cup (3 oz/90 g) orange marmalade

½ cup (3 oz/90 g) dried currants

Bran Muffins

These muffins are moist, flavorful, dark, and slightly sweet—they have a good measure of fiber, too. This recipe yields a lot; uneaten muffins can be stored in a tightly sealed plastic bag and will keep for several days.

Unsalted butter for greasing

2¹/₂ cups (6¹/₂ oz/200 g) wheat bran

1¹/₂ cups (7¹/₂ oz/235 g) whole-wheat (wholemeal) flour

¹/₄ cup (2 oz/60 g) firmly packed brown sugar

2¹/₂ teaspoons baking soda (bicarbonate of soda)

1 teaspoon salt

4 eggs

1 cup (8 fl oz/250 ml) buttermilk

¹/₃ cup (3 fl oz/80 ml) canola oil

¹/₄ cup (3 oz/90 g) molasses

¹/₄ cup (3 oz/90 g) honey

1 cup (6 oz/185 g) raisins

Preheat the oven to 400°F (200°C). Grease two 12-cup standard muffin pans.

In a bowl, stir together the bran, flour, brown sugar, baking soda, and salt. Set aside. In another bowl, whisk together the eggs, buttermilk, oil, molasses, and honey until smooth. Stir in the raisins. Add to the combined dry ingredients and stir just until blended.

Spoon the batter into the prepared muffin pans, filling each cup about two-thirds full. Bake until a toothpick inserted into the center of a muffin comes out clean, about 15 minutes. Let cool in the pan for 3–5 minutes, then remove.

Makes 24 muffins

Multibran Muffins with Golden Raisins

The widely reported health benefits of fiber have made bran muffins surge in popularity. This recipe features the three most widely available types of bran, all sold in well-stocked markets and health-food stores.

Preheat the oven to 400°F (200°C). Grease a 12-cup standard muffin pan.

In a bowl, stir together the flour, brans, baking powder, orange zest, and salt. Add the milk, honey, oil, and egg and stir just until the batter is evenly moistened but still slightly lumpy. Add the raisins and fold in gently.

Spoon the batter into the prepared muffin pan, filling each cup about two-thirds full. Bake until well risen and golden brown and a toothpick inserted into the center of a muffin comes out clean, 18–20 minutes. Let cool in the pan for 3–5 minutes, then remove. Serve warm. Freeze any left over muffins, as these dry out quickly.

Makes 12 muffins

Unsalted butter for greasing

1¹⁄₂ cups (7¹⁄₂ oz/235 g) all-purpose (plain) flour

¹⁄₄ cup (³⁄₄ oz/20 g) oat bran

¹⁄₄ cup (³⁄₄ oz/20 g) rice bran

¹⁄₄ cup (³⁄₄ oz/20 g) wheat bran

1 tablespoon baking powder

2 teaspoons grated orange zest (page 329)

¹⁄₄ teaspoon salt

1 cup (8 fl oz/250 ml) low-fat milk

¹⁄₂ cup (6 oz/185 g) honey

¹⁄₄ cup (2 fl oz/60 ml) canola oil

1 egg, beaten

¹⁄₂ cup (3 oz/90 g) golden raisins (sultanas)

Banana-Bran Muffins

Use only bananas that are fully ripe (the skins should be speckled with brown). After peeling, mash them vigorously with a potato masher or a fork into a smooth pulp. These muffins are moist and sweet, with a delicious banana flavor.

1 cup (5 oz/155 g) all-purpose (plain) flour

1 cup (2¹/₂ oz/75 g) wheat bran

1 teaspoon baking soda (bicarbonate of soda)

¹/₂ teaspoon salt

¹/₂ cup (2 oz/60 g) chopped walnuts or pecans

1 cup (8 oz/250 g) mashed ripe banana (2 large bananas)

¹/₂ cup (4 oz/125 g) unsalted butter, at room temperature, plus extra for greasing

¹/₂ cup (3¹/₂ oz/105 g) firmly packed brown sugar

1 egg

Preheat the oven to 375°F (190°C). Grease a 12-cup standard muffin pan.

In a bowl, stir together the flour, wheat bran, baking soda, salt, and nuts. Set aside. In another bowl, beat together the banana and butter until mixed—the mixture may look lumpy and curdled—then add the brown sugar and egg and beat until completely mixed; a hand-held mixer is useful for this step. Add the combined dry ingredients and stir just until blended.

Spoon the batter into the prepared muffin pan, filling each cup about three-fourths full. Bake until a toothpick inserted into the center of a muffin comes out clean, 15–20 minutes. Let cool in the pan for 3–5 minutes, then remove.

Makes 12 muffins

Oat-Bran Muffins

Oat bran muffins are lighter and more cakelike than those made with wheat bran. This recipe takes well to all kinds of additions, especially chopped dried fruit such as apricots, pears, or prunes; add up to 1 cup (6 oz/185 g) of any of these.

Preheat the oven to 425°F (220°C). Grease standard muffin pans to make 16 muffins, filling any unused cups with water to prevent warping.

In a bowl, stir together the oat bran, flour, brown sugar, baking powder, cinnamon, and salt. Set aside. In another bowl, whisk together the milk, eggs, and oil until smooth. Add the raisins and fold in gently. Add to the combined dry ingredients and stir just until blended.

Spoon the batter into the prepared muffin pans, filling each cup about two-thirds full. Bake until a toothpick inserted into the center of a muffin comes out clean, 15–18 minutes. Let cool in the pans for 3–5 minutes, then remove.

Makes 16 muffins

Unsalted butter for greasing

2 cups (6 oz/185 g) oat bran

1 cup (5 oz/155 g) all-purpose (plain) flour

1/2 cup (3 1/2 oz/105 g) firmly packed brown sugar

4 teaspoons baking powder

1 teaspoon ground cinnamon

1/2 teaspoon salt

1 1/4 cups (10 fl oz/310 ml) milk

2 eggs

1/3 cup (3 fl oz/80 ml) canola oil

1/2 cup (3 oz/90 g) raisins

Spice Muffins

The addition of heavy cream gives these muffins a fine, moist texture and a delicate crumb — and what could be a nicer accompaniment for your morning coffee or afternoon tea? You can substitute raisins for the currants, if you like.

2 cups (10 oz/315 g) all-purpose (plain) flour

2/3 cup (5 oz/155 g) sugar

1 tablespoon baking powder

1/2 teaspoon salt

2 teaspoons nutmeg, preferably freshly grated

1 teaspoon ground cinnamon

1/2 teaspoon ground cloves

1/2 teaspoon ground allspice

1 egg

1 cup (8 fl oz/250 ml) heavy (double) cream

1/2 cup (4 fl oz/125 ml) milk

1/3 cup (3 oz/90 g) unsalted butter, melted, plus extra for greasing

1/4 cup (1 1/2 oz/45 g) dried currants (optional)

Preheat the oven to 400°F (200°C). Grease a 12-cup standard muffin pan.

In a bowl, stir together the flour, sugar, baking powder, salt, nutmeg, cinnamon, cloves, and allspice. Set aside. In another bowl, whisk together the egg, cream, milk, melted butter, and the currants, if using. Add to the combined dry ingredients and stir just until blended.

Spoon the batter into the prepared muffin pan, filling each cup about two-thirds full. Bake until a toothpick inserted into the center of a muffin comes out clean, about 20 minutes. Let cool in the pan for 3–5 minutes, then remove.

Makes 12 muffins

Marion Cunningham's Fresh Ginger Muffins

These muffins pack a zesty punch, due to the addition of fresh ginger, lemon zest, and buttermilk, and they taste great with Pear-Ginger Jam (page 315). The recipe comes from cookbook author Marion Cunningham.

1 piece (4–5 oz/125–155 g) unpeeled fresh ginger

3/4 cup (6 oz/185 g) plus 3 tablespoons sugar

2 tablespoons finely grated lemon zest (page 329)

2 cups (10 oz/315 g) all-purpose (plain) flour

1/2 teaspoon salt

3/4 teaspoon baking soda (bicarbonate of soda)

1/2 cup (4 oz/125 g) unsalted butter, at room temperature, plus extra for greasing

2 eggs

1 cup (8 fl oz/250 ml) buttermilk

Preheat the oven to 375°F (190°C). Grease standard muffin pans to make 16 muffins, filling any unused cups with water to prevent warping.

Cut the unpeeled ginger into large chunks. In a food processor fitted with the metal blade, process the ginger until finely minced (or chop finely by hand). You should have about 1/4 cup (1 1/4 oz/35 g). In a small saucepan, combine the ginger and 1/4 cup (2 oz/60 g) of the sugar and cook over medium heat, stirring, until the sugar melts and the mixture is hot, about 2 minutes. Set aside to let cool until lukewarm.

In a small bowl, stir together the lemon zest and the 3 tablespoons sugar. Let stand for a few minutes, then add to the ginger mixture. Stir and set aside.

In a bowl, stir together the flour, salt, and baking soda. Set aside. In another bowl, beat the butter until smooth; a hand-held mixer is useful for this step. Add the remaining 1/2 cup (4 oz/125 g) sugar and beat until blended. Beat in the eggs and buttermilk. Add the combined dry ingredients and stir just until blended. Stir in the ginger-lemon mixture.

Spoon the batter into the prepared muffin pans, filling each cup about three-fourths full. Bake until a toothpick inserted into the center of a muffin comes out clean, 15–20 minutes. Let cool in the pans for 3–5 minutes, then remove.

Makes 16 muffins

Cinnamon Crunch Muffins

These streusel-topped muffins are reminiscent of a spicy coffeecake. The recipe makes plenty, so you can bake them on Sunday and enjoy them throughout the week, too. Serve with Strawberry Jam Butter (page 315).

Preheat the oven to 275°F (190°C). Grease standard muffin pans to make 18 muffins, filling any unused cups with water to prevent warping.

In a bowl, stir together the flour, brown sugar, salt, 1 teaspoon of the cinnamon, and the ginger. Add the shortening and mix the ingredients together—your fingertips are good tools for this job—until thoroughly combined and crumbly. Remove ²/₃ cup (3 oz/90 g) of the mixture to a small bowl and mix in the nuts and the remaining 1 teaspoon cinnamon. Set aside to use for the topping.

To the remaining flour mixture, add the baking powder and baking soda and stir to combine. Add the eggs and buttermilk and stir just until blended.

Spoon the batter into the prepared muffin pans, filling each cup about two-thirds full. Sprinkle each muffin with about 1 tablespoon of the reserved topping. Bake until a toothpick inserted into the center of a muffin comes out clean, 15–20 minutes. Let cool in the pans for 3–5 minutes, then remove. Serve with Strawberry Jam Butter, if desired.

Makes 18 muffins

Unsalted butter for greasing

3 cups (15 oz/470 g) all-purpose (plain) flour

1½ cups (10½ oz/330 g) firmly packed brown sugar

½ teaspoon salt

2 teaspoons ground cinnamon

1 teaspoon ground ginger

²/₃ cup (5 oz/155 g) vegetable shortening

½ cup (2 oz/60 g) chopped pecans or walnuts

2 teaspoons baking powder

½ teaspoon baking soda (bicarbonate of soda)

2 eggs, beaten

1 cup (8 fl oz/250 ml) buttermilk

Strawberry Jam Butter (page 315) (optional)

Sour Cream–Maple Muffins

The addition of sour cream balances the sweetness of these muffins while still allowing the sweet maple flavor to shine through. It also gives the muffins an incredible cakelike texture. Serve any extra sour cream alongside, if you like.

Preheat the oven to 400°F (200°C). Grease standard muffin pans to make 16 muffins, filling any unused cups with water to prevent warping.

In a bowl, stir together the flour, baking powder, baking soda, and salt. Set aside. In another bowl, beat the butter until smooth, then gradually add the maple syrup, beating constantly; a hand-held mixer is useful for this step. Beat in the sour cream and egg. Stir in the nuts. Add the combined dry ingredients and stir until blended.

Spoon the batter into the prepared muffin pans, filling each cup about two-thirds full. Bake until a toothpick inserted into the center of a muffin comes out clean, 15–18 minutes. Let cool in the pans for 3–5 minutes, then remove. Serve with sour cream, if desired.

Makes 16 muffins

1³/4 cups (9 oz/280 g) all-purpose (plain) flour

2 teaspoons baking powder

1 teaspoon baking soda (bicarbonate of soda)

1/2 teaspoon salt

1/2 cup (4 oz/125 g) unsalted butter, at room temperature, plus extra for greasing

3/4 cup (9 fl oz/280 ml) maple syrup

1 cup (8 fl oz/250 ml) sour cream, plus extra for serving (optional)

1 egg

1/2 cup (2 oz/60 g) chopped pecans

Poppy Seed Muffins

Poppy seeds have a subtle but unique flavor — earthy and a little spicy — and they add a nice crunch. Their flavor is complemented by sweet Lemon Glaze (page 317). If you like, omit the wheat germ and increase the flour to 2 cups (8 oz/250 g).

1¹⁄₂ cups (7¹⁄₂ oz/235 g) all-purpose (plain) flour

¹⁄₂ cup (1¹⁄₂ oz/45 g) toasted wheat germ

¹⁄₃ cup (1¹⁄₂ oz/45 g) poppy seeds

¹⁄₃ cup (3 oz/90 g) sugar

1 tablespoon baking powder

¹⁄₂ teaspoon salt

1 cup (8 fl oz/250 ml) milk

1 egg

¹⁄₄ cup (2 oz/60 g) unsalted butter, melted, plus extra for greasing

Lemon Glaze (page 317), optional

Lemon zest (page 329) for garnish (optional)

Preheat the oven to 400°F (200°C). Grease a 12-cup standard muffin pan.

In a bowl, stir together the flour, wheat germ, poppy seeds, sugar, baking powder, and salt. Set aside. In another bowl, whisk together the milk, egg, and melted butter until smooth. Add to the dry ingredients and stir just until blended.

Spoon the batter into the prepared muffin pan, filling each cup about two-thirds full. Bake until a toothpick inserted into the center of a muffin comes out clean, 15–18 minutes. Drizzle the Lemon Glaze, if using, over the muffins while they are still warm. Let cool in the pan for 3–5 minutes, then remove. Garnish with lemon zest, if using, and serve.

Makes 12 muffins

Peanut Butter Muffins

Fine-textured, moist, and golden, these muffins aren't too sweet and have a good nutty flavor—you could serve them with a curry or chicken dinner, or with roast pork. For breakfast, pass them with butter into which you've beaten a little honey.

Preheat the oven to 400°F (200°C). Grease standard muffin pans to make 16 muffins, filling any unused cups with water to prevent warping.

In a bowl, stir together the flour, brown sugar, baking powder, and salt. Set aside. In another bowl, beat the peanut butter and a few spoonfuls of the milk briefly, until smooth, and then beat in the remaining milk; a handheld mixer is useful for this step. Then beat in the melted butter and eggs. Stir in the peanuts. Add to the combined dry ingredients and stir just until blended.

Spoon the batter into the prepared muffin pans, filling each cup about three-fourths full. Bake until a toothpick inserted into the center of a muffin comes out clean, about 15 minutes. Let cool in the pans for 3–5 minutes, then remove.

Makes 16 muffins

2 cups (10 oz/315 g) all-purpose (plain) flour

1/3 cup (2 1/2 oz/75 g) firmly packed brown sugar

1 tablespoon baking powder

1/2 teaspoon salt

2/3 cup (6 oz/185 g) smooth peanut butter

1 1/3 cups (11 fl oz/330 ml) milk

1/4 cup (2 oz/60 g) unsalted butter, melted, plus extra for greasing

2 eggs

1/2 cup (2 oz/60 g) chopped, roasted peanuts, salted or unsalted

Triple-Chocolate Muffins

The different kinds of chocolate used here ensure a complex chocolate flavor for these dense, brownielike muffins. They are sturdy, perfect for transporting to potluck meals. Be sure not to overbake them; they should stay moist in the center.

3 squares (3 oz/90 g) unsweetened chocolate

3 squares (3 oz/90 g) semisweet (plain) chocolate

1/4 cup (2 oz/60 g) unsalted butter, plus extra for greasing

1/2 cup (2¹/2 oz/75 g) all-purpose (plain) flour

1/2 teaspoon baking powder

1/4 teaspoon salt

2 eggs

1/2 cup (4 oz/125 g) sugar

1 teaspoon vanilla extract (essence)

1 teaspoon instant coffee granules or powder

1/2 cup (3 oz/90 g) semisweet (plain) chocolate chips

1/2 cup (2 oz/60 g) walnuts

Preheat the oven to 350°F (180°C). Grease a 12-cup standard muffin pan.

Combine the chocolate squares and the butter in the top pan of a double boiler and place over (but not touching) simmering water. Stir frequently until melted and smooth. Set aside to let cool slightly.

In a bowl, stir together the flour, baking powder, and salt; set aside. In another bowl, combine the eggs, sugar, vanilla, and coffee granules. Beat until light and about doubled in volume; a hand-held mixer is useful for this step. Beat in the chocolate mixture and then the combined dry ingredients just until blended. Stir in the chocolate chips and walnuts. The mixture will be stiff, almost like a dough.

Spoon the batter into the prepared muffin pan, filling each cup about two-thirds full. Using moistened fingertips, smooth the top of each muffin. Bake until the muffins look dry on top, about 15 minutes. Do not overbake. Let cool in the pan for about 10 minutes, then remove.

Makes 12 muffins

Apple-Cheddar Muffins

Moist and flavorful, these muffins are especially delicious with pork, duck, or chicken. They also travel well, making them good lunch-box and picnic fare. If you like, substitute a pippin for the Golden Delicious apple.

1 large Golden Delicious apple

1¹/₂ cups (7¹/₂ oz/235 g) all-purpose (plain) flour

¹/₄ cup (1 oz/30 g) old-fashioned rolled oats

2 tablespoons sugar

2 teaspoons baking powder

¹/₂ teaspoon baking soda (bicarbonate of soda)

¹/₂ teaspoon salt

³/₄ cup (6 fl oz/180 ml) milk

2 eggs

¹/₄ cup (2 oz/60 g) unsalted butter, melted, plus extra for greasing

³/₄ cup (3 oz/90 g) finely grated Cheddar cheese

Preheat the oven to 400°F (200°C). Grease a 12-cup standard muffin pan.

Peel, halve, and core the apple. Cut it into ¹/₈-inch (3-mm) dice; set aside.

In a bowl, stir together the flour, oats, sugar, baking powder, baking soda, and salt. Set aside. In another bowl, whisk together the milk, eggs, and melted butter until smooth. Stir in the apple and cheese. Add to the combined dry ingredients and stir just until blended.

Spoon the batter into the prepared muffin pan, filling each cup about three-fourths full. Bake until a toothpick inserted into the center of a muffin comes out clean, about 20 minutes. Let cool in the pan for 3–5 minutes, then remove.

Makes 12 muffins

Cottage Cheese Muffins

Cottage cheese imparts a definite tang to these muffins. They have a substantial texture and pair nicely with a platter of grilled vegetables or a vegetable casserole for a balanced vegetarian meal.

Preheat the oven to 375°F (190°C). Grease standard muffin pans to make 16 muffins, filling any unused cups with water to prevent warping.

In a bowl, stir together the flour, sugar, baking powder, baking soda, and salt. Set aside. In another bowl, whisk together the egg, milk, melted butter, and dill until smooth. Add the cottage cheese and whisk until blended. Add to the combined dry ingredients and stir just until blended.

Spoon the batter into the prepared muffin pans, filling each cup about three-fourths full. Bake until a toothpick inserted into the center of a muffin comes out clean, about 20 minutes. Let cool in the pans for 3–5 minutes, then remove.

Makes 16 muffins

2 cups (10 oz/315 g) all-purpose (plain) flour

1 tablespoon sugar

2 1/2 teaspoons baking powder

1/2 teaspoon baking soda (bicarbonate of soda)

1/2 teaspoon salt

1 egg

1 cup (8 fl oz/250 ml) milk

1/4 cup (2 oz/60 g) unsalted butter, melted, plus extra for greasing

1 tablespoon chopped fresh dill or sage, or 1 teaspoon dried dill or sage

3/4 cup (6 oz/185 g) small-curd cottage cheese

Sun-Dried Tomato–Herb Muffins

These muffins are perfect partners for luncheon soups and salads. They are flecked with red and green and are full of tomato and cheese flavor, which gives them an Italian accent. Buy sun-dried tomatoes that are packed in olive oil; drain well before using.

Preheat the oven to 375°F (190°C). Grease a 12-cup standard muffin pan.

In a bowl, stir together the flour, baking powder, salt, and pepper. Set aside. In another bowl, whisk together the milk, egg, and oil until smooth. Add the cheese, tomatoes, and herb and stir until blended. Add to the combined dry ingredients and stir just until blended.

Spoon the batter into the prepared muffin pan, filling each cup about three-fourths full. Bake until a toothpick inserted into the center of a muffin comes out clean, about 20 minutes. Let cool in the pan for 3–5 minutes, then remove.

Makes 12 muffins

Unsalted butter for greasing

2 cups (10 oz/315 g) all-purpose (plain) flour

1 tablespoon baking powder

1/2 teaspoon salt

1/4 teaspoon freshly ground pepper

1 cup (8 fl oz/250 ml) milk

1 egg

1/4 cup (2 fl oz/60 ml) olive oil

1/2 cup (2 oz/60 g) freshly grated Parmesan cheese

1/4 cup (1 oz/30 g) olive oil–packed sun-dried tomatoes, drained and finely chopped

2 teaspoons chopped fresh thyme, oregano, or dill or 1 teaspoon dried thyme, oregano, or dill

Boston Brown Bread Muffins

From cookbook author Marion Cunningham, these muffins have much in common with old-fashioned steamed brown bread, but are much faster to make. Enjoy them hot from the oven for breakfast or supper.

Unsalted butter for greasing

1/2 cup (1 1/2 oz/45 g) rye flour

1/2 cup (2 1/2 oz/75 g) yellow cornmeal

1/2 cup (2 1/2 oz/75 g) whole-wheat (wholemeal) flour

1 1/2 teaspoons baking soda (bicarbonate of soda)

3/4 teaspoon salt

1 cup (8 fl oz/250 ml) buttermilk

1/3 cup (3 oz/90 g) firmly packed dark brown sugar

1/3 cup (3 fl oz/80 ml) canola oil

1/3 cup (4 oz/125 g) molasses

1 egg

1 cup (6 oz/185 g) raisins

Preheat the oven to 400°F (200°C). Grease a 12-cup standard muffin pan.

In a bowl, stir together the rye flour, cornmeal, whole-wheat flour, baking soda, and salt. Set aside. In another bowl, whisk together the buttermilk, brown sugar, oil, molasses, and egg until smooth. Add to the combined dry ingredients and stir just until blended. Stir in the raisins.

Spoon the batter into the prepared muffin pan, filling each cup about two-thirds full. Bake until a toothpick inserted into the center of a muffin comes out clean, about 15 minutes. Let cool in the pan for 3–5 minutes, then remove.

Makes 12 muffins

Chili-Corn Muffins

Moist and rich, these muffins are perfection when warm from the oven and spread with butter. For a lively brunch, serve with huevos rancheros. Roasted, peeled, and diced green chiles are readily available in cans.

Preheat the oven to 400°F (200°C). Grease a 12-cup standard muffin pan.

In a bowl, stir together the flour, cornmeal, baking powder, baking soda, salt, and chili powder. Set aside. In another bowl, whisk together the sour cream, eggs, and melted butter until smooth. Stir in the chiles and cheese. Add to the combined dry ingredients and stir just until blended.

Spoon the batter into the prepared muffin pan, filling each cup about two-thirds full. Bake until a toothpick inserted into the center of a muffin comes out clean, about 15 minutes. Let cool in the pan for 3–5 minutes, then remove.

Makes 12 muffins

3/4 cup (4 oz/125 g) all-purpose (plain) flour

3/4 cup (4 oz/125 g) yellow or white cornmeal

2 teaspoons baking powder

1/2 teaspoon baking soda (bicarbonate of soda)

1/2 teaspoon salt

1 1/2 teaspoons chili powder

3/4 cup (6 fl oz/180 ml) sour cream

2 eggs

1/4 cup (2 oz/60 g) unsalted butter, melted, plus extra for greasing

1/4 cup (2 oz/60 g) roasted, peeled, and diced green chiles

1/2 cup (2 oz/60 g) finely grated Cheddar cheese

Cornmeal Nugget Muffins

In this unusual twist on standard corn muffins, the cornmeal is cooked and toasted, and then crumbled and added to the buttery batter like tiny nuggets of gold. These taste great alongside a main course of soup, stew, or chili.

1 cup (8 fl oz/250 ml) boiling water

1/2 cup (2 1/2 oz/75 g) yellow cornmeal

1 teaspoon salt

2 cups (10 oz/315 g) all-purpose (plain) flour

3 tablespoons sugar

2 teaspoons baking powder

1/2 teaspoon baking soda (bicarbonate of soda)

1 cup (8 fl oz/250 ml) buttermilk

1 egg

1/3 cup (3 oz/90 g) unsalted butter, melted, plus extra for greasing

Preheat the oven to 375°F (190°C). Grease a 12-cup standard muffin pan and a baking sheet.

In a small bowl, stir together the boiling water, cornmeal, and 1/2 teaspoon of the salt; don't worry if some small lumps remain in the mixture. Spread evenly in a thin layer on the prepared baking sheet. Bake until golden brown and toasted, about 25 minutes. Let cool completely, then crumble into small pieces. Set aside.

In a bowl, stir together the flour, sugar, baking powder, baking soda, and remaining 1/2 teaspoon salt. Set aside. In another bowl, whisk together the buttermilk, egg, and melted butter until smooth. Add to the combined dry ingredients, along with the cornmeal nuggets, and stir just until blended.

Spoon the batter into the prepared muffin pan, filling each cup about three-fourths full. Bake until a toothpick inserted into the center of a muffin comes out clean, about 20 minutes. Let cool in the pan for 3–5 minutes, then remove.

Makes 12 muffins

Buttermilk-Bacon Muffins

Apples and smoked bacon are a wonderful combination anytime, especially in these great-tasting muffins. Serve these for breakfast with fried or scrambled eggs or with a bowl of hot cereal.

Unsalted butter for greasing

6 slices bacon

2 cups (10 oz/315 g) all-purpose (plain) flour

2 tablespoons sugar

2 teaspoons baking powder

1/2 teaspoon baking soda (bicarbonate of soda)

1/2 teaspoon salt

1 cup (8 fl oz/250 ml) buttermilk

1/3 cup (3 fl oz/80 ml) corn oil

1 egg

1 small Golden Delicious apple, peeled, cored, and finely chopped

Preheat the oven to 400°F (200°C). Grease a 12-cup standard muffin pan.

In a frying pan, fry the bacon over high heat until crisp, about 5 minutes. Transfer to paper towels to drain and let cool. Crumble the bacon and set aside.

In a bowl, stir together the flour, sugar, baking powder, baking soda, and salt. Set aside. In another bowl, whisk together the buttermilk, oil, and egg until smooth. Add to the combined dry ingredients, along with the apple and the crumbled bacon, and stir just until blended.

Spoon the batter into the prepared muffin pan, filling each cup about three-fourths full. Bake until a toothpick inserted into the center of a muffin comes out clean, about 20 minutes. Let cool in the pan for 3–5 minutes, then remove.

Makes 12 muffins

Corn Kernel–Bacon Muffins

Crisp bacon gives these muffins a hearty flavor, while cornmeal and corn kernels lend an earthy texture. You can substitute canola oil for the bacon drippings, but the flavor will be slightly diminished.

Preheat the oven to 400°F (200°C). Grease standard muffin pans to make 16 muffins, filling any unused cups with water to prevent warping.

In a frying pan, fry the bacon over high heat until crisp, about 5 minutes. Transfer to paper towels to drain and let cool. Reserve about ¼ cup (2 fl oz/60 ml) of the drippings from the pan. Crumble the bacon and set aside.

In a bowl, stir together the flour, cornmeal, sugar, baking powder, and salt. Set aside. In another bowl, whisk together the milk, egg, corn kernels, and reserved bacon drippings until blended. Add to the combined dry ingredients, along with the crumbled bacon, and stir just until blended.

Spoon the batter into the prepared muffin pans, filling each cup about two-thirds full. Bake until a toothpick inserted into the center of a muffin comes out clean, about 15 minutes. Let cool in the pans for 3–5 minutes, then remove.

Makes 16 muffins

Unsalted butter for greasing

6 slices bacon

1 cup (5 oz/155 g) all-purpose (plain) flour

1 cup (5 oz/155 g) yellow or white cornmeal

3 tablespoons sugar

1 tablespoon baking powder

½ teaspoon salt

1 cup (8 fl oz/250 ml) milk

1 egg

½ cup (3 oz/90 g) fresh corn kernels or thawed frozen corn kernels

Potato Muffins

Potato starch produces slightly chewy breads with a subtle potato flavor. These muffins are excellent companions to chicken and meat dishes. Piquant Caper-Mustard Butter (page 313) provides a nice contrast to their delicate flavor.

Preheat the oven to 400°F (200°C). Grease a 12-cup standard muffin pan.

In a bowl, stir together the flour, potato starch, sugar, baking powder, salt, and thyme. Set aside. In another bowl, whisk together the milk and mashed potatoes until smooth, then add the egg, melted butter, and cheese, and whisk until well blended. Add to the combined dry ingredients and stir just until blended.

Spoon the batter into the prepared muffin pan, filling each cup about three-fourths full. Bake until a toothpick inserted into the center of a muffin comes out clean, 15–18 minutes. Let cool in the pan for 3–5 minutes, then remove. Serve with the Caper-Mustard Butter, if desired.

Makes 12 muffins

1 cup (5 oz/155 g) all-purpose (plain) flour

1 cup (4 oz/125 g) potato starch (potato flour)

1 tablespoon sugar

1 tablespoon baking powder

1/2 teaspoon salt

1 1/2 teaspoons chopped fresh thyme or 1/2 teaspoon dried thyme

1 cup (8 fl oz/250 ml) milk

1/2 cup (4 oz/125 g) warm mashed potatoes

1 egg

1/4 cup (2 oz/60 g) unsalted butter, melted, plus extra for greasing

1/3 cup (1 1/2 oz/45 g) finely grated Swiss or Cheddar cheese

Caper-Mustard Butter (page 313) (optional)

Quick Breads

Lemon Bread

This recipe carries a double dose of lemon, with grated zest in the batter and lemon syrup poured over the top after baking. For a fancy presentation, trim away the sides of the loaf and garnish the plate with fresh berries and mint sprigs.

1/2 cup (4 oz/125 g) vegetable shortening, plus extra for greasing

1 cup (8 oz/250 g) granulated sugar

2 eggs

1¼ cups (6½ oz/200 g) all-purpose (plain) flour, plus extra for dusting

1 teaspoon baking powder

1/2 teaspoon salt

1/2 cup (4 fl oz/125 ml) milk

1 tablespoon finely grated lemon zest (page 329)

1/2 cup (2 oz/60 g) chopped pecans (optional)

FOR THE LEMON SYRUP:

1/4 cup (2 oz/60 g) granulated sugar

3 tablespoons fresh lemon juice

Confectioners' (icing) sugar for dusting (optional)

Preheat the oven to 350°F (180°C). Grease an 8 1/2-by-4 1/2-inch (21.5-by-11.5-cm) loaf pan and dust with flour.

In a bowl, combine the shortening and sugar and beat until blended; a hand-held mixer is useful for this step. Add the eggs, one at a time, beating well after each addition. In another bowl, stir together the flour, baking powder, and salt. Add to the shortening mixture, along with the milk and lemon zest, and beat until completely blended and smooth. Stir in the pecans, if using. Pour and scrape the batter into the prepared pan and spread evenly. Bake until a thin wooden skewer inserted into the center of the loaf comes out clean, about 1 hour.

While the bread bakes, make the lemon syrup: Combine the sugar and lemon juice in a small bowl. Set aside, stirring occasionally; don't worry if the sugar does not dissolve completely.

Remove the bread from the oven and, using a fork, gently poke the top in several places. Stir the syrup, then slowly drizzle it over the hot bread. Let cool in the pan for 15 minutes, then turn out onto a wire rack to cool completely. Dust with the confectioners' sugar before serving, if desired.

Makes 1 medium loaf

Holiday Fruit Bread

This moist bread has so much flavor and texture that it could replace the usual fruit cake. If you want a round loaf rather than the conventional shape, bake the batter in a springform pan and decorate with dried fruit.

1 3/4 cups (9 oz/280 g) all-purpose (plain) flour, plus extra for dusting

1/2 cup (4 oz/125 g) sugar

1 tablespoon baking powder

1/2 teaspoon salt

3/4 cup (6 fl oz/180 ml) milk

2 eggs

1/3 cup (3 oz/90 g) unsalted butter, melted, plus extra for greasing

3/4 cup (5 oz/155 g) finely chopped dried apricots

3/4 cup (5 oz/155 g) finely chopped pitted prunes

1/2 cup (2 oz/60 g) chopped walnuts or almonds

Preheat the oven to 350°F (180°C). Grease an 8 1/2-by-4 1/2-inch (21.5-by-11.5-cm) loaf pan or a 7-inch (18-cm) springform pan and dust with flour.

In a bowl, stir together the flour, sugar, baking powder, and salt. In another bowl, whisk together the milk, eggs, and melted butter until smooth. Stir in the apricots, prunes, and nuts. Add to the combined dry ingredients and stir just until blended.

Pour and scrape the batter into the prepared pan and spread evenly. Bake until a thin wooden skewer inserted into the center of the loaf comes out clean, about 1 hour. Let cool in the pan for 10 minutes, then turn out onto a wire rack and allow to cool completely.

Makes 1 medium loaf

Currant Scones

Traditionally triangular in shape, these small Irish-Scottish cakes were at one time always cooked on a griddle. Delicious for breakfast or afternoon tea, scones are at their best served warm from the oven.

Preheat the oven to 375°F (190°C). Grease a baking sheet and dust with flour.

In a bowl, sift together the flour, baking powder, salt, and sugar. Using your finger-tips, rub in the butter until the mixture resembles fine meal. Stir in the currants. Make a well in the center of the flour mixture and pour in the milk. Using a rubber spatula, quickly mix together to form a soft dough. (Do not overmix.)

Turn out the dough onto a lightly floured work surface and cut in half. Place each half on the prepared baking sheet. Lightly form each half into a round about ¹/₂ inch (12 mm) thick. Brush the tops with the egg-yolk mixture. Then, using a sharp knife, score each round into 10 equal wedges, cutting about halfway through.

Bake until well risen and golden brown, 15–17 minutes. Transfer to a wire rack and let cool slightly, then cut apart. Serve warm.

Makes 20 scones

Unsalted butter, at room temperature, for greasing

2 cups (10 oz/315 g) all-purpose (plain) flour, plus extra for dusting

1 teaspoon baking powder

¹/₄ teaspoon salt

¹/₃ cup (3 oz/90 g) sugar

¹/₄ cup (2 oz/60 g) cold unsalted butter, cut into pieces

¹/₂ cup (3 oz/90 g) dried currants

¹/₂ cup (4 fl oz/125 ml) milk

1 egg yolk beaten with 1 teaspoon water

Spiced Fruit Loaf

This easy soda bread is an ideal holiday treat for those who cannot tolerate wheat. Both brown-rice flour and xanthan gum powder (a natural product that adds "stretch" to gluten-free flours) can be found at natural-food stores.

Place a baking sheet in the oven and preheat to 425°F (220°C).

In a bowl, mix together the rice flour, cornstarch, salt, sugar, xanthan gum powder, baking soda, baking powder, cloves, and nutmeg. Using your fingertips, lightly rub in the butter until the mixture resembles a coarse meal. Add the currants, raisins, and orange zest and stir to distribute evenly.

In another bowl, stir together the egg and yogurt until well blended. Pour the egg mixture into the flour mixture. Using a rubber spatula, quickly mix together to form a soft dough. Gather the dough together and turn it out onto a work surface lightly dusted with brown-rice flour. Form into a ball, then quickly knead a few times until smooth. Cut in half. Using a rolling pin, roll out each half into a 9-by-7-inch (23-by-18-cm) oval. Fold each oval lengthwise, with the top layer just slightly narrower than the bottom layer, forming a "step." Using a large spatula, transfer the ovals to the baking sheet.

Bake until well risen and golden brown, and a thin wooden skewer inserted into the center of the loaves comes out clean, about 25 minutes. Transfer the loaves to a wire rack to cool completely. Dust with confectioners' sugar before serving.

Makes two 18-oz (560-g) loaves

2 cups (10 oz/315 g) brown-rice flour, plus extra for dusting

2/3 cup (2 1/2 oz/75 g) cornstarch (cornflour)

1/2 teaspoon salt

3 tablespoons granulated sugar

2 teaspoons xanthan gum powder

1 teaspoon baking soda (bicarbonate of soda)

1/2 teaspoon baking powder

1/4 teaspoon ground cloves

1/4 teaspoon ground nutmeg

1/4 cup (2 oz/60 g) cold unsalted butter, cut into pieces

1/2 cup (3 oz/90 g) dried currants

1/2 cup (3 oz/90 g) golden raisins (sultanas)

Grated zest of 1 small orange (page 329)

1 egg

1 cup (8 oz/250 g) plain yogurt

Confectioners' (icing) sugar for dusting

Fig-Date Bread

This dark, firm-textured bread with hearty character is delicious thinly sliced and topped with cream cheese and a scattering of chopped dates. It will keep for several days if it is stored in a tightly sealed container.

1 cup (6 oz/185 g) chopped pitted dates

1 cup (6 oz/185 g) chopped dried figs

1/4 cup (2 oz/60 g) unsalted butter, at room temperature, plus extra for greasing

1 1/2 teaspoons baking soda (bicarbonate of soda)

1 cup (8 fl oz/250 ml) boiling water

1/2 cup (4 oz/125 g) sugar

1/2 cup (2 oz/60 g) chopped walnuts

2 eggs

3/4 cup (4 oz/125 g) all-purpose (plain) flour, plus extra for dusting

3/4 cup (4 oz/125 g) whole-wheat (wholemeal) flour

1/2 teaspoon baking powder

1/2 teaspoon salt

In a bowl, combine the dates, figs, butter, and baking soda. Pour in the boiling water, stir well, and let stand for 15 minutes.

Preheat the oven to 350°F (180°C). Grease an 8 1/2-by-4 1/2-inch (21.5-by-11.5-cm) loaf pan and dust with flour.

Beat the sugar, walnuts, and eggs into the date mixture; a hand-held mixer is useful for this step. Set aside. In another bowl, stir together the flours, baking powder, and salt. Add to the date mixture and stir just until blended.

Pour and scrape the batter into the prepared pan and spread evenly. Bake until a thin wooden skewer inserted into the center of the loaf comes out clean, about 1 hour. Allow to cool in the pan for 10 minutes, then turn out onto a wire rack to let cool completely.

Makes 1 medium loaf

Oatmeal-Raisin Bread

This easy-to-make bread is golden, cakelike, and spicy. It will taste all the better with peanut butter or simple Strawberry Jam (page 315) spread on each piece. If it becomes a little stale, simply toast before serving.

In a bowl, stir together the buttermilk and oatmeal. Let stand for 30 minutes.

Preheat the oven to 350°F (180°C). Grease an 8 1/2-by-4 1/2-inch (21.5-by-11.5-cm) loaf pan and dust with flour

In another bowl, stir together the flour, cinnamon, ginger, baking soda, baking powder, and salt. Set aside. Add the sugar, melted butter, eggs, and raisins to the oatmeal mixture and beat until blended; a hand-held mixer is useful for this step. Add the combined dry ingredients and beat just until blended.

Pour and scrape the batter into the prepared pan and spread evenly. Bake until a thin wooden skewer inserted into the center of the loaf comes out clean, about 1 hour. Let cool in the pan for 10 minutes, then turn out onto a wire rack and cool completely. Serve with the Strawberry Jam, if desired.

Makes 1 medium loaf

1¼ cups (10 fl oz/310 ml) buttermilk

½ cup (1½ oz/45 g) old-fashioned rolled oats

1½ cups (7½ oz/235 g) all-purpose (plain) flour, plus extra for dusting

1 teaspoon ground cinnamon

1 teaspoon ground ginger

1 teaspoon baking soda (bicarbonate of soda)

1 teaspoon baking powder

½ teaspoon salt

½ cup (4 oz/125 g) sugar

½ cup (4 oz/125 g) unsalted butter, melted, plus extra for greasing

2 eggs

½ cup (3 oz/90 g) raisins

Strawberry Jam (page 315) for serving (optional)

Sour Cream–Raisin Bread

A spicy brown sugar topping crowns this rich bread. For an even more delectable treat, top it with cinnamon-laced Whipped Cream (page 316). Serve it for a Sunday brunch, or whenever you want an indulgent loaf.

1½ cups (12 fl oz/375 ml) sour cream

1½ teaspoons baking soda (bicarbonate of soda)

½ cup (4 oz/125 g) unsalted butter, melted, plus extra for greasing

1 cup (4 oz/125 g) granulated sugar

2 eggs

½ cup (3 oz/90 g) raisins

1¾ cups (9 oz/280 g) all-purpose (plain) flour, plus extra for dusting

2 teaspoons baking powder

2 teaspoons ground cinnamon

½ teaspoon salt

¼ cup (2 oz/60 g) firmly packed brown sugar

¼ cup (1 oz/30 g) chopped walnuts

Preheat the oven to 350°F (180°C). Grease a 9-by-5-inch (23-by-13-cm) loaf pan and dust with flour.

In a bowl, stir together the sour cream and baking soda. Set aside for 5 minutes. Add the melted butter, granulated sugar, eggs, and raisins and whisk until blended. Set aside.

In another bowl, stir together the flour, baking powder, half of the cinnamon, and the salt. Add to the sour cream mixture and stir just until blended.

Pour and scrape the batter into the prepared pan and spread evenly. Stir together the remaining 1 teaspoon cinnamon, the brown sugar, and walnuts. Sprinkle over the batter. Bake until a thin wooden skewer inserted into the center of the loaf comes out clean, 65–75 minutes. Let cool in the pan for 15 minutes, then turn out onto a wire rack to cool completely.

Makes 1 large loaf

Whole-Wheat Pumpkin Bread

This pumpkin bread is moist, dark, and spicy, and the cornmeal gives it an interesting texture. It is especially festive and satisfying for holiday breakfasts, and makes for good sandwiches of holiday leftovers, too.

Preheat the oven to 350°F (180°C). Grease two 8 1/2-by-4 1/2-inch (21.5-by-11.5-cm) loaf pans and dust with flour.

In a bowl, stir together the flour, cornmeal, baking soda, ginger, cinnamon, cloves, nutmeg, and salt. Set aside. In another bowl, beat together the butter and sugar until blended; a hand-held mixer is useful for this step. Beat in the pumpkin, eggs, and water until completely mixed. Add the combined dry ingredients and stir just until blended. Stir in the raisins and walnuts.

Pour and scrape the batter into the 2 prepared pans and spread evenly. Bake until a thin wooden skewer inserted into the center of the loaves comes out clean, about 1 hour. Allow to cool in the pans for 10 minutes, then turn out onto a wire rack to cool completely.

Makes 2 medium loaves

2 1/2 cups (12 1/2 oz/390 g) whole-wheat (wholemeal) flour, plus extra for dusting

1/2 cup (2 1/2 oz/75 g) yellow or white cornmeal

2 teaspoons baking soda (bicarbonate of soda)

1 teaspoon ground ginger

1 1/2 teaspoons ground cinnamon

1/2 teaspoon ground cloves

1/2 teaspoon ground nutmeg

1/2 teaspoon salt

2/3 cup (5 oz/155 g) unsalted butter, at room temperature, plus extra for greasing

2 cups (1 lb/500 g) sugar

2 cups (1 lb/500 g) mashed cooked pumpkin or canned pumpkin

4 eggs

2/3 cup (5 fl oz/160 ml) water

1 cup (6 oz/185 g) raisins

1/2 cup (2 oz/60 g) chopped walnuts

Patsy's Honey Nut Bread

Dense, moist, and golden, this bread comes from San Francisco–based cook Patsy McFetridge. Serve it with fruit salads, compotes, a bowl of yogurt, or honey-swirled butter for breakfast. The bread is even better the day after it is baked.

1 cup (8 fl oz/250 ml) milk

1 cup (12 oz/375 g) honey

1/2 cup (4 oz/125 g) sugar

2 1/2 cups (12 1/2 oz/390 g) all-purpose (plain) flour, plus extra for dusting

1 teaspoon baking soda (bicarbonate of soda)

1 teaspoon salt

1/4 cup (2 oz/60 g) unsalted butter, melted, plus extra for greasing

2 egg yolks

1/2 cup (2 oz/60 g) chopped walnuts

Preheat the oven to 325°F (165°C). Grease a 9-by-5-inch (23-by-13-cm) loaf pan or a 7-inch (18-cm) springform pan and dust with flour.

In a saucepan, bring the milk to a simmer over medium heat. Add the honey and sugar and stir until the sugar dissolves. Set aside to cool to lukewarm.

Meanwhile, in a bowl, stir together the flour, baking soda, and salt. Set aside. Add the melted butter and egg yolks to the cooled honey mixture and whisk until blended. Add to the combined dry ingredients and beat until thoroughly blended. Stir in the walnuts.

Pour and scrape the batter into the prepared pan and spread evenly. Bake until a thin wooden skewer inserted into the center of the loaf comes out clean, about 65 minutes. Allow to cool in the pan for 15 minutes, then turn out onto a wire rack to cool completely.

Makes 1 large loaf

Whole-Wheat Banana Nut Bread

A slice or two of this dark, rich, and sweet bread is good for breakfast, toasted and spread with softened cream cheese. This recipe makes two loaves; make the entire recipe and freeze one of the loaves to enjoy later.

Preheat the oven to 350°F (180°C). Grease two 8 1/2-by-4 1/2-inch (21.5-by-11.5-cm) loaf pans and dust with flour.

In a bowl, stir together the flour, baking soda, and salt. Set aside. In another bowl, beat together the butter and sugar until blended; a hand-held mixer is useful for this step. Beat in the banana, then beat in the eggs until completely mixed; don't worry if the mixture looks lumpy and curdled. Stir in the nuts. Add the combined dry ingredients and stir just until blended.

Pour and scrape the batter into the 2 prepared pans and spread evenly. Bake until a thin wooden skewer inserted into the center of the loaves comes out clean, about 1 hour. Allow to cool in the pans for 10 minutes, then turn out onto a wire rack to cool completely.

Makes 2 medium loaves

2 1/2 cups (12 1/2 oz/390 g) whole-wheat (wholemeal) flour, plus extra for dusting

2 teaspoons baking soda (bicarbonate of soda)

1 teaspoon salt

1 cup (8 oz/250 g) unsalted butter, at room temperature, plus extra for greasing

2 cups (1 lb/500 g) sugar

2 cups (1 lb/500 g) mashed ripe banana (4 large bananas)

4 eggs

1 cup (4 oz/125 g) chopped walnuts or pecans

Chocolate-Pecan Bread

This loaf doesn't rise very high, but it has a sophisticated flavor and a lovely, moist texture. Cut it into generous slices and serve with Chocolate Whipped Cream (page 317) to make a simple yet elegant dessert appropriate for any occasion.

5 eggs, separated, at room temperature

3/4 cup (6 oz/185 g) sugar

1/4 cup (2 oz/60 g) unsalted butter, melted and cooled slightly, plus extra for greasing

1 teaspoon vanilla extract (essence)

1 cup (4 oz/125 g) all-purpose (plain) flour, sifted before measuring, plus extra for dusting

1/4 teaspoon ground cinnamon

3 oz (90 g) unsweetened chocolate, finely chopped (scant 2/3 cup)

1 cup (4 oz/125 g) ground pecans, almonds, or toasted hazelnuts (filberts) (page 326)

3 cups (24 fl oz/750 ml) Chocolate Whipped Cream (page 317)

Preheat the oven to 375°F (190°C). Grease an 8 1/2-by-4 1/2-inch (21.5-by-11.5-cm) loaf pan and dust with flour.

Place the egg whites and about half of the sugar in a clean bowl. Using an electric mixer set on high speed, beat until stiff and shiny, but not dry. Set aside.

In another bowl, combine the egg yolks and the remaining sugar and beat on high speed until thick and light-colored, 3–5 minutes. Beat in the melted butter and vanilla.

Sift together the sifted flour and cinnamon into a large bowl. Stir into the yolk mixture, mixing until completely incorporated. Stir in half the beaten egg whites, then gently fold in the remaining egg whites. Fold in the chocolate and nuts. Pour and scrape the batter into the prepared pan. Smooth the top with a rubber spatula, mounding the batter slightly higher along the center.

Bake until a thin wooden skewer inserted into the center of the loaf comes out clean and dry, 45–50 minutes. Let cool in the pan for 15 minutes, then turn out onto a wire rack to cool completely. Serve with the Chocolate Whipped Cream.

Makes 1 medium loaf

Whole-Wheat Walnut Bread

The wheaty flavor and crunch of walnuts makes this eggless bread a good accompaniment to soups and stews, main-course salads, or fruit and cheese. A very good bread for very little effort, it makes nice breakfast toast, too.

1¹/₂ cups (7¹/₂ oz/235 g) whole-wheat (wholemeal) flour

1 cup (5 oz/155 g) all-purpose (plain) flour, plus extra for dusting

1 teaspoon baking powder

1 teaspoon baking soda (bicarbonate of soda)

¹/₂ teaspoon salt

1¹/₂ cups (12 fl oz/375 ml) buttermilk

¹/₃ cup (3 fl oz/80 ml) canola oil, plus extra for greasing

¹/₃ cup (4 oz/125 g) molasses

1 cup (4 oz/125 g) chopped walnuts, toasted (page 326)

Preheat the oven to 350°F (180°C). Grease a 9-by-5-inch (23-by-13-cm) loaf pan and dust with flour.

In a bowl, stir together the flours, baking powder, baking soda, and salt. Set aside. In another bowl, whisk together the buttermilk, oil, and molasses until smooth. Stir in the walnuts. Add to the combined dry ingredients and stir just until blended.

Pour and scrape the batter into the prepared pan and spread evenly. Bake until a thin wooden skewer inserted into the center of the loaf comes out clean, about 55 minutes. Let cool in the pan for 10 minutes, then turn out onto a wire rack to cool completely.

Makes 1 large loaf

Nutted Squash Bread

Golden and fine-textured, this slightly sweet bread has cold-weather appeal. Serve it with hearty soups, stews, or baked beans. Use any mashed cooked winter squash, such as acorn, Hubbard, or butternut, or cooked or canned pumpkin.

2 cups (10 oz/315 g) all-purpose (plain) flour, plus extra for dusting

2 teaspoons baking powder

1/4 teaspoon baking soda (bicarbonate of soda)

1/2 teaspoon salt

1/2 teaspoon ground nutmeg

1 cup (8 oz/250 g) mashed cooked winter squash

1/3 cup (3 fl oz/80 ml) milk

1/3 cup (3 oz/90 g) unsalted butter, melted, plus extra for greasing

2 eggs

1/2 cup (2 oz/60 g) firmly packed brown sugar

1/2 teaspoon vanilla extract (essence)

1/2 cup (2 oz/60 g) chopped toasted walnuts or pecans (page 326)

1/4 cup (1.5 oz/45 g) raisins

Preheat the oven to 350°F (180°C). Grease an 8 1/2-by-4 1/2-inch (21.5-by-11.5-cm) loaf pan and dust with flour.

In a bowl, stir together the flour, baking powder, baking soda, salt, and nutmeg. Set aside. In another bowl, whisk together the squash, milk, melted butter, eggs, brown sugar, and vanilla until smooth. Stir in the nuts and raisins. Add to the combined dry ingredients and stir just until blended.

Pour and scrape the batter into the prepared pan and spread evenly. Bake until a thin wooden skewer inserted into the center of the loaf comes out clean, about 1 hour. Allow to cool in the pan for 10 minutes, then turn out onto a wire rack to cool completely.

Makes 1 medium loaf

Cheese-and-Grits Bread

Hominy grits look like coarse cornmeal and are made from dried, ground corn kernels that have had the hull and germ removed. This rough-hewn bread scented with rosemary is best warm, spread with butter.

1 cup (5 oz/155 g) all-purpose (plain) flour

1 cup (6 oz/185 g) quick-cooking hominy grits

1 tablespoon sugar

2 teaspoons chopped fresh rosemary or 1 teaspoon crumbled dried rosemary

1 teaspoon baking soda (bicarbonate of soda)

1/2 teaspoon salt

1 1/2 cups (12 fl oz/375 ml) buttermilk

1 egg

1/3 cup (3 oz/90 g) unsalted butter, melted, plus extra for greasing

1 cup (4 oz/125 g) finely grated Cheddar or Swiss cheese, or a mixture

Preheat the oven to 400°F (200°C). Grease an 8-inch (20-cm) square pan.

In a bowl, stir together the flour, grits, sugar, rosemary, baking soda, and salt. Set aside. In another bowl, whisk together the buttermilk, egg, and melted butter until smooth. Stir in the cheese. Add to the combined dry ingredients and stir just until blended.

Pour and scrape the batter into the prepared pan and spread evenly. Bake until a thin wooden skewer inserted into the center of the bread comes out clean, 25–30 minutes. Cut into 2-inch (5-cm) squares and serve warm from the pan.

Makes 16 squares

Pistachio-Olive Bread

Pistachios, black olives, and olive oil give this bread flecks of color and an enticing flavor and aroma. Tender and cakelike, it goes well with egg dishes. Greek olives are pungent and quite salty, so a few go a long way.

Preheat the oven to 350°F (180°C). Grease an 8 1/2-by-4 1/2-inch (21.5-by-11.5-cm) loaf pan and dust with flour.

In a bowl, stir together the flour, sugar, baking powder, and salt. In another bowl, whisk together the milk, olive oil, and eggs until smooth. Stir in the pistachios and olives. Add to the combined dry ingredients and stir just until blended.

Pour and scrape the batter into the prepared pan and spread evenly. Bake until a thin wooden skewer inserted into the center of the loaf comes out clean, about 50 minutes. Let cool in the pan for 10 minutes, then turn out onto a wire rack to cool completely.

Makes 1 medium loaf

1 1/2 cups (7 1/2 oz/235 g) all-purpose (plain) flour, plus extra for dusting

1 tablespoon sugar

2 1/2 teaspoons baking powder

1/2 teaspoon salt

3/4 cup (6 fl oz/180 ml) milk

1/4 cup (2 fl oz/60 ml) olive oil, plus extra for greasing

2 eggs

1/3 cup (1 1/2 oz/45 g) chopped pistachios

3 tablespoons chopped pitted Greek olives

Vegetable-Nut Bread

This flavorful bread is hearty and healthful. You can use other chopped cooked vegetables instead of spinach, and vary the cheese as well. This bread does not keep, so freeze what you will not use within a day.

1 cup (5 oz/155 g) whole-wheat (wholemeal) flour

1 cup (5 oz/155 g) all-purpose (plain) flour, plus extra for dusting

1 tablespoon baking powder

1/4 teaspoon baking soda (bicarbonate of soda)

1/2 teaspoon ground ginger

1 teaspoon salt

1 cup (8 fl oz/250 ml) milk

3 tablespoons honey

3 tablespoons olive oil, plus extra for greasing

1 egg

1/2 cup (3 1/2 oz/105 g) cooked drained spinach, chopped

1/2 cup (2 oz/60 g) chopped walnuts or almonds, toasted (page 326)

1/2 cup (2 oz/60 g) freshly grated Parmesan or Swiss cheese

Preheat the oven to 375°F (190°C). Grease an 8 1/2-by-4 1/2-inch (21.5-by-11.5-cm) loaf pan and dust with flour.

In a bowl, stir together the flours, baking powder, baking soda, ginger, and salt. Set aside. In another bowl, whisk together the milk, honey, olive oil, and egg. Stir in the spinach, nuts, and cheese. Add to the dry ingredients and stir just until blended.

Pour and scrape the batter into the prepared pan and spread evenly. Bake until a thin wooden skewer inserted into the center of the loaf comes out clean, about 55 minutes. Let cool in the pan for 10 minutes, then turn out onto a wire rack to cool completely.

Makes 1 medium loaf

Whole-Wheat Bulgur Bread

Bulgur is cracked wheat, and although the bits are quite hard and crunchy, soaking them briefly softens them. It adds a unique flavor to this whole-wheat loaf. Try it with Tomato-Basil Butter (page 313).

In a small bowl, stir together the bulgur and boiling water. Let the mixture stand for about 30 minutes, then fluff the grains with a fork.

Meanwhile, preheat the oven to 350°F (180°C). Grease a 9-by-5-inch (23-by-13-cm) loaf pan and dust with flour.

In a bowl, stir together the flours, baking powder, salt, and brown sugar and set aside. In another bowl, whisk together the milk, eggs, and melted shortening until smooth. Stir in the bulgur and the pecans. Add to the combined dry ingredients and stir just until blended.

Pour and scrape the batter into the prepared pan and spread evenly. Bake until a thin wooden skewer inserted into the center of the loaf comes out clean, about 1 hour. Allow to cool in the pan for 10 minutes, then turn out onto a wire rack to cool completely.

Makes 1 large loaf

1/2 cup (3 oz/90 g) bulgur

3/4 cup (6 fl oz/180 ml) boiling water

1 1/2 cups (7 1/2 oz/235 g) whole-wheat (wholemeal) flour

1/2 cup (2 1/2 oz/75 g) all-purpose (plain) flour, plus extra for dusting

1 tablespoon baking powder

1 teaspoon salt

1/4 cup (2 oz/60 g) firmly packed brown sugar

1 1/2 cups (12 fl oz/375 ml) milk

2 eggs

1/3 cup (3 oz/80 g) vegetable shortening, melted, plus extra for greasing

1/2 cup (2 oz/60 g) chopped pecans, toasted (page 326)

Herbed Cheese and Beer Bread

Beer gives bread a yeasty flavor and aroma, even when there is no active yeast added. With no milk or eggs, this is also a very easy loaf to make. It is good with all manner of soups and salads, and, thinly sliced, makes great ham-and-cheese sandwiches.

Preheat the oven to 375°F (190°C). Grease a 9-by-5-inch (23-by-13-cm) loaf pan and dust with flour.

In a bowl, stir together the flour, sugar, baking powder, baking soda, salt, and sage. Stir in the beer and cheese until completely blended.

Pour and scrape the batter into the prepared pan and spread evenly. Bake until a thin wooden skewer inserted into the center of the loaf comes out clean, about 50 minutes. Let cool in the pan for 10 minutes, then turn out onto a wire rack to cool completely.

Makes 1 large loaf

Unsalted butter for greasing

2½ cups (12½ oz/390 g) all-purpose (plain) flour, plus extra for dusting

2 tablespoons sugar

1 tablespoon baking powder

1½ teaspoons baking soda (bicarbonate of soda)

1 teaspoon salt

1 tablespoon chopped fresh sage or 1½ teaspoons dried sage

1½ cups (12 fl oz/375 ml) beer, freshly opened

1 cup (4 oz/125 g) finely grated Cheddar cheese

Irish Soda Bread

Irish wheat flour is very soft; adding rolled oats and bran to the harder American wheat flour helps to approximate the correct texture for this traditional bread of Ireland. It is best served warm, just after baking.

2¼ cups (11½ oz/360 g) unbleached bread flour, plus extra for dusting

½ cup (1½ oz/45 g) old-fashioned rolled oats

¼ cup (½ oz/15 g) wheat bran

1½ teaspoons baking soda (bicarbonate of soda)

1 teaspoon salt

¼ cup (2 oz/60 g) cold unsalted butter, cut into small pieces

1½ cups (12 oz/375 g) plain low-fat yogurt

Place a baking sheet in the oven and preheat to 425°F (220°C).

In a large bowl, combine the flour, oats, bran, baking soda, and salt. Add the butter and rub it in with your fingertips until the mixture resembles coarse meal. Add the yogurt and stir to blend as evenly as possible, forming a rough ball. (The dough will start rising as soon as the baking soda comes in contact with the yogurt, so work quickly to mix and form the dough and bake at once.)

Turn out the dough onto a lightly floured work surface and knead gently for about 30 seconds, dusting with just enough flour to avoid sticking. The dough should feel quite soft to the touch.

Sprinkle a little flour on a clean work surface and set the ball of dough on it. Flatten slightly into a 7-inch (18-cm) dome and sprinkle with flour, spreading it lightly over the surface with your fingertips. Using a sharp knife, cut a shallow **X** from one side of the loaf to the other. Using a large spatula, transfer the loaf to the preheated baking sheet and bake until well risen, brown, crusty, and the loaf sounds hollow when tapped on the bottom, 30–35 minutes. Transfer the loaf to a wire rack to cool. Since soda bread is best fresh, freeze what will not be used immediately.

Makes one 1 ¼-lb (625-g) loaf

Buckwheat Kasha Bread

Buckwheat flour imparts a dark, earthy character and a unique, claylike aroma to this bread. Kasha, roasted buckwheat groats, is milled from the same seed as the flour, but it is more coarsely ground.

In a small bowl, stir together the kasha and boiling water. Let stand for 15 minutes.

Preheat the oven to 350°F (180°C). Grease an 8 1/2-by-4 1/2-inch (21.5-by-11.5-cm) loaf pan and dust with flour.

In a bowl, stir together the flours, brown sugar, baking powder, baking soda, and salt. Set aside. In another bowl, whisk together the buttermilk, egg, and oil until smooth. Stir in the nuts and the kasha. Add to the combined dry ingredients and stir just until blended.

Pour and scrape the batter into the prepared pan and spread evenly. Bake until a thin wooden skewer inserted into the center of the loaf comes out clean, about 1 hour. Allow to cool in the pan for 10 minutes, then turn out onto a wire rack to cool completely.

Makes 1 medium loaf

1/4 cup (2 oz/50 g) kasha

1/3 cup (3 fl oz/80 ml) boiling water

1 cup (5 oz/155 g) buckwheat flour

1 cup (4 oz/125 g) all-purpose (plain) flour, plus extra for dusting

1/3 cup (2 1/2 oz/75 g) firmly packed brown sugar

1 teaspoon baking powder

1 teaspoon baking soda (bicarbonate of soda)

1/2 teaspoon salt

1 cup (8 fl oz/250 ml) buttermilk

1 egg

1/4 cup (2 fl oz/60 ml) canola oil or olive oil

1/2 cup (2 oz/60 g) chopped hazelnuts (filberts) or walnuts

Nine-Grain Bread

Nine-grain cereal usually contains cracked rye, barley, rice, corn, oats, millet, flax, soy, and triticale. It is coarse and earthy and valued for its fiber and nutrients. Look for it in health-food stores or well-stocked grocery stores.

½ cup (3 oz/90 g) 9-grain cereal

¾ cup (6 fl oz/180 ml) boiling water

1¾ cups (9 oz/280 g) whole-wheat (wholemeal) flour, plus extra for dusting

½ cup (2 oz/60 g) cake (soft-wheat) flour

2 teaspoons baking powder

1 teaspoon baking soda (bicarbonate of soda)

1 teaspoon salt

1½ cups (12 fl oz/375 ml) buttermilk

⅓ cup (4 oz/125 g) honey

⅓ cup (3 fl oz/80 ml) canola oil, plus extra for greasing

1 egg

In a small bowl, stir together the cereal and boiling water. Let stand for 20 minutes, then drain off any remaining water.

Meanwhile, preheat the oven to 350°F (180°C). Grease a 9-by-5-inch (23-by-13-cm) loaf pan and dust with flour.

In a bowl, stir together the flours, baking powder, baking soda, and salt. Set aside. In another bowl, whisk together the buttermilk, honey, oil, and egg until smooth. Stir in the cereal. Add to the combined dry ingredients and stir just until blended.

Pour and scrape the batter into the prepared pan and spread evenly. Bake until a thin wooden skewer inserted into the center of the loaf comes out clean, about 1 hour. Allow to cool in the pan for 10 minutes, then turn out onto a wire rack to cool completely.

Makes 1 large loaf

Oat-Flour Bread

Oat flour, also called oatmeal flour, is simply whole oats ground to a powder. It lends this bread the subtle taste of oatmeal and a sturdy, chewy character. The loaf is crumbly when warm, and will cut more easily at room temperature.

Preheat the oven to 375°F (190°C). Grease a 8 1/2-by-4 1/2-inch (21.5-by-11.5-cm) loaf pan and dust with flour.

In a bowl, stir together the flours, brown sugar, baking powder, baking soda, and salt. Set aside. In another bowl, whisk together the buttermilk, egg, and olive oil until smooth. Stir in the raisins and nuts. Add to the combined dry ingredients and stir just until blended.

Pour and scrape the batter into the prepared pan and spread evenly. Bake until a thin wooden skewer inserted into the center of the loaf comes out clean, about 50 minutes. Let cool in the pan for 10 minutes, then turn out onto a wire rack to cool completely.

Makes 1 medium loaf

1 cup (5 oz/155 g) all-purpose (plain) flour, plus extra for dusting

1 cup (5 oz/155 g) oat flour

1/4 cup (2 oz/60 g) firmly packed brown sugar

2 teaspoons baking powder

1/2 teaspoon baking soda (bicarbonate of soda)

1/2 teaspoon salt

1 cup (8 fl oz/250 ml) buttermilk

1 egg

1/4 cup (2 fl oz/60 ml) olive oil, plus extra for greasing

1/4 cup (1 1/2 oz/45 g) raisins

1/4 cup (1 oz/30 g) chopped walnuts or almonds

Beaten Biscuits

A century or more ago, the dough for these rustic biscuits was actually beaten with a hammer, developing the flour's gluten to produce very crisp, flaky results. Today, the action of a food processor's metal blades yields the same result.

Unsalted butter, at room temperature, for greasing

2 cups (10 oz/315 g) all-purpose (plain) flour

1 tablespoon baking powder

1 teaspoon sugar

1/2 teaspoon salt

1/2 cup (4 oz/125 g) cold unsalted butter, cut into 1/2-inch (12-mm) pieces

3/4 cup (6 fl oz/180 ml) cold whole or low-fat milk

Preheat the oven to 425°F (220°C). Lightly grease 2 baking sheets.

In a food processor fitted with the metal blade, combine the flour, baking powder, sugar, and salt. Pulse several times to combine. Add the butter and pulse again several times until the mixture resembles coarse crumbs. With the motor running, add the milk; continue processing just until the dough forms a ball.

Turn out the dough onto a lightly floured work surface and knead gently a few times. Pat it out to an even thickness of about 1/2 inch (12 mm). Using a round biscuit cutter 2 inches (5 cm) in diameter, cut out the biscuits. Arrange them evenly spaced on the prepared baking sheets.

Bake the biscuits until they are golden brown, 15–20 minutes. Serve hot.

Makes about 24 biscuits

Yeast Breads

Sticky Buns

In a large bowl or the bowl of an electric stand mixer, combine 1 1/2 cups (7 1/2 oz/235 g) of the flour, the granulated sugar, salt, and yeast. In a saucepan over low heat, combine the milk, 1/2 cup (4 fl oz/125 ml) water, and 1/4 cup (2 oz/60 g) of the butter and heat to lukewarm (110°F/43°C). Gradually beat the milk mixture into the flour mixture. Beat in the eggs, then gradually stir in 2 1/2 cups (12 1/2 oz/390 g) more flour to make a soft dough that holds its shape.

Knead by hand or with a dough hook, adding flour as needed. Knead by hand until smooth and elastic, about 10 minutes; knead by hook until the dough is not sticky and pulls cleanly from the bowl sides, 6–7 minutes. Form the dough into a ball and place in a clean, greased bowl, turning to coat all sides. Cover and let rise in a warm place until doubled, 1 1/4–1 3/4 hours.

Turn out the dough onto a lightly floured work surface. Cut in half. Using a rolling pin, roll out each half into an 8-by-15-inch (20-by-37.5-cm) rectangle. Spread the rectangles with 1/4 cup of the remaining butter, dividing it equally. In a bowl, mix 1/2 cup (3 1/2 oz/110 g) of the brown sugar, the cinnamon, and the raisins, and sprinkle half of it over the dough pieces. Starting at a long side, roll up tightly and pinch the seams to seal (page 319). Cut each log crosswise into 10 equal slices.

Butter one 9-inch (23-cm) round and one 8-inch (20 cm) square cake pan. Add the remaining 1/2 cup brown sugar and 1/4 cup butter to the remaining brown sugar mixture; stir well. Toss in the pecans and sprinkle over the pan bottoms. Place 9 dough slices, cut sides down and almost touching, in the square pan. Place 11 dough slices in the round pan. Cover with a kitchen towel and let rise until doubled, 60–75 minutes. Preheat the oven to 350°F (180°C). Uncover the loaves and bake until golden brown, 30–35 minutes. Invert the pans and serve warm.

Makes 2 pull-apart loaves, about 1 1/2 lb (750 g) each

4 1/2–5 cups (22 1/2–25 oz/700–780 g) unbleached bread flour

1/2 cup (4 oz/125 g) granulated sugar

1 teaspoon salt

1 package (2 1/4 teaspoons) quick-rise yeast

1/2 cup (4 fl oz/125 ml) milk

3/4 cup (6 oz/185 g) unsalted butter, at room temperature

2 eggs, at room temperature

1 cup (7 oz/220 g) firmly packed brown sugar

1 teaspoon ground cinnamon

2/3 cup (4 oz/125 g) raisins

2/3 cup (2 1/2 oz/75 g) coarsely chopped pecans

Hot Cross Buns

1 package (2¼ teaspoons) active dry yeast

3½–4 cups (17½–20 oz/ 545–625 g) unbleached bread flour

1¼ cups (10 fl oz/310 ml) luke-warm milk (110°F/43°C)

1 teaspoon salt

3 tablespoons firmly packed golden brown sugar

½ teaspoon ground nutmeg

½ teaspoon ground cinnamon

¼ teaspoon ground cloves

¼ teaspoon ground allspice

2 eggs, at room temperature

3 tablespoons unsalted butter, at room temperature, cut into small pieces, plus extra for greasing

½ cup (3 oz/90 g) dried currants

½ cup (3 oz/90 g) golden raisins (sultanas)

¼ cup (2 fl oz/60 ml) milk and ½ cup (4 oz/125 g) granulated sugar, heated to bubbling

In a small bowl, whisk the yeast and ½ cup (2½ oz/75 g) of the flour into the luke-warm milk and let stand until bubbles start to rise, about 10 minutes. In a large bowl or the bowl of an electric stand mixer, combine 3 cups (15 oz/470 g) of the flour, the salt, brown sugar, nutmeg, cinnamon, cloves, and allspice. Stir in the yeast mixture. Beat in the eggs, one at a time, then beat in the butter.

Knead by hand or with a dough hook, adding flour as needed. Knead by hand until smooth and elastic, about 10 minutes; knead by hook until dough is not sticky and pulls cleanly from the bowl sides, 6–7 minutes. The dough will be soft.

Form the dough into a ball and place in a clean, greased bowl, turning to coat all sides. Cover with greased plastic wrap and let rise in a warm place until doubled, about 1½–2 hours.

Turn out the dough onto a lightly floured work surface and press flat. Scatter the currants and raisins over the dough. Fold in half, then knead to distribute the fruits. Dust lightly with flour and let rest for 10 minutes.

Grease and flour a baking sheet. On the work surface, roll the dough into a log 9 inches (23 cm) long. Cut crosswise into 18 equal pieces. Knead each piece into a ball. Arrange the balls, well spaced, on the prepared baking sheet. Cover with a clean kitchen towel and let rise until doubled, about 40 minutes.

Preheat the oven to 400°F (200°C). Place a shallow pan of boiling water on the oven floor. Using a sharp knife, slash a cross ½ inch (12 mm) deep on each bun. Bake until golden brown, 15–20 minutes. Transfer the buns to a wire rack and immediately brush with the sugar syrup. Serve slightly warm.

Makes 18 buns

Pandolce Genovese

In the bowl of an electric stand mixer, dissolve 1 teaspoon of the yeast in the luke-warm water. Let stand until bubbles start to rise, about 5 minutes. Add 3 cups (15 oz/470 g) of the flour and stir well. Knead with a dough hook until the dough is no longer sticky and pulls cleanly from the bowl sides, about 5 minutes.

Form the dough into a ball and place in a warmed, greased bowl, turning to coat all sides. Cover with greased plastic wrap and let rise in a warm place until doubled, 50–60 minutes.

Wash and dry the mixer bowl and hook. In the bowl, dissolve the remaining yeast in the milk. Let stand until bubbles start to rise, about 5 minutes. Stir in 2 1/2 cups (12 1/2 oz/390 g) of the flour, the salt, 1/2 cup melted butter, sugar, orange water, vanilla, and aniseeds. Add the risen dough and knead with the hook, adding flour as needed, until smooth and elastic, about 12 minutes. Place in a clean, greased bowl, turning to coat all sides. Cover and let rise until doubled, 1 1/2–2 hours.

Turn out the dough onto a work surface and press flat. Scatter the nuts, raisins, and candied peel over the dough. Roll up like a jelly roll (page 319) and knead briefly to distribute the fruit and nuts evenly. Let rest for 10 minutes.

Grease two 8-inch (20-cm) round cake pans and dust with flour. Cut the dough in half and form 2 balls, stretching the sides down and under (page 319). Place the ball in the center of each prepared pan, cover with greased plastic wrap, and let rise until more than doubled and the dough reaches the pan sides, about 1 1/2 hours. Preheat the oven to 375°F (190°C). Using a sharp knife, slash a large triangle on each loaf.

Bake until dark golden brown, 35–40 minutes. Transfer to a rack, glaze the hot loaves with the 1 tablespoon melted butter, and let cool.

Makes two 1 3/4-lb (875-g) loaves

1 package (2 1/4 teaspoons) quick-rise yeast

1 cup (8 fl oz/250 ml) luke-warm water (110°F/43°C)

5 1/2–6 cups (27 1/2–30 oz/860–940 g) unbleached bread flour

1 cup (8 fl oz/250 ml) luke-warm milk (110°F/43°C)

1 1/2 teaspoons salt

1/2 cup (4 oz/125 g) plus 1 tablespoon unsalted butter, melted and cooled to luke-warm (110°F/43°C)

1/2 cup (4 oz/125 g) sugar

2 tablespoons orange flower water or 2 teaspoons grated orange zest (page 329)

2 teaspoons vanilla extract (essence)

1 teaspoon aniseeds

1/4 cup (1 1/2 oz/45 g) pine nuts, lightly toasted (page 326)

1 cup (6 oz/185 g) golden raisins (sultanas), soaked in 1/4 cup (2 fl oz/60 ml) Marsala wine for 30 minutes, then drained and patted dry

1/2 cup (3 oz/90 g) chopped Candied Lemon or Orange Peel (page 314)

Swedish Cardamom Twist

3½–4 cups (17½–20 oz/ 545–625 g) unbleached bread flour

¼ teaspoon salt

¼ cup (2 oz/60 g) sugar

1 package (2¼ teaspoons) quick-rise yeast

½ cup (4 fl oz/125 ml) milk

¼ cup (2 oz/60 g) unsalted butter

Seeds from 12 cardamom pods, crushed (page 328)

FOR THE FILLING:

¼ cup (2 oz/60 g) unsalted butter, at room temperature, cut into pieces

¼ cup (2 oz/60 g) sugar

¾ teaspoon ground cinnamon

1 egg yolk beaten with 1 teaspoon water

In a large bowl, combine 1 cup (5 oz/155 g) of the flour, the salt, sugar, and yeast. In a saucepan over low heat, combine the milk, butter, ½ cup (4 fl oz/125 ml) water, and the cardamom seeds. Heat to lukewarm (110°F/43°C). Beat the milk mixture into the flour mixture until smooth. Gradually beat in 2½ cups (12½ oz/ 390 g) more flour to make a soft dough that holds its shape.

Knead by hand or with a dough hook, adding flour as needed. Knead by hand until smooth and elastic, about 10 minutes; knead by hook until dough is not sticky and pulls cleanly from the bowl sides, 6–7 minutes. Form the dough into a ball and place in a clean, greased bowl, turning to coat all sides. Cover with greased plastic wrap and let rise in a warm place until doubled, about 1½–2 hours.

Meanwhile, make the filling: In a small bowl, cream together the butter, sugar, and cinnamon.

Turn out the dough onto a floured work surface and press flat. Form into a ball and knead for about 1 minute until smooth and shiny. Let rest for 10 minutes. Using a rolling pin, roll out the dough into a 9-by-12-inch (23-by-30-cm) rectangle. Spread the filling evenly over the dough, leaving a 1-inch (2.5-cm) border on all sides. Starting at the long side, roll up tightly and pinch the seams to seal (page 319). Dust a baking sheet with flour. Place the roll, seam side down, on the prepared baking sheet. Using scissors and cutting at an angle, snip the roll at ½-inch (12-mm) intervals, cutting almost halfway through. With the fingers of both hands, pull and push the snipped sections of dough alternately to the left and right, twisting each section slightly in the process, to expose the spiral inside.

Cover and let rise in a warm place until doubled, about 1 hour.

Preheat the oven to 375°F (190°C). Brush the loaf with the egg-yolk mixture. Bake until golden brown, 25–30 minutes. Transfer to a wire rack to cool.

Makes one 1¾-lb (875-g) loaf

Round Currant Loaf

Lightly spiced and studded with tiny currants, this round bread is excellent toasted and spread with butter for a morning or afternoon treat. If you would like to make more than one loaf at a time, the recipe can easily be doubled.

In a bowl, combine 1 1/2 cups (7 1/2 oz/235 g) of the flour, the sugar, salt, cloves, cinnamon, and yeast. In a saucepan over low heat, combine the milk, 1/2 cup (4 fl oz/125 ml) water, and butter. Heat briefly, stirring often, until lukewarm (110°F/43°C). Stir the milk mixture into the flour mixture, then beat hard with a wooden spoon until smooth, about 2 minutes, scraping down the sides of the bowl occasionally. Add the egg and 1/2 cup (2 1/2 oz/75 g) more flour. Beat with an electric mixer set on high speed, or by hand, until smooth, about 2 minutes. If needed, gradually stir in more flour to make a batter that almost holds its shape. (If it is too stiff, stir in a little warm water.) Cover with greased plastic wrap and let rise in a warm place until doubled, 1–1 1/2 hours.

Grease a 1-qt (1-l) porcelain soufflé dish, tinned steel charlotte mold, or any round 1-qt (1-l) mold. Uncover the bowl and stir the batter to deflate. Stir in the currants. Spoon the batter into the prepared dish and smooth the top with a rubber spatula. Cover with a clean kitchen towel and let rise until the bread reaches the top of the mold, 30–40 minutes.

Preheat the oven to 375°F (190°C).

Uncover the dough and bake until well browned and a dome forms at the top, 30–40 minutes. Unmold the loaf and transfer to a wire rack to cool.

Makes one 1 1/2-lb (750-g) loaf

2–2 1/2 cups (10–12 1/2 oz/ 310–390 g) unbleached bread flour

1/4 cup (2 oz/60 g) sugar

1/2 teaspoon salt

1/4 teaspoon ground cloves

1/4 teaspoon ground cinnamon

1 1/2 teaspoons quick-rise yeast

1/2 cup (4 fl oz/125 ml) milk

2 tablespoons unsalted butter, plus extra for greasing

1 egg, at room temperature

1/2 cup (3 oz/90 g) dried currants or raisins

Honey and Bran Bread

Unlike typical high-fiber loaves, which can be dense and heavy, this bread is quite light in texture and has a delicate, nutty flavor. Serve it alongside a salad with avocados for dinner, or spread with Strawberry Jam Butter (page 315) for a snack.

1 package (2¼ teaspoons) quick-rise yeast

2½ cups (20 fl oz/625 ml) lukewarm water (110°F/43°C)

3 cups (15 oz/470 g) whole-wheat (wholemeal) flour

2–2½ cups (10–12½ oz/ 315–390 g) unbleached bread flour

2 cups (5 oz/155 g) wheat bran

¼ cup (3 oz/90 g) honey

1 tablespoon corn oil

1½ teaspoons salt

1 egg yolk beaten with 1 teaspoon water

In a small bowl, dissolve the yeast in ½ cup (4 fl oz/125 ml) of the lukewarm water and let stand until bubbles start to rise, about 5 minutes. In a large bowl or the bowl of an electric stand mixer, combine the whole-wheat flour, 1 cup (5 oz/155 g) of the bread flour, and the bran. Stir in the remaining 2 cups (16 fl oz/500 ml) lukewarm water, honey, oil, salt, and yeast mixture. Gradually stir in enough of the remaining bread flour to make a soft dough that holds its shape.

Knead by hand or with a dough hook, adding bread flour as needed. Knead by hand until smooth and elastic, about 10 minutes; knead by hook until the dough pulls cleanly from the bowl sides, 6–7 minutes. Form the dough into a ball and place in a clean, greased bowl, turning the dough to coat all sides. Cover with greased plastic wrap and let rise in a warm place until doubled, 45–60 minutes.

Grease two 8½-by-4½-inch (21.5-by-11.5-cm) loaf pans. Turn out the dough onto a lightly floured work surface and press flat. Cut in half. Using a rolling pin, roll out each half into a 12-by-7-inch (30-by-18-cm) rectangle. Starting at a long side, roll up tightly and pinch the seams to seal (page 319). Place in the prepared pans, seam sides down. Cover with a clean kitchen towel and let rise in a warm place until doubled, about 45–60 minutes. Preheat the oven to 375°F (190°C).

Brush the loaves with the egg-yolk mixture. Bake until well browned and a thin wooden skewer inserted into the center of the loaf comes out clean, 30–35 minutes. Transfer the loaves to a wire rack to cool.

Makes two 23-oz (720-g) loaves

Walnut Bread

Scented with walnut oil and studded with chopped walnuts, this easy-to-make batter bread is delicious served in thin slices alongside a selection of gourmet cheeses. Using unsulfured dark molasses will give the bread a more mild flavor.

In a large bowl, combine the whole-wheat flour, 1 cup (5 oz/155 g) of the bread flour, the salt, and yeast. In a small bowl, stir together the warm water, egg, molasses, and walnut oil. Stir the water mixture into the flour mixture. Using and electric mixer set on medium speed, beat until smooth, about 2 minutes. Gradually beat in enough of the remaining bread flour to form a batter that almost holds its shape. (If it is too stiff, stir in a little warm water.) Cover with greased plastic wrap and let rise in a warm place until doubled, 45–60 minutes.

Grease a 1-qt (1-l) tinned steel charlotte mold, porcelain soufflé dish, or any round 1-qt (1-l) mold with walnut oil. Uncover the bowl and stir the batter to deflate. Stir in the walnuts. Spoon the batter into the prepared mold and smooth the top with a rubber spatula. Scatter walnuts evenly over the top, if you like. Cover with a clean kitchen towel and let rise until doubled, 30–45 minutes.

Preheat the oven to 375°F (190°C).

Uncover the dough and bake until golden brown, 30–40 minutes. Unmold the loaf and transfer to a wire rack to cool.

Makes one 1 1/4-lb (625-g) loaf

1 cup (5 oz/155 g) whole-wheat (wholemeal) flour

1³/₄–2 cups (9–10 oz/ 280–315 g) unbleached bread flour

1/2 teaspoon salt

1¹/₂ teaspoons quick-rise yeast

1 cup (8 fl oz/250 ml) warm water (125°F/52°C)

1 egg, at room temperature

1 tablespoon dark molasses

2 tablespoons walnut oil, plus extra for greasing

2 tablespoons chopped walnuts, plus extra for sprinkling (optional)

1 bay leaf

¹/₄ teaspoon mahaleb
(page 326) (optional)

¹/₂ teaspoon ground cinnamon

¹/₂ teaspoon aniseeds

1 teaspoon grated lemon zest
(page 329)

¹/₂ cup (4 fl oz/125 ml) milk

¹/₂ cup (4 oz/125 g) unsalted
butter

3 eggs, beaten

¹/₂ cup (4 oz/125 g) sugar

1 teaspoon salt

1 package (2¹/₄ teaspoons)
quick-rise yeast

6¹/₂–7 cups (32–35 oz/1–1.1 kg)
unbleached bread flour

2 hard-boiled eggs, dyed red

1 egg white beaten with
1 teaspoon water

2 tablespoons sesame seeds

Greek Easter Bread

In a small saucepan, combine the bay leaf, mahaleb (if using), cinnamon, aniseeds, lemon zest, and ¹/₂ cup (4 fl oz/125 ml) water. Bring to a boil, remove from the heat, and let cool to lukewarm (110°F/43°C). Discard the bay leaf. In another saucepan, combine ¹/₂ cup (4 fl oz/125 ml) water, the milk, and the butter and heat to lukewarm (110°F/43°C).

In a large bowl or the bowl of an electric stand mixer, combine the beaten eggs, the milk mixture, and the spice mixture. Stir in the sugar, salt, and yeast. Gradually stir in 5 cups (25 oz/780 g) of the flour to make a soft dough that holds its shape.

Knead by hand or with a dough hook, adding flour as needed. Knead by hand until smooth and elastic, about 15 minutes; knead by hook until the dough is not sticky and pulls cleanly from the bowl sides, 6–7 minutes.

Form the dough into a ball and place in a clean, greased bowl, turning to coat all sides. Cover and let rise in a warm place until doubled, 1 ¹/₂–2 hours.

Turn out the dough onto a lightly floured work surface and press flat. Cut off one-fifth. Cut the larger piece in half and form into 2 rounds each 8 inches (20 cm) in diameter. Cut the small piece into 8 equal pieces and roll each into a rope 12 inches (30 cm) long. Twist pairs of the ropes together. Make an indentation on top of each loaf and place a red egg in each. Crisscross 2 ropes over each egg; secure them under the loaf. Place each loaf on a floured baking sheet, cover with a clean kitchen towel, and let rise until doubled, 60–70 minutes. Preheat the oven to 350°F (180°C).

Uncover the loaves, brush with the egg-white mixture (avoiding the red eggs), and sprinkle with the sesame seeds. Bake until golden brown, 40–45 minutes. Transfer to a wire rack to cool.

Makes two 30-oz (940-g) loaves

Egg Braid

In a large bowl or the bowl of an electric stand mixer, combine 4 cups (20 oz/625 g) of the flour, the salt, and the yeast. In a saucepan over low heat, combine 1 cup (8 fl oz/250 ml) water, the saffron, and the butter. Heat to warm (125°F/52°C). Stir the water mixture into the flour mixture, then beat in the eggs. Gradually stir in enough of the remaining flour to make a soft dough that holds its shape.

Knead by hand or with a dough hook, adding flour as needed. Knead by hand until smooth and elastic, about 10 minutes; knead by hook until the dough is not sticky and pulls cleanly from the bowl sides, about 6–7 minutes.

Turn out the dough onto a lightly floured work surface and press flat. Cut in half and form each half into a ball. Let rest for 5 minutes. Roll each ball into a log about 9 inches (23 cm) long and about 2 1/4 inches (5.5 cm) in diameter. Cut one-third off the end of each log. Cut the larger section of 1 log into three equal pieces, then roll each piece into a rope 12 inches (30 cm) long. Pinch the ropes together at one end. Braid them by alternately twisting the left- and right-hand ropes over the center. Pinch the ends to seal. Cut the smaller section into thirds and repeat to make a thinner braid. Set the small braid on top of the large one. Repeat to form a second loaf. Place the loaves on a baking sheet. Cover with greased plastic wrap and let rise until doubled, 30–40 minutes. Preheat the oven to 400°F (200°C).

Uncover the loaves, brush with the egg-yolk mixture, and sprinkle with the poppy seeds. Bake until well browned and the loaves sound hollow when tapped on the bottoms, 35–45 minutes. Transfer the loaves to a wire rack to cool.

Makes two 18-oz (560-g) loaves

6–6 1/2 cups (30–32 oz/ 940 g–1 kg) unbleached bread flour

2 teaspoons salt

1 package (2 1/4 teaspoons) quick-rise yeast

Large pinch of saffron threads

1/4 cup (2 oz/60 g) unsalted butter

4 eggs, at room temperature

1 egg yolk beaten with 1 teaspoon water

2 teaspoons poppy seeds

Bagels

1 package (2¼ teaspoons) quick-rise yeast

2½–3 cups (12½–15 oz/ 390–470 g) unbleached bread flour

1 cup (8 fl oz/250 ml) luke- warm milk (110°F/43°C)

¼ cup (2 fl oz/60 ml) corn oil, plus extra for greasing

1 teaspoon regular salt

1 egg, separated

1 tablespoon sugar

Poppy seeds, sesame seeds, or coarse salt crystals for sprinkling

In a large bowl or the bowl of an electric stand mixer, combine the yeast and ½ cup (2½ oz/75 g) of the flour. Stir in the milk and let stand until frothy, about 10 minutes. Using a wooden spoon, beat in the oil, the regular salt, the egg yolk, and the sugar. Gradually beat in enough of the remaining flour to make a stiff but workable dough.

Knead by hand or with a dough hook, adding flour as needed. Knead by hand until smooth and elastic, about 10 minutes; knead by hook until the dough is not sticky and pulls cleanly from the bowl sides, 6–7 minutes. Form the dough into a ball and place in a clean, greased bowl, turning to coat all sides. Cover with greased plastic wrap and let rise in a warm place until doubled, 45–60 minutes.

Turn out the dough onto a lightly floured work surface and press flat. Roll into a log about 8 inches (20 cm) long and cut into 16 equal pieces. Cover with a clean kitchen towel. One at a time, form each piece into a ball, then flatten it into a round 2½ inches (6 cm) in diameter. Using the handle of a wooden spoon, make a hole through the center of each round, then gently widen the hole to 1 inch (2.5 cm) in diameter. Place the rounds on the work surface, cover with a clean kitchen towel, and let rise until doubled, about 20 minutes. Preheat the oven to 375°F (190°C). Grease a baking sheet.

In a pot, bring 3 qt (3 l) water to a boil. Reduce the heat to low. Slip 3 bagels at a time into the simmering water. Poach, turning once, for 3 minutes on each side; reform the holes if necessary. Using a slotted spoon, transfer to the prepared sheet.

Lightly beat the egg white and brush over the bagels. Sprinkle with the seeds or coarse salt. Bake until golden brown, about 30 minutes. Transfer the bagels to wire racks to cool.

Makes 16 bagels

English Muffins

If you don't have muffin rings, fold 7-by-12-inch (18-by-30-cm) sheets of aluminum foil in half and then in thirds lengthwise, forming 6 layers in all. Bend into circles 3½ inches (9 cm) in diameter and secure with tape at the top.

Preheat the oven to 250°F (120°C). Pour the flour into a large ovenproof bowl and place it in the oven until warm to the touch, about 10 minutes. Then turn off the oven. Dissolve the yeast in the lukewarm water and let stand until bubbles start to rise, about 5 minutes.

Add the salt and sugar to the warmed flour. Stir in the lukewarm milk, oil, and yeast mixture and beat until smooth, making an almost pourable batter. Cover and let rise in a warm place until doubled, 60–70 minutes.

Place a griddle or 2 heavy frying pans in the cold oven. Turn on the oven to its lowest setting, heat for 5 minutes, then turn off the heat. Remove the griddle or pans and sprinkle with cornmeal. Butter eight 3 ½-inch (9-cm) muffin rings (see note) on the inside and sprinkle with cornmeal, tilting and tapping to coat the bottom and sides evenly. Arrange the rings on the griddle or pans.

Stir the batter to deflate and scoop about ¼ cup (2 fl oz/60 ml) into each ring. Place the muffins in the still barely warm oven and let rise, uncovered, until doubled in size, about 30 minutes.

Set the griddle or pans over medium-low heat. Cook slowly, loosening the muffins with a spatula after about 5 minutes to prevent sticking, until the bottoms are a very pale brown, 8–10 minutes. Gently remove the rings and turn the muffins over. Lightly brown on the second side, about 8 minutes.

Transfer the muffins to a wire rack to cool. Using a fork, split the muffins in half and then toast them.

Makes 8 muffins

3 cups (15 oz/470 g) unbleached bread flour

1½ teaspoons active dry yeast

¾ cup (6 fl oz/180 ml) plus 2 tablespoons lukewarm water (110°F/43°C)

2 teaspoons salt

1 teaspoon sugar

¾ cup (6 fl oz/180 ml) plus 2 tablespoons lukewarm milk (110°F/43°C)

2 tablespoons corn oil

Cornmeal for sprinkling

French Baguettes

The dough for these traditional loaves can be quite soft. If you do not have a mixer, lift and turn the dough with a pastry scraper until can be kneaded by hand. This recipe makes 4 loaves; leftovers will keep for several days, if tightly covered.

5–5½ cups (25–27½ oz/ 780–855 g) unbleached bread flour

2 teaspoons salt

1 package (2¼ teaspoons) quick-rise yeast

2 cups (16 fl oz/500 ml) luke- warm water (110°F/43°C)

Boiling water, as needed

Canola oil for greasing

Cornmeal for sprinkling

1 egg white (page 324) beaten with a pinch of salt

In the bowl of an electric stand mixer, combine 4 cups (20 oz/625 g) of the flour, the salt, yeast, and lukewarm water. Knead with the dough hook until the dough is elastic and pulls cleanly from the bowl sides, about 10 minutes. The dough will be very soft. Turn out onto a lightly floured surface and knead for 1 minute. Form a ball and place in a clean, lightly greased bowl. Dust the dough lightly with flour, cover with greased plastic wrap, and let rise until doubled, 45–60 minutes.

Turn the dough out onto a lightly floured work surface. Press flat, knead for a few seconds, and return to the bowl. Cover with greased plastic wrap and let rise again until doubled, 20–30 minutes.

Line each of 2 double baguette pans (4 molds total), each 18 inches (45 cm) long and 6 inches (15 cm) wide, with a clean kitchen towel and sprinkle with flour, rubbing it into the fabric. Turn out the dough onto a lightly floured work surface and press flat. Cut into 4 equal pieces, knead into balls, and let rest for 5 minutes. Press each ball flat and fold into thirds. Roll each into a rope 16 inches (40 cm) long with tapered ends. Place in the towel-lined pans. Cover with a clean kitchen towel and let rise until doubled, about 20 minutes. Preheat the oven to 450°F (230°C).

Place a shallow pan of boiling water on the floor of the preheated oven. Pull the pans out from under the dough-filled towels. Grease the pans and sprinkle with cornmeal. One at a time, flip the loaves into the pans, underside up. Brush with the egg-white mixture. Using a sharp knife, make three ¼-inch (6 mm) deep diagonal slashes on each loaf. Bake until brown and crusty, 20–25 minutes. Transfer to a wire rack to cool. Serve warm or at room temperature.

Makes four ½-lb (250-g) baguettes

German Pumpernickel Bread

In a bowl, whisk together the rye flour, bran, and 2 cups (10 oz/315 g) of the bread flour. In a large bowl or the bowl of an electric stand mixer, combine the yeast, $^{1}/_{2}$ cup (2 oz/60 g) of the flour mixture, and the lukewarm water; let stand until bubbles start to rise, about 10 minutes. Stir in the molasses, oil, salt and yogurt. Gradually stir in 4 cups (16 oz/500 g) of the remaining flour mixture to make a stiff but workable dough. The dough will be sticky.

Knead by hand or with a dough hook, adding the remaining flour mixture and more bread flour as needed. Knead by hand until smooth and elastic, about 15 minutes; knead by hook until the dough is not sticky and pulls cleanly from the bowl sides, about 10 minutes. The dough will be slightly heavy. Form the dough into a ball and place in a clean, greased bowl, turning to coat all sides. Cover with greased plastic wrap and let rise in a warm place until doubled, 60–75 minutes.

Turn out the dough onto a lightly floured work surface and press flat. Cut in half, knead briefly, and form each half into a ball, stretching the sides down and under (page 319). Sprinkle a baking sheet with cornmeal and place the loaves on it. Cover with a clean kitchen towel and let rise in a warm place until doubled, 45–60 minutes. Preheat the oven to 350°F (180°C).

Uncover and bake until browned and the loaves sound hollow when tapped on the bottoms, about 1 hour. Transfer to a wire rack to cool.

Makes two 21-oz (655-g) loaves

3 cups (9 oz/280 g) rye flour

1 cup (2$^{1}/_{2}$ oz/75 g) wheat bran

2$^{1}/_{2}$–3 cups (12$^{1}/_{2}$–15 oz/ 390–470 g) unbleached bread flour

1 package (2$^{1}/_{4}$ teaspoons) quick-rise yeast

$^{1}/_{2}$ cup (4 fl oz/125 ml) luke-warm water (110°F/43°C)

2 tablespoons dark or light molasses

3 tablespoons corn oil

2 teaspoons salt

2 cups (1 lb/500 g) plain low-fat yogurt, warmed to 110°F (43°C)

Cornmeal for sprinkling

Russian-Style Black Bread

In a bowl, whisk together the rye flour and 2 3/4 cups (14 oz/440 g) of the bread flour. In another bowl, combine 1 cup (4 oz/125 g) of the flour mixture, the sugar, salt, bran, cocoa powder, caraway seeds, fennel seeds, and yeast.

In a saucepan over low heat, combine 1 1/2 cups (12 fl oz/375 ml) water, the vinegar, molasses, and butter. Heat to lukewarm (110°F/43°C); the butter does not need to be entirely melted. Stir into the bran mixture. Add 1/2 cup (2 oz/60 g) of the flour mixture and beat until smooth. Gradually stir in the remaining flour mixture to make a stiff dough.

Knead until smooth and elastic, about 15 minutes, adding bread flour as needed. The dough will be heavy and slightly sticky. Form the dough into a ball and place in a clean, greased bowl, turning to coat all sides. Cover with greased plastic wrap and let rise in a warm place until doubled, 45–60 minutes.

Grease two 8-inch (20-cm) round cake pans. Turn out the dough onto a floured work surface and press flat. Knead for 1 minute. Cut in half and form each half into a 6-inch (15-cm) round, stretching the sides down and under (page 319). Place in the prepared pans. Cover with a clean kitchen towel and let rise until doubled, 40–45 minutes.

Preheat the oven to 350°F (180°C). Bake the loaves for 45 minutes. Put the cornstarch mixture in a saucepan over medium heat and cook, stirring, until it boils, turns clear, and thickens, about 1 minute. Remove the loaves from the oven, then remove from the pans. Brush with the cornstarch mixture and return to the oven, placing the loaves directly on the rack. Bake until the glaze sets and the loaves are browned and sound hollow when tapped on the bottoms, about 3 minutes longer. Transfer to a wire rack to cool.

Makes two 1-lb (500-g) loaves

2 1/4 cups (6 1/2 oz/200 g) rye flour

2 3/4–3 1/4 cups (14–16 1/2 oz/ 440–515 g) unbleached bread flour

1 teaspoon sugar

1 teaspoon salt

3/4 cup (2 oz/60 g) wheat bran

2 tablespoons unsweetened cocoa powder

1 1/2 teaspoons caraway seeds, crushed

1 teaspoon fennel seeds, crushed

1 package (2 1/4 teaspoons) quick-rise yeast

1 tablespoon red wine vinegar

3 tablespoons dark molasses

1/4 cup (2 oz/60 g) unsalted butter, plus extra for greasing

1 teaspoon cornstarch (cornflour) dissolved in 1/2 cup (4 fl oz/125 ml) water

Cornish Saffron Bread

This slightly sweet bread of England's West Country, stuffed with raisins, currants, and bits of Candied Lemon Peel (page 314), is often served with tea. If available use saffron threads instead of saffron powder for the best flavor.

1/4 teaspoon saffron threads

1/3 cup (3 fl oz/80 ml) boiling water

1 package (2 1/4 teaspoons) quick-rise yeast

6 tablespoons (3 oz/90 g) unsalted butter, plus extra for greasing

2/3 cup (5 fl oz/160 ml) milk

3–3 1/2 cups (15–17 1/2 oz/ 470–545 g) unbleached bread flour

3 tablespoons sugar

1 teaspoon salt

1/2 teaspoon ground nutmeg

1/2 cup (3 oz/90 g) golden raisins (sultanas)

1/2 cup (3 oz/90 g) dried currants

1/4 cup (1 1/2 oz/45 g) chopped Candied Lemon Peel (page 314)

1 egg yolk mixed with 1 teaspoon water

Crumble the saffron into a bowl and add the boiling water. Let cool for 15 minutes. Add the yeast and stir to dissolve. In a saucepan over low heat, combine the butter and milk. Heat until the butter melts, then let cool to lukewarm (110°F/43°C).

In a large bowl or the bowl of an electric stand mixer, combine 2 1/2 cups (12 1/2 oz/ 390 g) of the flour, the sugar, salt, and nutmeg. Stir in the saffron mixture and the butter mixture. Stir in enough of the remaining flour to make a soft dough.

Knead by hand or with a dough hook, adding flour as needed. Knead by hand until smooth and elastic, about 10 minutes; knead by hook until the dough is not sticky and pulls cleanly from the bowl sides, 6–7 minutes. Form the dough into a ball and place in a clean, greased bowl, turning to coat all sides. Cover with greased plastic wrap and let rise in a warm place until doubled, 60–75 minutes.

Grease two 8 1/2-by-4 1/2-inch (21.5-by-11.5-cm) loaf pans. Turn out the dough onto a lightly floured work surface and press flat. Scatter the raisins, currants, and lemon peel over the dough. Roll up like a jelly roll (page 319) and knead to distribute the fruits. Use a rolling pin to roll out each half into a 12-by-7-inch (30-by-18-cm) rectangle. Starting at a short side, roll each rectangle and pinch the seams to seal. Place in the prepared pans, seam sides down. Cover with a clean kitchen towel and let rise until doubled, about 1 hour. Preheat the oven to 400°F (200°C).

Brush the loaves with the egg-yolk mixture. Bake for 10 minutes, then reduce the oven temperature to 375°F (190°C) and bake until well browned and the loaves sound hollow when tapped on the bottoms, 25–30 minutes longer. Transfer to a wire rack to cool.

Makes two 22-oz (690-g) loaves

Old English Oatmeal Bread

These golden brown, oat-sprinkled round loaves are based on a traditional old English country recipe. Sprinkling the oats on top of the loaves makes them even more rustic and adds a deliciously satisfying texture to every bite.

Place the oats in a large bowl or the bowl of an electric stand mixer. In a saucepan over low heat, combine the milk, 3/4 cup (6 fl oz/180 ml) water, and the butter and bring to a boil. Pour over the oats and let stand until lukewarm (110°F/43°C), about 30 minutes; stir often to hasten cooling. Stir in the molasses, 1 1/2 cups (7 1/2 oz/ 235 g) of the flour, the salt, and the yeast. Gradually stir in enough of the remaining flour to make a soft dough that holds its shape.

Knead by hand or with a dough hook, adding flour as needed. Knead by hand until smooth and elastic, about 10 minutes; knead by hook until the dough is not sticky and pulls cleanly from the bowl sides, 6–7 minutes.

Form the dough into a ball and place in a clean, greased bowl, turning to coat all sides. Cover with greased plastic wrap and let rise in a warm place until doubled, 45–60 minutes.

Dust a baking sheet with flour. Turn out the dough onto a lightly floured work surface and press flat. Cut in half, knead briefly, and form each half into a ball, stretching the sides down and under (page 319). Place well apart on the prepared baking sheet and flatten slightly. Cover with a clean kitchen towel and let rise until doubled, 20–30 minutes. Preheat the oven to 425°F (220°C).

Uncover the loaves, brush with the egg-yolk mixture and sprinkle with oats. Bake until golden brown and the loaves sound hollow when tapped on the bottoms, 25–30 minutes. Unmold the loaves and transfer to a wire rack to cool.

Makes two 13-oz (410-g) loaves

1 cup (3 oz/90 g) old-fashioned rolled oats, plus extra for sprinkling

3/4 cup (6 fl oz/180 ml) milk

1/4 cup (2 oz/60 g) unsalted butter

1 tablespoon dark molasses

2–2 1/2 cups (10–12 1/2 oz/ 315–390 g) unbleached bread flour

1 teaspoon salt

1 package (2 1/2 teaspoons) quick-rise yeast

1 egg yolk mixed with 1 teaspoon water

New Mexico Pueblo Bread

New Mexico's Pueblo Indians bake these wonderfully crusty loaves for festivals and holy days. The unique shape of the bread is traditional and makes for easy serving because the wedges pull apart so easily.

5–5½ cups (25–27 oz/
780–860 g) all-purpose
(plain) flour

8 tablespoons (4 oz/125 g)
unsalted butter, melted and
cooled, plus extra for greasing

3 tablespoons sugar

1 tablespoon active dry yeast

2 teaspoons salt

1½ cups (12 fl oz/375 ml) warm
water (125°F/52°C)

In a large bowl or the bowl of an electric stand mixer, combine 1 ½ cups (7 ½ oz/ 235 g) of the flour, 2 tablespoons of the butter, the sugar, yeast, and salt. Add the warm water and beat until well mixed. Beat in 3–3 ½ cups (15–17 ½ oz/470–545 g) of the remaining flour to make a dough that is semisoft and no longer sticky.

Knead by hand or with a dough hook, adding flour as needed. Knead by hand until smooth and elastic, about 10 minutes; knead by hook until the dough is not sticky and pulls cleanly from the bowl sides, 6–7 minutes. Form the dough into a ball and place in a clean bowl greased with 2 tablespoons of the butter, turning to coat all sides. Cover with greased plastic wrap and let rise in a warm place until doubled, about 2 hours.

Turn out the dough onto a lightly floured work surface. Knead until smooth, 2–3 minutes. Divide the dough in half. Roll out each half into a round 8 inches (20 cm) in diameter. Brush each round with 2 tablespoons of the butter. Fold each round in half and press gently to close. Grease a baking sheet with butter and place the loaves on it. Using a sharp knife, make 2 equidistant cuts crosswise, in a slight V, if desired, through each loaf, cutting only two-thirds of the way to the back of the dough. Cover with a clean kitchen towel and let rise until doubled, about 1 hour.

Preheat the oven to 375°F (190°C). Bake until the loaves are golden brown and sound hollow when tapped on the bottoms, about 45 minutes. Let cool briefly on a wire rack, then pull apart at each section to serve.

Makes 2 loaves

Portuguese Corn Bread

Unlike American corn bread, which is traditionally cut into squares, the Portuguese variety is baked in large, round loaves. It tastes delicious torn into pieces, spread with butter, and served alongside a hearty soup.

In a large bowl or the bowl of an electric stand mixer, combine ¹/₂ cup (2 ¹/₂ oz/75 g) of the cornmeal, the salt, and the boiling water. Stir until smooth. Stir in the corn oil and let cool to lukewarm (110°F/43°C). Stir in the remaining ¹/₂ cup (2 ¹/₂ oz/ 75 g) cornmeal, ¹/₂ cup (2 ¹/₂ oz/75 g) of the flour, and the yeast. Cover with greased plastic wrap and let rise in a warm place until doubled, 30–45 minutes.

Stir to deflate the dough and gradually stir in 1 cup (5 oz/155 g) more flour.

Knead by hand or with a dough hook, adding flour as needed. Knead by hand until smooth and elastic, about 10 minutes; knead by hook until the dough is not sticky and easily pulls cleanly from the bowl sides, 6–7 minutes. The dough should be firm but not stiff.

Form the dough into a ball, stretching the sides down and under (page 319). Sprinkle a baking sheet with cornmeal and place the dough on it. Cover loosely with greased plastic wrap and let rise until doubled, 45–60 minutes.

Preheat the oven to 375°F (190°C).

Uncover the loaf and place the baking sheet in the oven. Using a spray bottle, spritz the oven floor and sides with water (this creates steam to help form a crisp crust). Bake until golden brown and the loaf sounds hollow when tapped on the bottom, 35–45 minutes. Transfer the loaf to a wire rack to cool.

Makes one 15-oz (470-g) loaf

1 cup (5 oz/155 g) yellow corn-meal, plus extra for sprinkling

1 teaspoon salt

1 cup (8 fl oz/250 ml) boiling water

1 tablespoon corn oil

1¹/₂–2 cups (7¹/₂–10 oz/ 235–315 g) unbleached bread flour

1¹/₂ teaspoons quick-rise yeast

Scottish Floury Baps

A traditional breakfast bread in Scotland, these soft, oval rolls always delight visitors to that country. Serve warm with butter and Dundee marmalade, heather honey, or any variety of jam and honey. Try it with Strawberry Jam (page 315).

3½–4 cups (17½–20 oz/545–625 g) unbleached bread flour, plus extra for dusting

1 teaspoon salt

1 package (2¼ teaspoons) quick-rise yeast

1 cup (8 fl oz/250 ml) milk

¼ cup (2 oz/60 g) unsalted butter

In a large bowl or the bowl of an electric stand mixer, combine 3 cups (15 oz/470 g) of the flour, the salt, and the yeast. In a saucepan over low heat, combine the milk and butter. Heat briefly, stirring often, until warm (125°F/52°C). Make a well in the center of the flour mixture, pour in the milk mixture, and stir until combined.

Knead by hand or with a dough hook, adding flour as needed. Knead by hand until smooth and elastic, about 10 minutes; knead by hook until the dough is not sticky and pulls cleanly from the bowl sides, 6–7 minutes.

Form the dough into a ball and place in a clean, greased bowl, turning to coat all sides. Cover with greased plastic wrap and let rise in a warm place until doubled, 45–60 minutes.

Turn out the dough onto a lightly floured work surface and press flat. Let rest for 5 minutes. Roll into a log 10 inches (25 cm) long, then cut into 10 equal pieces. Knead each piece into a ball, then form each ball into an oval ½ inch (12 mm) thick. Lightly dust a baking sheet with flour and place the rolls on it, spaced well apart. Cover loosely a clean kitchen towel and let rise until doubled, about 20 minutes. Preheat the oven to 425°F (220°C).

Uncover the rolls, press each one gently in the center with 3 fingers to prevent the tops from splitting, then lightly dust flour over the tops. Bake until well risen and lightly browned, 15–18 minutes. Serve warm.

Makes 10 rolls

Rye Bread

Wonderful for making a variety of savory, deli-style sandwiches, this robust, dark bread is also good spread with cream cheese and topped with lox, dill, red onion, and a squeeze of lemon for a weekend brunch.

2½ cups (7½ oz/235 g) rye flour

1–1½ cups (5–7½ oz/155–235 g) unbleached bread flour

1 cup (5 oz/155 g) whole-wheat (wholemeal) flour

2 teaspoons salt

2 teaspoons caraway seeds

1 package (2¼ teaspoons) quick-rise yeast

1½ cups (12 fl oz/375 ml) warm water (125°F/52°C)

1 tablespoon canola oil

⅓ cup (3 fl oz/80 ml) dark molasses

Cornmeal for sprinkling

1 egg yolk beaten with 1 teaspoon water

In a large bowl or the bowl of an electric stand mixer, combine the rye flour, ¾ cup (4 oz/125 g) of the bread flour, and the whole-wheat flour. Add the salt, caraway seeds, and yeast and mix well. In another bowl, stir together the warm water, oil, and molasses. Pour into the flour mixture and stir to make a soft dough.

Knead by hand or with a dough hook, adding bread flour as needed. Knead by hand until smooth and elastic, about 15 minutes; knead by hook until the dough is not sticky and pulls cleanly from the bowl sides, about 10 minutes. The dough will be heavy. Form the dough into a ball and place in a clean, greased bowl, turning to coat all sides. Cover with greased plastic wrap and let rise in a warm place until doubled, 1–1½ hours.

Turn out the dough onto a lightly floured work surface and press flat. Cut in half and form each half into a ball, stretching the sides down and under (page 319). Let rest for 5 minutes. Flatten each ball slightly and roll into a tapered log about 10 inches (25 cm) long. Sprinkle a baking sheet with cornmeal and place the loaves on it. Cover with a clean kitchen towel and let rise until doubled, 20–30 minutes. Preheat the oven to 375°F (190°C).

Brush the loaves with the egg-yolk mixture. Bake until browned and the loaves sound hollow when tapped on the bottoms, 25–30 minutes. Transfer to a wire rack to cool completely.

Makes two 18-oz (560-g) loaves

Scandinavian Beer Bread

This glossy, richly flavored rye bread is particularly good for open-faced sandwiches and as an accompaniment to soups and stews. Use a favorite stout beer for this recipe; one of high-quality will enhance the flavor.

In a large bowl, dissolve the yeast into the lukewarm water and let stand until bubbles start to rise, about 5 minutes. Stir in the beer, salt, rye flour, and 1 cup (5 oz/155 g) of the bread flour. Cover with a clean kitchen towel and let stand in a warm place for 1 hour.

In a small saucepan over low heat, melt the butter. Stir in the corn syrup and let cool to lukewarm (110°F/43°C), then add to the flour mixture. Gradually stir in 1 1/2 cups (7 1/2 oz/235 g) more bread flour to make a stiff but workable dough. Cover with greased plastic wrap and let rest for 30 minutes.

Knead by hand or with a dough hook, adding bread flour as needed. Knead by hand until smooth and elastic, about 15 minutes; knead by hook until the dough is not sticky and pulls cleanly from the bowl sides, about 10 minutes. Form the dough into a ball and place in a clean, greased bowl, turning to coat all sides. Cover with greased plastic wrap and let rise until doubled, 60–70 minutes.

Dust a baking sheet with flour. Turn out the dough onto a lightly floured work surface and press flat. Cut in half and form each half into a ball, stretching the sides down and under (page 319), then flatten slightly. Place on the prepared baking sheet. Cover with a clean kitchen towel and let rise until doubled, 45–60 minutes.

Preheat the oven to 350°F (180°C). Brush the loaves with the egg-white mixture. Bake until browned and the loaves sound hollow when tapped on the bottoms, 35–40 minutes. Wrap in kitchen towels to promote a soft crust and place on a wire rack to cool.

Makes two 14-oz (440-g) loaves

1 package (2¹/₄ teaspoons) active dry yeast

³/₄ cup (6 fl oz/180 ml) lukewarm water (110°F/43°C)

1 cup (8 fl oz/250 ml) dark beer, warmed to 110°F (43°C)

1 teaspoon salt

2 cups (6 oz/185 g) rye flour

3–3¹/₃ cups (15–17¹/₂ oz/ 470–545 g) unbleached bread flour

¹/₄ cup (2 oz/60 g) unsalted butter

¹/₄ cup (2¹/₂ fl oz/70 ml) dark corn syrup

1 egg white, well beaten

San Francisco Sourdough Bread

The dough for these loaves must rise slowly to develop the characteristic porous crumb, crisp crust, and wonderful sour tang. In San Francisco, this bread is often found next to a steaming bowl of clam chowder or a platter of fresh crabmeat.

In a large bowl or the bowl of an electric stand mixer, dissolve the yeast in the lukewarm water and let stand until bubbles start to rise, about 5 minutes. Stir in the sourdough starter, salt, and 2 1/2 cups (12 1/2 oz/390 g) of the flour. Gradually stir in enough of the remaining flour to make a soft dough that holds its shape.

Knead by hand or with a dough hook, adding flour as needed. Knead by hand until smooth and elastic, about 10 minutes; knead by hook until the dough is not sticky and pulls cleanly from the bowl sides, 5–6 minutes.

Form the dough into a ball and place in a clean, greased bowl, turning to coat all sides. Cover with greased plastic wrap and let rise in a warm place until tripled in size, 2–3 hours.

Sprinkle a baking sheet with cornmeal. Turn out the dough onto a lightly floured work surface and press flat. Knead twice and cut in half. Form each half into a ball, stretching the sides down and under (page 319). Flatten each ball into a round loaf 8 inches (20 cm) in diameter. Place on the prepared baking sheet, cover with a clean kitchen towel, and let rise until doubled, about 1 hour.

Preheat the oven to 450°F (230°C).

Place a shallow pan of boiling water on the floor of the preheated oven. Using a sharp knife, slash a diagonal grid pattern on top of each loaf. Bake for 15 minutes, then reduce the heat to 350°F (180°C) and bake until well browned and the loaves sound hollow when tapped on the bottoms, 20–25 minutes longer. Transfer the loaves to a wire rack to cool.

Makes two 1-lb (500-g) loaves

1 package (2 1/4 teaspoons) active dry yeast

1 cup (8 fl oz/250 ml) lukewarm water (110°F/43°C)

2 cups (16 fl oz/500 ml) Sourdough Starter (page 312), at room temperature

2 teaspoons salt

4–4 1/2 cups (20–22 1/2 oz/ 625–700 g) unbleached bread flour

Cornmeal for sprinkling

Boiling water, as needed

Sourdough Olive Bread

1 teaspoon active dry yeast

1/2 cup (4 fl oz/125 ml) luke-warm water (110°F/43°C)

1/2 cup (3 oz/90 g) Tapenade (page 313)

2 cups (16 fl oz/500 ml) Sourdough Starter (page 312), at room temperature

1/2 teaspoon salt

3 1/2–4 cups (17 1/2–20 oz/ 545–625 g) unbleached bread flour

Boiling water, as needed

Canola oil for greasing

Cornmeal for sprinkling

1 egg white beaten with a pinch of salt

In a large bowl or the bowl of an electric stand mixer, dissolve the yeast in the luke-warm water and let stand until bubbles start to rise, about 5 minutes. Stir in the tapenade, sourdough starter, and salt. Gradually stir in 2 1/2 cups (12 1/2 oz/390 g) of the flour to make a soft dough that holds its shape.

Knead by hand or with a dough hook, adding flour as needed. Knead by hand until smooth and elastic, about 10 minutes; knead by hook until the dough pulls cleanly from the bowl sides, 5–6 minutes. The dough will feel slightly sticky to the touch. Form the dough into a ball and place in a clean, greased bowl, turning to coat all sides. Cover with greased plastic wrap and let rise in a warm place until almost tripled in size, 1 1/2–2 hours.

Line each of 2 double baguette pans (4 molds total), each 18 inches (45 cm) long and 6 inches (15 cm) wide, with a clean kitchen towel and sprinkle with flour, rubbing it into the fabric. Turn out the dough onto a lightly floured work surface and press flat. Cut into 4 equal pieces, knead into balls, and let rest for 5 minutes. Press each ball flat and fold into thirds. Roll each into a rope 14 inches (35 cm) long with tapered ends. Place in the towel-lined pans. Cover with a clean kitchen towel and let rise until doubled, about 30 minutes. Preheat the oven to 450°F (230°C).

Place a shallow pan of boiling water on the floor of the preheated oven. Pull the pans out from under the dough-filled towels. Grease the pans and sprinkle with cornmeal. One at a time, flip the loaves into the pans, underside up. Brush with the egg-white mixture. Using a sharp knife, make 3 diagonal slashes, each 1/2 inch (12 mm) deep, in each loaf. Bake until brown and crusty, 20–25 minutes. Transfer to a wire rack to cool.

Makes four 1/2-lb (250-g) baguettes

2–2¹/₂ cups (10–12¹/₂ oz/
315–390 g) unbleached
bread flour

1 package (2¹/₄ teaspoons)
active dry yeast

2 cups (16 fl oz/500 ml) lukewarm water (110F/43°C)

2 tablespoons corn oil

2 tablespoons dark or light
molasses

2 teaspoons salt

2 cups (10 oz/315 g) whole-
wheat (wholemeal) flour

¹/₂ cup (1¹/₂ oz/45 g) rye flour

¹/₂ cup (1¹/₄ oz/40 g) oat bran

2 teaspoons aniseeds

Unsalted butter for greasing

Three-Grain Bread

In a large bowl or the bowl of an electric stand mixer, combine ¹/₄ cup (1¹/₂ oz/45 g) of the bread flour, the yeast, and ¹/₂ cup (4 fl oz/125 ml) of the lukewarm water and mix well. Let stand until bubbles start to rise, about 10 minutes. In another bowl, stir together the remaining 1¹/₂ cups (12 fl oz/375 ml) lukewarm water, the oil, molasses, and salt. Add this mixture to the yeast mixture and stir well. Stir in 1¹/₂ cups (7¹/₂ oz/235 g) of the remaining bread flour, the whole-wheat flour, the rye flour, and the bran. Add the aniseeds and stir briefly to mix.

Knead by hand or with a dough hook, adding bread flour as needed. Knead by hand until smooth and elastic, about 15 minutes; knead by hook until the dough is not sticky and pulls cleanly from the bowl sides, about 10 minutes. Form the dough into a ball and place in a clean, greased bowl, turning to coat all sides. Cover with greased plastic wrap and let rise in a warm place until doubled, 1¹/₂–2 hours.

Grease two 8¹/₂-by-4¹/₂-inch (21.5-by-11.5-cm) loaf pans. Turn out the dough onto a lightly floured work surface and press flat. Cut in half. Using a rolling pin, roll out each half into a 12-by-7-inch (30-by-18-cm) rectangle. Starting at a long side, roll up tightly and pinch the seams to seal (page 319). Place in the prepared pans, seam sides down. Cover and let rise in a warm place until doubled, about 1 hour.

Preheat the oven to 375°F (190°C). Uncover and bake until brown and the loaves sound hollow when tapped on the bottoms, about 1 hour. Transfer to a wire rack to cool completely.

Makes two 1¹/₄-lb (625-g) loaves

Potato Bread

In a saucepan, combine the potatoes with water to cover. Bring to a boil and cook until tender, 20–25 minutes. Using a slotted spoon, transfer the potatoes to a large bowl and reserve the water in the pan. Mash the potatoes until smooth; let cool. Pour ¹/₂ cup (4 fl oz/125 ml) of the potato water into another large bowl and let cool to lukewarm (110°F/43°C). Stir in the yeast and then 3 tablespoons of the flour. Let stand until bubbles start to rise, about 15 minutes.

Rewarm ¹/₂ cup (4 fl oz/125 ml) of the remaining potato water to lukewarm and add to the bowl along with the oil, salt, mashed potatoes, and 3 cups (15 oz/470 g) of the flour. Stir well. Gradually stir in enough of the remaining flour to a make a soft dough.

Knead until smooth and elastic, about 10 minutes, adding flour as needed. Form the dough into a ball and place in a clean, greased bowl, turning to coat all sides. Cover with greased plastic wrap and let rise in a warm place until doubled, 1–1 ¹/₂ hours.

Grease a baking sheet and dust with flour. Turn out the dough onto a lightly floured work surface, press flat, and knead for 2 minutes. Form into a ball and stretch the sides down and under (page 319). Flatten into a round 10 inches (25 cm) in diameter and place on the prepared baking sheet. Cover with a clean kitchen towel and let rise until doubled, 30–40 minutes. Preheat the oven to 425°F (220°C).

Uncover the loaf and bake for 15 minutes, then reduce the heat to 375°F (190°C) and continue to bake until browned and the loaf sounds hollow when tapped on the bottom, 35–40 minutes. Transfer to a wire rack to cool.

Makes one 22-oz (685-g) loaf

2 russet potatoes, about ¹/₂ lb (250 g) total weight, peeled and quartered

1 package (2¹/₄ teaspoons) quick-rise yeast

3¹/₂–4 cups (17¹/₂–20 oz/ 545–625 g) unbleached bread flour

1 tablespoon corn oil, plus extra for greasing

1¹/₂ teaspoons salt

Rustic Country Bread

Three risings give this free-form loaf an airy texture and a crisp crust. The dusting of flour on the top not only enhances the presentation but the texture of the final product as well. This is a very versatile loaf, making it great for everyday use.

In a large bowl or the bowl of an electric stand mixer, combine 1 cup (5oz/155 g) of the bread flour, the gluten flour, the salt, and the yeast. Add the lukewarm water and stir well. Gradually stir in enough of the remaining flour to make a soft dough that holds its shape.

Knead by hand or with a dough hook, adding bread flour as needed. Knead by hand until smooth and elastic, about 10 minutes; knead by hook until the dough is not sticky and pulls cleanly from the bowl sides, 5–6 minutes. Form the dough into a ball and place in a clean, greased bowl, turning to coat all sides. Cover with greased plastic wrap and let rise in a warm place until doubled, 45–60 minutes.

Turn out the dough onto a slightly floured work surface and press flat. Knead for 1 minute, form into a ball and return to the greased bowl, turning to coat all sides. Cover and let rise again until doubled, 30–45 minutes.

Turn out the dough onto a lightly floured surface and press flat. Form into a ball, stretching the sides down and under, then form into a plump oval. Sprinkle a baking sheet with cornmeal, place the loaf on it, and cover with a clean kitchen towel. Let rise until doubled, about 30 minutes. Preheat the oven to 400°F (200°C).

Uncover the loaf and sprinkle with bread flour. Using a sharp knife, make 3 parallel diagonal cuts, each 1/2 inch (12 mm) deep, across the top. Using a spray bottle, spritz the oven sides and floor with water (this creates steam to help form a crisp crust). Bake until the bread is brown and crusty and sounds hollow when tapped on the bottom, 30–35 minutes. Transfer to a wire rack to cool.

Makes one 1 1/2-lb (750-g) oval loaf

2 3/4–3 1/4 cups (14–16 1/2 oz/ 440–515 g) unbleached bread flour, plus extra for sprinkling

3/4 cup (4 oz/125 g) gluten flour

1 tablespoon salt

1 package (2 1/4 teaspoons) quick-rise yeast

2 cups (16 fl oz/500 ml) luke-warm water (110°F/43°C)

Cornmeal for sprinkling

Whole-Wheat Bread

4¹/₂ cups (22¹/₂ oz/705 g) whole-wheat (wholemeal) flour

2¹/₂–3 cups (12¹/₂–15 oz/ 390–470 g) unbleached bread flour

2 teaspoons salt

1 package (2¹/₄ teaspoons) quick-rise yeast

1 cup (8 fl oz/250 ml) milk

¹/₄ cup (3 fl oz/90 ml) dark molasses

¹/₄ cup (2 oz/60 g) unsalted butter, plus extra for greasing

1 egg yolk beaten with 1 teaspoon water

In a bowl, whisk together the whole-wheat flour and 2 ¹/₂ cups (12 ¹/₂ oz/390 g) of the bread flour. In a large bowl or the bowl of an electric stand mixer, combine 2 cups (10 oz/315 g) of the flour mixture, the salt, and the yeast. In a saucepan over low heat, combine 1 cup (8 fl oz/250 ml) water, the milk, molasses, and butter. Heat to lukewarm (110°F/43°C). Stir the water mixture into the yeast mixture, then beat hard until smooth. Gradually stir in the remaining flour mixture.

Knead by hand or with a dough hook, adding bread flour as needed. Knead by hand until smooth and elastic, about 10 minutes; knead by hook until the dough pulls cleanly from the bowl sides, 6–7 minutes. The dough will be slightly heavy. Form into a ball and place in a clean, greased bowl, turning the dough to coat all sides. Cover with greased plastic wrap and let rise in a warm place until doubled, 1–1 ¹/₂ hours.

Grease two 8 ¹/₂-by-4 ¹/₂-inch (21.5-by-11.5-cm) loaf pans. Turn out the dough onto a lightly floured work surface and press flat. Cut in half. Using a rolling pin, roll out each half into a 12-by-7-inch (30-by-18-cm) rectangle. Starting at a long side, roll up tightly and pinch the seams to seal (page 319). Place in the prepared pans, seam sides down. Cover with a clean kitchen towel and let rise in a warm place until doubled, 45–60 minutes. Preheat the oven to 375°F (190°C).

Brush the loaves with the egg-yolk mixture. Bake until golden brown and the loaves sound hollow when tapped on the bottoms, 30–40 minutes. Transfer to a wire rack to cool.

Makes two 22-oz (685-g) loaves

Polenta and Chestnut Flour Bread

In a saucepan over medium heat, bring 1 cup (8 fl oz/250 ml) water to a boil. Pour in the polenta, stirring vigorously. Cook, stirring, until thickened, about 5 minutes. Spoon into a large bowl or the bowl of an electric stand mixer. Stir in the milk and oil. Let cool to lukewarm (110°F/43°C). Meanwhile, in a frying pan over medium heat, toast the chestnut flour, stirring until tan and fragrant, 3 minutes. Let cool.

In a small bowl, dissolve the yeast in the lukewarm water; let stand until bubbles start to rise, about 5 minutes. Stir the yeast mixture, salt, brown sugar, and toasted chestnut flour into the polenta. Gradually stir in 3 cups (15 oz/470 g) of the bread flour to make a soft dough.

Knead by hand or with a dough hook, adding bread flour as needed. Knead by hand until smooth and elastic, about 10 minutes; knead by hook until the dough pulls cleanly from the bowl sides, 5–6 minutes. The dough will be slightly heavy.

Form the dough into a ball and place in a clean, greased bowl, turning to coat all sides. Cover with greased plastic wrap and let rise in a warm place until doubled, 1 1/4–1 3/4 hours.

Turn out the dough onto a work surface dusted with chestnut flour and press flat. Cut in half, knead briefly, and form each half into a ball, stretching the sides down and under (page 319). Elongate into two 8-by-3-inch (20-by-7.5-cm) ovals. Roll in chestnut flour. Dust a baking sheet with polenta and place the loaves on it. Cover with a clean kitchen towel and let rise until doubled, 45–60 minutes.

Preheat the oven to 425°F (220°C). Using a sharp knife, slash a grid pattern across each loaf, no more than 1/4 inch (6 mm) deep. Bake for 10 minutes, then reduce the heat to 350°F (180°C) and bake until browned and the loaves sound hollow when tapped on the bottoms, 25–30 minutes. Transfer to a wire rack to cool.

Makes two 1 1/4-lb (625-g) loaves

1/2 cup (3 1/2 oz/105 g) polenta, plus extra for sprinkling

1 cup (8 fl oz/250 ml) milk

1 tablespoon corn oil

1 cup (3 1/2 oz/105 g) chestnut flour, plus extra for dusting

1 package (2 1/4 teaspoons) quick-rise yeast

1/2 cup (4 fl oz/125 ml) luke-warm water (110°F/43°C)

2 teaspoons salt

2 tablespoons firmly packed dark brown sugar

3–3 1/2 cups (15–17 1/2 oz/ 470–545 g) unbleached bread flour

Harvest Wheat Sheaf Bread

This bread makes a wonderful centerpiece for a Thanksgiving dinner. Its creative design also simplifies serving; pieces will pull apart easily into perfectly-sized portions for everyone at the table.

1 package (2¼ teaspoons) quick-rise yeast

3½–4 cups (17½–20 oz/ 545–625 g) unbleached bread flour

1 cup (8 fl oz/250 ml) luke-warm water (110°F/43°C)

2 teaspoons salt

1 tablespoon canola oil

1 egg beaten with 2 teaspoons water

In a large bowl or the bowl of an electric stand mixer, combine the yeast, ½ cup (2½ oz/75 g) of the flour, and 1 cup (8 fl oz/250 ml) of the lukewarm water. Let stand until bubbles start to rise, about 10 minutes. Stir in the salt, oil, and 2 cups (10 oz/315 g) more flour until well combined. Gradually stir in enough of the remaining flour to make a soft dough that holds its shape.

Knead by hand or with a dough hook, adding flour as needed. Knead by hand until smooth and elastic, about 10 minutes; knead by hook until the dough is not sticky and pulls cleanly from the bowls sides, 6–7 minutes. Form the dough into a ball and place in a clean, greased bowl, turning to coat all sides. Cover with greased plastic wrap and let rise in a warm place until doubled, 60–75 minutes.

Turn out the dough a lightly floured work surface and press flat. Divide into thirds and form each portion into a ball. Let rest for 10 minutes. Grease a baking sheet and dust with flour.

To make the wheat sheaf base, roll out 1 ball of dough into an oval 12 inches (30 cm) long and 9 inches (23 cm) wide. Cut away a small rectangle measuring 2-by-3 inches (5-by-7.5 cm) from opposite sides on one end of the oval, forming a tall mushroom shape. Transfer to the prepared baking sheet. Decorate the wheat sheaf following the directions on page 319. Cover with a clean kitchen towel and let rise until puffy, about 30 minutes. Preheat the oven to 400°F (200°C).

Brush the loaf with the remaining egg mixture. Bake until well risen and golden brown, 40–45 minutes. Transfer to a wire rack to cool.

Makes one 22-oz (685-g) loaf

Rosemary Batter Bread

This savory batter bread goes well with simple, Mediterranean-style food, such as spit-roasted lamb, charbroiled poultry, or fish steaks. The pine nuts make a lovely topping that also adds to the delicious taste.

In a large bowl, combine the whole-wheat flour, 1 cup (5 oz/155 g) of the bread flour, the salt, and the yeast and mix well. In a small bowl, stir together the warm water, the olive oil, the egg, and the rosemary. Stir the water mixture into the flour mixture, then beat with an electric mixer set on medium speed or beat hard with a wooden spoon until smooth, about 2 minutes, scraping down the sides of the bowl occasionally. Gradually beat in enough of the remaining bread flour to make a stiff batter that almost holds its shape. Beat at high speed or hard by hand until smooth, about 2 minutes. Cover with greased plastic wrap and let rise in a warm place until doubled, 40–50 minutes.

Grease a 1-qt (1-l) tinned steel charlotte mold, porcelain soufflé dish, or any round 1-qt (1-l) mold and sprinkle with cornmeal. Uncover the bowl and stir the batter to deflate. Spoon the batter into the prepared mold and smooth the top with a rubber spatula. Scatter the pine nuts evenly over the top. Cover with a clean kitchen towel and let rise until doubled, 30–45 minutes.

Preheat the oven to 375°F (190°C).

Uncover the dough and bake until golden and well risen, 35–40 minutes. (If the nuts start to overbrown, cover the loaf loosely with aluminum foil.) Unmold the loaf and transfer to a wire rack to cool.

Makes one 1 1/4-lb (625-g) loaf

1/2 cup (2 1/2 oz/75 g) whole-wheat (wholemeal) flour

1 3/4–2 cups (9–10 oz/280–315 g) unbleached bread flour

2 teaspoons salt

1 package (2 1/4 teaspoons) quick-rise yeast

1 cup (8 fl oz/250 ml) warm water (125°F/52°C)

2 tablespoons olive oil, plus extra for greasing

1 egg, at room temperature

1 teaspoon chopped fresh rosemary

Cornmeal for sprinkling

2 teaspoons pine nuts

Dinner Rolls

4¹/₂–5 cups (22¹/₂–25 oz/ 700–780 g) unbleached bread flour

2 teaspoons salt

1 package (2¹/₄ teaspoons) quick-rise yeast

1¹/₂ cups (12 fl oz/375 ml) warm water (125°F/52°C)

¹/₄ cup (2 oz/60 g) unsalted butter, at room temperature

Cornmeal for sprinkling

1 egg white beaten with 2 teaspoons cold water

Poppy seeds for sprinkling

In a large bowl or the bowl of an electric stand mixer, combine 1 cup (5 oz/155 g) of the flour, the salt, and the yeast. Using a wooden spoon or the paddle attachment of the mixer set on medium speed, beat in the warm water and butter until smooth. Add 1 cup (5 oz/155 g) of the remaining flour and continue beating until smooth. Gradually beat in enough of the remaining flour to make a soft dough.

Knead by hand or with a dough hook, adding flour as needed. Knead by hand until smooth and elastic, about 10 minutes; knead by hook until the dough is not sticky and pulls cleanly from the bowl sides, 6–7 minutes. Form the dough into a ball and place in a clean, greased bowl, turning to coat all sides. Cover with greased plastic wrap and let rise in a warm place until doubled, 45–60 minutes.

Turn out the dough onto a lightly floured work surface and press flat. Form into a ball and let rest for 5 minutes. Cut the dough in half. Roll each half into a log 9 inches (23 cm) long. Cut each crosswise into 9 equal pieces. Knead each piece into a ball. Sprinkle 2 baking sheets with the cornmeal and place the rolls on them, spaced well apart. Cover with a clean kitchen towel and let rise until doubled, about 35 minutes. Preheat the oven to 425°F (220°C).

Brush the rolls with the egg-white mixture and sprinkle with poppy seeds. Using a spray bottle, spritz the oven sides and floor with water. Bake until golden brown, 15–20 minutes; switch pan positions halfway through baking. Transfer the rolls to a wire rack to cool.

Makes 18 rolls

Golden Sesame Bread Sticks

In a large bowl or the bowl of an electric stand mixer, combine 2 cups (10 oz/315 g) of the flour, the salt, and the yeast. Stir in the lukewarm water. Gradually stir in enough of the remaining flour to make a soft dough that holds its shape.

Knead by hand or with a dough hook, adding flour as needed. Knead by hand until smooth and elastic, about 10 minutes; knead by hook until the dough pulls cleanly from the bowl sides, 6–7 minutes. Form the dough into a ball and place in a clean, greased bowl, turning to coat all sides. Cover with greased plastic wrap and let rise in a warm place until doubled, 45–60 minutes.

Turn out the dough onto a lightly floured work surface and press flat. Let rest for 5 minutes. Grease 2 baking sheets. Using a rolling pin, roll out the dough into a 10-by-12-inch (25-by-30-cm) rectangle about $1/2$ inch (12 mm) thick. Using a sharp knife, cut lengthwise into 20 strips, each $1/2$ inch (12 mm) wide. Using the palms of your hands, roll out and elongate to form ropes 14 inches (35 cm) long. Place on the prepared sheets about 1 inch (2.5 cm) apart, cover with a clean kitchen towel, and let rest for 20 minutes. Preheat the oven to 300°F (150°C).

Uncover and bake until lightly golden, about 25 minutes; switch pan positions halfway through baking. Transfer the breadsticks to a work surface. Brush with the egg-yolk mixture and sprinkle with sesame seeds on all sides. Return the bread sticks to the baking sheets. Continue to bake until deep gold and crisp, 14–17 minutes longer. Transfer to a wire rack to cool.

Makes twenty 14-inch (35-cm) breadsticks

3–3$1/2$ cups (15–17$1/2$ oz/470–545 g) unbleached bread flour

2 teaspoons salt

1 package (2$1/4$ teaspoons) quick-rise yeast

1 cup (8 fl oz/250 ml) luke-warm water (110°F/43°C)

1 egg yolk beaten with 2 teaspoons water and $1/2$ teaspoon salt

1 cup (3 oz/90 g) sesame seeds

Flat Breads & Pizzas

Focaccia

This flat Italian bread is delectable served warm from the oven with cheese, fruit, and a glass of wine. Or split it lengthwise for making great sandwiches. When you prepare it, keep in mind that it is best eaten the same day it is made.

1 package (2¹/₄ teaspoons) quick-rise yeast

1¹/₄ cups (10 fl oz/310 ml) lukewarm water (110°F/43°C)

2 tablespoons olive oil, plus extra for greasing and brushing

2 teaspoons table salt

3–3¹/₂ cups (15–17¹/₂ oz/ 470–545 g) unbleached bread flour

Coarse sea salt for sprinkling

In a large bowl or the bowl of an electric stand mixer, dissolve the yeast in the lukewarm water. Stir in the olive oil and the table salt. Gradually stir in 3 cups (15 oz/470 g) of the flour to make a soft dough that holds its shape.

Knead by hand or with a dough hook, adding flour as needed. Knead by hand until smooth and elastic, about 10 minutes; knead by hook until the dough is not sticky and pulls cleanly from the bowl sides, 6–7 minutes.

Form the dough into a ball and place in a clean, greased bowl, turning to coat all sides. Cover and let rise in a warm place until doubled, 45–60 minutes.

Using olive oil, grease an 11-by-17-inch (28-by-43-cm) heavy baking sheet with 1-inch (2.5-cm) sides. Turn out the dough onto a lightly floured work surface and press flat. Again form into a ball. Place on the prepared baking sheet and let rest for 5 minutes. Using your fingers, stretch out the dough so that it evenly covers the pan bottom. Cover with a clean kitchen towel and let rise until puffy, about 30 minutes. Preheat the oven to 400°F (200°C).

Using your fingertips, make a pattern of dimples at 2-inch (5-cm) intervals over the entire surface of the dough. Brush the surface with olive oil and lightly sprinkle with sea salt.

Bake until golden brown, 15–20 minutes. Serve warm.

Makes one 1-lb (500-g) flat bread

Focaccia with Onions

1 package (2¼ teaspoons) quick-rise yeast

1¼ cups (10 fl oz/310 ml) lukewarm water (110°F/43°C)

3 tablespoons olive oil, plus extra for greasing

2½ teaspoons salt

3–3½ cups (15–17½ oz/ 470–545 g) unbleached bread flour

½ cup (4 oz/125 g) unsalted butter

2 lb (1 kg) yellow onions, thinly sliced

1 teaspoon sugar

In a large bowl or the bowl of an electric stand mixer, dissolve the yeast in the luke-warm water. Stir in the olive oil and 2 teaspoons of the salt. Gradually stir in 3 cups (15 oz/470 g) of the flour to make a soft dough that holds its shape.

Knead by hand or with a dough hook, adding flour as needed. Knead by hand until smooth and elastic, about 10 minutes; knead by hook until the dough is not sticky and pulls cleanly from the bowl sides, 6–7 minutes.

Form the dough into a ball and place in a clean, greased bowl, turning to coat all sides. Cover and let rise in a warm place until doubled, 45–60 minutes.

In 2 sauté pans over medium-low heat, melt the butter, dividing it equally. Add half of the onions to each pan and season with the sugar and the remaining ½ teaspoon salt. Cook, stirring, until soft but not browned, about 10 minutes. Let cool.

Using olive oil, grease an 11-by-17-inch (28-by-43-cm) heavy baking sheet with 1-inch (2.5-cm) sides. Turn out the dough onto a lightly floured work surface and press flat. Again form into a ball. Place on the prepared baking sheet and let rest for 5 minutes. Using your fingers, stretch the dough so that it evenly covers the pan bottom. Cover with a clean kitchen towel and let rise until puffy, 45–60 minutes. Preheat the oven to 400°F (200°C).

Using your fingertips, make a pattern of dimples at 2-inch (5-cm) intervals over the entire surface of the dough. Cover the surface with the onions.

Bake until golden brown, 15–17 minutes. Serve warm.

Makes one 1½-lb (750-g) flat bread

Herb and Olive Focaccia

In a large bowl or the bowl of a stand mixer, dissolve the yeast in the lukewarm water. Add 2 tablespoons of the olive oil, 1 tablespoon of the oregano, the salt, and a generous grinding of pepper. Gradually stir in 3 cups (15 oz/470 g) of the flour to make a soft dough that holds its shape.

Knead by hand or with a dough hook, adding flour as needed. Knead by hand until smooth and elastic, about 10 minutes; knead by hook until the dough is not sticky and pulls cleanly from the bowl sides, 6–7 minutes.

Form the dough into a ball and place in a clean, greased bowl, turning to coat all sides. Cover and let rise in a warm place until doubled, 45–60 minutes.

Combine the onion, the remaining 2 tablespoons oregano, the olives, and 1 table-spoon of the remaining olive oil; mix well. Set aside.

Using olive oil, grease an 11-by-17-inch (28-by-43-cm) heavy baking sheet with 1-inch (2.5-cm) sides. Turn out the dough onto a lightly floured work surface and press flat. Again form into a ball. Place on the prepared baking sheet and let rest for 5 minutes. Using your fingers, stretch the dough so that it evenly covers the pan bottom. Cover with a clean kitchen towel and let rise until puffy, 30–40 minutes. Preheat the oven to 425°F (220°C).

Using your fingertips, make a pattern of dimples at 2-inch (5-cm) intervals over the entire surface of the dough. Brush with the remaining 1/2 tablespoon oil. Sprinkle on the olive mixture.

Bake until golden brown, 18–20 minutes. Serve warm.

Makes one 1 1/2-lb (750-g) flat bread

1 package (2¼ teaspoons) quick-rise yeast

1¼ cups (10 fl oz/310 ml) lukewarm water (110°F/43°C)

3½ tablespoons olive oil, plus extra for greasing

3 tablespoons chopped fresh oregano, rosemary, or sage

1 teaspoon salt

Freshly ground pepper

3½–4 cups (17½–20 oz/ 545–625 g) unbleached bread flour

1 small yellow onion, quartered and sliced

24 oil-cured black olives, pitted and chopped

Crusty Corn Focaccia

This delicious wheat-free bread is made with corn flour, which is finely ground white or yellow cornmeal, and brown-rice flour. Xanthan gum powder is added to provide stretch. All three of these products can be found in natural-food stores.

Line a baking sheet with parchment (baking) paper and set aside. In a large bowl, whisk together the rice flour, corn flour, cornstarch, salt, xanthan gum powder, and yeast. In another bowl, beat together the warm water, eggs, and corn oil. Add the egg mixture to the flour mixture and beat with a wooden spoon until smooth.

Using a rubber spatula, spread the dough into 2 circles, each 8 inches (20 cm) in diameter, on the prepared baking sheet, mounding them slightly in the center. Cover loosely with greased plastic wrap and let rise in a warm place until doubled, 1–1 1/2 hours. Preheat the oven to 425°F (220°C).

Brush the dough with the egg-yolk mixture. Dust with corn flour and, using a sharp knife or single-edged razor blade, slash the dough with a 2-inch (5-cm) diamond-grid pattern. Bake until light golden brown, 14–18 minutes. Serve warm.

Makes two 10-oz (315-g) loaves

1 cup (5 oz/155 g) brown-rice flour

1 cup (5 1/2 oz/170 g) corn flour, plus extra for dusting

1/2 cup (2 oz/60 g) cornstarch (cornflour)

1 teaspoon salt

2 teaspoons xanthan gum powder

1 1/2 teaspoons active dry yeast

1 1/2 cups (12 fl oz/375 ml) lukewarm water (110°F/43°C)

2 eggs, at room temperature

2 tablespoons corn oil

1 egg yolk mixed with 1 teaspoon water

Focaccia with Pancetta

This tasty bread, which contains little nuggets of pancetta (Italian bacon), tastes best when served warm from the oven. For a first course at a dinner party, try complementing this dish with cool, fresh crudites and vinaigrette for dipping.

1 package (2¼ teaspoons) quick-rise yeast

½ cup (4 fl oz/125 ml) lukewarm water (110°F/43°C)

¾ cup (6 fl oz/180 ml) lukewarm milk (110°F/43°C)

1 tablespoon olive oil, plus extra for greasing

1 teaspoon salt

3½–4 cups (17½–20 oz/ 545–625 g) unbleached bread flour

¼ lb (125 g) pancetta, diced, lightly fried, drained, and cooled

In a large bowl or the bowl of an electric stand mixer, dissolve the yeast in the lukewarm water. Stir in the lukewarm milk, the olive oil, and the salt. Gradually stir in 3 cups (15 oz/470 g) of the flour to make a soft dough that holds its shape.

Knead by hand or with a dough hook, adding flour as needed. Knead by hand until smooth and elastic, about 10 minutes; knead by hook until the dough is not sticky and pulls cleanly from the bowl sides, 6–7 minutes.

Form the dough into a ball and place in a clean, greased bowl, turning to coat all sides. Cover and let rise in a warm place until doubled, 45–60 minutes.

Using olive oil, grease an 11-by-17-inch (28-by-43-cm) baking sheet with 1-inch (2.5-cm) sides. Turn out the dough onto a lightly floured work surface and press flat. Sprinkle with the pancetta and knead gently to distribute evenly. Again form into a ball and place on the prepared baking sheet and let rest for 10 minutes. Using your fingers, stretch out the dough so that it evenly covers the pan bottom. Cover with a clean kitchen towel and let rise until puffy, 45–60 minutes. Preheat the oven to 400°F (200°C).

Using your fingertips, make a pattern of dimples at 2-inch (5-cm) intervals over the entire surface of the dough. Bake until golden brown, 15–17 minutes. Serve warm.

Makes one 1½-lb (750-g) flat bread

Sweet Focaccia with Grapes

In a bowl, dissolve 1 teaspoon of the yeast in 1 cup (8 fl oz/250 ml) of the lukewarm water. Stir in 1 cup (5 oz/155 g) of the flour and the 1 tablespoon sugar. Cover with a clean kitchen towel and let rise in a warm place until doubled, 45–60 minutes. (This is known as the "sponge.")

Meanwhile, stem the grapes, rinse them well, and pat dry. Place in a bowl and toss with the $^1/_2$ cup (4 oz/125 g) sugar.

In a large bowl or the bowl of an electric stand mixer, dissolve the remaining $1^1/_4$ teaspoons yeast in the remaining $^1/_2$ cup (4 fl oz/125 ml) lukewarm water. Stir in the sponge, the olive oil, and the salt. Gradually stir in $2^1/_2$ cups ($12^1/_2$ oz/390 g) more flour to make a soft dough that holds its shape.

Knead by hand or with a dough hook, adding flour as needed. Knead by hand until smooth and elastic, about 10 minutes; knead by hook until the dough is not sticky and pulls cleanly from the bowl sides, 6–7 minutes.

Form the dough into a ball and place in a clean, greased bowl, turning to coat all sides. Cover and let rise in a warm place until doubled, 45–60 minutes.

Using olive oil, grease 2 pizza pans, each 12–14 inches (30–35 cm) in diameter, or 2 baking sheets. Turn out the dough onto a lightly floured work surface and press flat. Cut in half and form each half into a ball. Dust with flour and let rest for 5 minutes. Using a rolling pin, roll out each half into a round 12–14 inches (30–35 cm) in diameter. Place the rounds on the prepared pans and sprinkle evenly with the sugared grapes. Cover loosely with greased plastic wrap and let rise until doubled, 25–35 minutes. Preheat the oven to 400°F (200°C).

Uncover the rounds and bake until golden brown, about 20 minutes. Serve warm.

Makes two $1^1/_2$-lb (750-g) flat breads

1 package ($2^1/_4$ teaspoons) quick-rise yeast

$1^1/_2$ cups (12 fl oz/375 ml) lukewarm water (110°F/43°C)

$3^1/_2$–4 cups ($17^1/_2$–20 oz/ 545–625 g) unbleached bread flour

1 tablespoon plus $^1/_2$ cup (4 oz/125 g) sugar

2 lb (1 kg) seedless red grapes such as Thompson Red Flame

2 tablespoons olive oil, plus extra for greasing

$^1/_2$ teaspoon salt

Scottish Oatcakes

The traditional bread of Scotland, oatcakes are thin oatmeal crackers baked on a griddle. Highland oatcakes are quite plain; this richer version from border country includes wheat and butter and is oven baked.

1 cup (3 oz/90 g) old-fashioned rolled oats

1/3 cup (2 oz/60 g) whole-wheat (wholemeal) flour

1/2 teaspoon sugar

1/4 teaspoon salt

1/4 teaspoon baking soda (bicarbonate of soda)

1/4 cup (2 oz/60 g) cold unsalted butter, cut into pieces

2–3 tablespoons water

Honey or marmalade for serving (optional)

Preheat the oven to 325°F (165°C).

In a food processor fitted with the metal blade, process the oats to a fine meal. Add the flour, sugar, salt, baking soda, and butter and process briefly to mix well. With the motor running, add 2 tablespoons of the water and process for 20 seconds to form a crumbly dough, adding as much of the remaining 1 tablespoon water as needed to achieve the desired texture.

Turn out the dough onto a lightly floured work surface. Knead a couple of times to incorporate any crumbs, then form into a ball. Cut in half. Using a rolling pin, roll out each half into a round 6 inches (15 cm) in diameter and 1/4 inch (6 mm) thick. Crimp the edges using your finger and thumb to make a fluted border. Using a metal spatula, transfer the rounds to a baking sheet and cut each one into 4 equal wedges. Separate the wedges slightly, then prick the top of each one 3 or 4 times with a fork.

Bake until pale and tan and no longer soft, 25–30 minutes. Transfer the oatcakes to a wire rack to cool. Serve with honey or marmalade, if desired.

Makes 8 oatcakes

Swedish Limpa

A mainstay in Sweden, these flat, light brown loaves are cut into wedges and then split for serving plain, with butter, or as a base for sandwiches. Try serving them with crisp cucumber slices and dill sprigs.

In a large bowl or the bowl of an electric stand mixer, whisk together the rye flour, 3 1/2 cups (17 1/2 oz/545 g) of the bread flour, the salt, aniseeds, cardamom, and yeast. In a saucepan over low heat, combine the butter and milk. Heat briefly, stirring to melt the butter, until lukewarm (110°F/43°C). Add the lukewarm water and corn syrup. Stir the milk mixture into the flour mixture.

Knead by hand or with a dough hook, adding bread flour as needed. Knead by hand until smooth and elastic, about 15 minutes; knead by hook until the dough is not sticky and pulls cleanly from the bowl sides, about 10 minutes.

Form the dough into a ball and place in a clean, greased bowl, turning to coat all sides. Cover and let rise in a warm place until doubled, 45–60 minutes.

Turn out the dough onto a lightly floured work surface and press flat. Cut in half and form each half into a ball. Let rest for 10 minutes. Dust a baking sheet with bread flour. Flatten each ball into a round 9 inches (23 cm) in diameter and place them on the prepared baking sheet. Cover with a clean kitchen towel and let rise until doubled, 35–45 minutes. Preheat the oven to 350°F (180°C).

Prick the loaves all over with a fork at 2-inch (5-cm) intervals. Bake until golden brown and the loaves sound hollow when tapped on the bottoms, 35–40 minutes. Using a spray bottle, mist the tops of the loaves with water. Wrap in kitchen towels to promote a soft crust and place on a wire rack to cool.

Makes two 1 1/4-lb (625-g) loaves

2 cups (6 oz/185 g) rye flour

4–4 1/2 cups (20–22 1/2 oz/ 625–700 g) unbleached bread flour

1 teaspoon salt

1 teaspoon aniseeds

Seeds from 12 cardamom pods, crushed (page 328)

1 package (2 1/4 teaspoons) quick-rise yeast

1/4 cup (2 oz/60 g) unsalted butter

1 cup (8 fl oz/250 ml) milk

1 cup (8 fl oz/250 ml) luke-warm water (110°F/43°C)

2 tablespoons dark corn syrup

Tomato and Cheese Pizza

Pizza dough can be made quickly in a food processor, and with so many ways to top it, the possibilities for a quick, satisfying dinner are practically endless. Using bread flour here yields more crust than a dough made of all-purpose flour would.

FOR THE DOUGH:

Olive oil for greasing

2¹/₂–3 cups (12¹/₂–15 oz/ 390–470 g) unbleached bread flour

1 teaspoon quick-rise yeast

¹/₂ teaspoon salt

1 cup (8 fl oz/250 ml) luke-warm water (110°F/43°C)

FOR THE TOPPING:

6 ripe tomatoes, about 2 lb (1 kg), sliced

2 tablespoons well-drained capers

4 teaspoons chopped fresh oregano or 2 teaspoons dried oregano

1 lb (500 g) mozzarella, Monterey jack, or Swiss cheese, thinly sliced

2 cans (2 oz/60 g *each*) anchovies packed in oil, drained and cut in half lengthwise (optional)

4 teaspoons olive oil

To make the dough, lightly grease a large bowl with olive oil. In a food processor fitted with the metal blade, combine 2¹/₂ cups (12¹/₂ oz/390 g) of the flour, the yeast, and the salt. Pulse briefly to combine. With the motor running, pour in the lukewarm water and process until the mixture clings together, about 25 seconds. If it is too wet, add as much of the remaining flour, ¹/₄ cup (1¹/₂ oz/45 g) at a time, as needed to form a mass.

Turn out the dough onto a lightly floured work surface and gather it into a loose ball. (The dough will be slightly soft and sticky.) Place it in the greased bowl and turn to coat all sides. Cover with greased plastic wrap and let rise in a warm place until doubled, 35–45 minutes.

Oil 2 pizza pans or baking sheets. Turn out the dough onto a lightly floured work surface and press flat. Cut in half and form each half into a ball. Dust lightly with flour and let rest for 5 minutes. Using a rolling pin, roll out each ball into a 12-inch (30-cm) round, making the edges a little thicker than the center. Lay each round on a prepared pan, cover lightly with greased plastic wrap, and let rise again in a warm place until puffy, 15–20 minutes. Preheat the oven to 400°F (200°C).

Uncover the dough rounds and top evenly with the tomato slices to within ¹/₂ inch (12 mm) of the edge. Sprinkle evenly with the capers and oregano. Top evenly with the cheese. If using the anchovies, arrange them in a lattice pattern on each pizza. Sprinkle evenly with the olive oil.

Bake until the crust is golden and crispy around the edges, about 20 minutes. Cut into wedges and serve immediately.

Makes two 12-inch (30-cm) pizzas; serves 4–6

Pizza Marinara

Serve these small pizzas as hors d'oeurves or as companions to soups or salads. You can alter this recipe to make a 9-inch thick-crust or 12-inch thin-crust pizza by following all of the instructions given for the Basic Pizza Dough.

Make the pizza dough through the first rising.

Shape the dough into 8 hors d'oeuvre-sized rounds and let rise again as directed. Preheat the oven to 450°F (220°C). If using a baking stone or tiles, place in the oven now. Oil a pizza pan or baking sheet.

Sprinkle with the garlic, oregano, and salt and pepper to taste. Drizzle 3 tablespoons of the olive oil evenly over the top. Bake for 10 minutes. Reduce the oven temperature to 400°F (200°C) and bake until the crust is golden, 10 minutes longer. Drizzle the remaining 1 tablespoon olive oil over the top and serve immediately.

Makes 8 small pizzas

Basic Pizza Dough (page 312)

8 cloves garlic, minced

1 teaspoon dried oregano

Salt and freshly ground pepper

4 tablespoons (2 fl oz/60 ml) extra-virgin olive oil, plus extra for greasing

Pizza with Smoked Gouda, Spicy Peppers, and Cilantro

To give this easy-to-make pizza an Italian accent, substitute an equal amount of basil and balsamic vinegar for the cilantro and lime juice. If you prefer to make your own dough, make a double recipe of the Basic Pizza Dough on page 312.

2 tablespoons fresh lime juice

3 tablespoons extra-virgin olive oil

Salt and freshly ground pepper

3/4 lb (375 g) cherry tomatoes, halved

2 9-inch (23-cm) store-bought partially baked pizza crusts

6 oz (185 g) smoked Gouda cheese, coarsely shredded

1/2 red bell pepper (capsicum), seeded, deribbed, and cut into long, very narrow strips

1/2 green bell pepper (capsicum), seeded, deribbed, and cut into long, very narrow strips

1 fresh jalapeño or serrano chile pepper, seeded and minced

1/4 cup (1/3 oz/10 g) coarsely chopped fresh cilantro (fresh coriander) leaves

Position 2 racks near the center of the oven and preheat to 500°F (260°C).

In a bowl, whisk together the lime juice, olive oil, and salt and pepper to taste. Add the tomatoes, turn to coat, and set aside.

Place each pizza crust on a baking sheet. Sprinkle half of the cheese evenly over each round to within 1/2 inch (12 mm) of the edge. Then top each round with half of the red and green bell peppers and half of the minced chile pepper.

Bake until the crusts are crisp and golden, 10–12 minutes; switch pan positions halfway through baking. Remove the pizzas from the oven and distribute half of the tomatoes and cilantro over each one. Cut into wedges and serve immediately.

Makes two 9-inch (23-cm) pizzas; serves 4–6

Pizza with Onions, Peppers, and Olives

Basic Pizza Dough (page 312)

2 tablespoons olive oil, plus extra for greasing

3 yellow onions, sliced

2 cloves garlic, minced

1 red bell pepper (capsicum), roasted and peeled (page 322), then sliced into narrow strips

Salt and freshly ground pepper

20 oil-cured olives, halved

Make the pizza dough through the first rising.

Meanwhile, in a frying pan over medium heat, warm the olive oil. Add the onions and sauté until soft, 6–7 minutes. Add the garlic and bell pepper and sauté until soft, about 3 minutes. Season to taste with salt and pepper. Remove from the heat and set aside.

Shape the dough into a large round and let rise again as directed. Preheat the oven to 400°F (200°C). If using a baking stone or tiles, place in the oven now. Using olive oil, grease a pizza pan or baking sheet.

When the second rising is complete, transfer the dough to the prepared pan. Spoon the onion mixture over the dough to within $^1/_2$ inch (12 mm) of the edge and sprinkle with the olives. Bake until golden brown around the edges, about 20 minutes. Cut into wedges and serve immediately.

Makes one 12-inch (30-cm) pizza; serves 6–8 as a first course, 2–3 as a main course

Pepperoni and Mushroom Pizza

Make the pizza dough through the first rising, assembling each batch separately.

Meanwhile, make the sauce: In a saucepan over medium heat, warm the olive oil. Add the onion and sauté, stirring often, until transparent, about 3 minutes. Add the garlic and sauté for 1 minute longer. Remove from the heat. Add the tomato purée, ¹/₄ cup (2 fl oz/60 ml) water, the sugar, oregano, and basil. Season to taste with salt and pepper. Bring to a boil over very high heat, stirring constantly. Reduce the heat to low and simmer, stirring occasionally, for 30 minutes. Taste and adjust the seasoning. Remove from the heat and set aside.

Shape each batch of dough into a large round and let rise again as directed. Preheat the oven to 500°F (260°C). If using a baking stone or tiles, place in the oven now. Using olive oil, grease 2 pizza pans or baking sheets.

When the second rising is complete, transfer each dough round to a prepared pan. Spoon half of the sauce evenly over each round, spreading it to within ¹/₂ inch (12 mm) of the edge. Sprinkle the mozzarella and then the Parmesan evenly over the sauce. Drizzle ¹/₂ tablespoon olive oil over each pizza. Divide the pepperoni and mushroom slices among the pizzas, distributing them evenly over the top. Bake until the cheese is melted and the crust is lightly browned, about 10 minutes. Cut into wedges and serve immediately.

Makes two 12-inch (30-cm) pizzas; serves 12–16 as a first course, 4–6 as a main course

2 recipes Basic Pizza Dough (page 312)

FOR THE SAUCE:

1 tablespoon olive oil

1 small yellow onion

1 large garlic clove, minced

1 can (15 oz/470 g) tomato purée

1¹/₂ teaspoons sugar

1 teaspoon dried oregano

1 teaspoon dried basil

Salt and freshly ground pepper

FOR THE TOPPING:

8 oz (250 g) mozzarella cheese, coarsely shredded

¹/₄ cup (1 oz/30 g) grated Parmesan cheese

1 tablespoon olive oil, plus extra for greasing

¹/₄ pound pepperoni, thinly sliced

2 oz (60 g) white mushrooms, brushed clean and thinly sliced (about ³/₄ cup)

Cookies, Bars & Brownies

Strawberry Shortcakes

Here the classic summer dessert turns into a delicate sandwich cookie. For an even prettier presentation, use a second, smaller cutter to cut a window in the top of each cookie before baking to allow the colorful preserves to show.

2¼ cups (11½ oz/360 g) all-purpose (plain) flour

¼ cup (1 oz/30 g) cornstarch (cornflour)

¼ teaspoon salt

¾ cup (6 oz/185 g) unsalted butter, at room temperature, plus extra for greasing

1½ teaspoons vanilla extract (essence)

1½ teaspoons grated lemon zest (page 329)

1 cup (8 oz/250 g) granulated sugar

1 whole egg

1 egg yolk (page 324)

About 2 cups (22 oz/680 g) Strawberry Jam (page 315)

Confectioners' (icing) sugar for dusting (optional)

Sift together the flour, cornstarch, and salt into a bowl; set aside. Combine the butter, vanilla, and zest in another bowl and, using an electric mixer set on high speed, beat until light. Add the granulated sugar and continue to beat until completely incorporated. Add the whole egg and egg yolk and beat until light and fluffy. Reduce the speed to low, add the flour mixture, and mix until incorporated. Gather the dough into a ball, then divide into thirds. Flatten each third into a disk. Wrap the disks in separate sheets of waxed paper and chill until firm, at least 1 hour or up to overnight.

Preheat the oven to 350°F (180°C). Lightly grease baking sheets.

Dust 1 dough disk with flour and place between 2 large sheets of waxed paper. Roll out the dough ⅛ inch (3 mm) thick. Using a 3-inch (7.5-cm) decoratively shaped cutter, cut out cookies. Transfer the cookies to the prepared baking sheets, spacing them ½ inch (12 mm) apart. Refrigerate for 10 minutes. Gather up the scraps, wrap them in waxed paper, and chill as well.

Bake until the edges are golden, about 10 minutes. Transfer the cookies to wire racks to cool. Repeat with the remaining 2 dough portions. Finally, roll out the scraps and cut, chill, and bake in the same manner.

Spread the preserves on the bottoms of half of the cookies, spreading only lightly at the edges. Top with the remaining cookies, bottom sides down. Dust confectioners' sugar over the tops, if desired. Store refrigerated in an airtight container for up to 1 week.

Makes about 3 dozen sandwich cookies

Orange-Coconut Macaroons

Preheat the oven on to 350°F (180°C). Line baking sheets with the parchment (baking) paper.

In a bowl, combine the zest, coconut, sweetened condensed milk, and almond and vanilla extracts. Using a wooden spoon, stir the ingredients until well mixed.

Drop the mixture by scant tablespoonfuls onto the prepared baking sheets, spacing the mounds about 1 inch (2.5 cm) apart. If necessary, wet your fingers with cool water and gently shape and press each mound to make it neat.

Bake until lightly browned, 10–15 minutes. Transfer to wire racks and let the macaroons cool completely on the baking sheets.

Makes about 40

Grated zest of 1 orange
(page 329)

3¹/₂ cups (14 oz/440 g) flaked
coconut

1 can (14 fl oz/430 ml)
sweetened condensed milk

2 teaspoons almond extract
(essence)

1 teaspoon vanilla extract
(essence)

Lemon Crisps

Preheat the oven to 375°F (190°C). Generously grease 2 baking sheets with shortening.

In a bowl, combine the butter and sugar. With an electric mixer set on medium-high speed, beat until well blended. Add the egg and lemon extract and beat until the mixture is fluffy, stopping occasionally to scrape down the sides of the bowl. Reduce the speed to low, add the flour, and mix just until incorporated.

Drop a tablespoonful of the batter at one end of the prepared baking sheet. Dip the blade of an icing spatula into cool water and spread the batter into a thin circle 3½–4 inches (9–10 cm) in diameter. Make another circle on the baking sheet, spacing it well apart from the first. Repeat this process, using all the batter and both baking sheets.

Bake until the edges are just beginning to brown, about 6 minutes. Transfer the baking sheets to wire racks and let cool for 1 minute. Using a metal spatula, transfer the cookies to the racks to cool completely.

Makes about 16

Vegetable shortening for greasing

½ cup (4 oz/125 g) unsalted butter, at room temperature

⅓ cup (3 oz/90g) sugar

1 egg

1 teaspoon lemon extract (essence)

¾ cup (4 oz/125 g) all-purpose (plain) flour

Vanilla Cookie-Press Ribbons

A touch of cardamom adds an unusual accent to what is essentially a vanilla cookie. Use the ribbon-design plate in the cookie press to make festive ribbons. Be sure to use a large egg for this recipe so that the dough has the proper consistency.

Preheat the oven to 375°F (190°C).

In a bowl, combine the butter and granulated sugar. Using an electric mixer set on high speed, beat until light and fluffy. Beat in the egg, vanilla, cardamom, and salt. Using a wooden spoon, stir in the flour until well mixed.

Pack the dough into a cookie press. Fit with the ribbon-design plate. Press the dough out onto ungreased baking sheets in strips 4 inches (10 cm) long.

Bake until golden brown, about 10 minutes. Gently transfer the cookies to wire racks. Sprinkle with vanilla sugar, if desired, and let cool. Store in an airtight container at room temperature for up to 4 days.

Makes about 3 dozen

1 cup (8 oz/250 g) unsalted butter, at room temperature

1 cup (8 oz/250 g) granulated sugar

1 egg

2$\frac{1}{2}$ teaspoons vanilla extract (essence)

$\frac{1}{2}$ teaspoon ground cardamom

$\frac{1}{2}$ teaspoon salt

2$\frac{1}{2}$ cups (10 oz/315 g) all-purpose (plain) flour, sifted before measuring

Vanilla Sugar (page 315) for sprinkling (optional)

Pecan-Lemon Shortbread Hearts

These pretty, delicate cookies are perfect with coffee or as the finish to a romantic meal. Use other shapes, if you like, and sprinkle with Vanilla Sugar to liven them up. It is fun to use several sizes of cutters, too.

1½ cups (7½ oz/235 g) all-purpose (plain) flour

½ cup (4 oz/125 g) granulated sugar

¼ cup (1 oz/30 g) cornstarch (cornflour)

1 tablespoon plus 1 teaspoon grated lemon zest (page 329)

¼ teaspoon salt

¾ cup (6 oz/185 g) cold unsalted butter, cut into ½-inch (12-mm) pieces

½ teaspoon vanilla extract (essence)

1 cup (4 oz/125 g) pecans

Vanilla Sugar (page 315) for sprinkling (optional)

Preheat the oven to 350°F (180°C).

In a food processor fitted with the metal blade, combine the flour, granulated sugar, cornstarch, lemon zest, and salt. Process briefly until well mixed. Add the butter and vanilla and, using rapid off-on pulses, process until the mixture resembles a fine meal. Add the pecans and process until finely chopped.

Transfer the mixture to a large sheet of waxed paper and gather together into a flat disk. Top with a second sheet of waxed paper. Roll out the dough ¼ inch (6 mm) thick. Using a 3-inch (7.5-cm) or 1½-inch (4-cm) heart-shaped cutter, cut out the cookies. Transfer the cookies to ungreased baking sheets, spacing them ½ inch (12 mm) apart. Gather up the scraps, roll out again, and cut out additional cookies. Sprinkle the cookies with Vanilla Sugar, if desired.

Bake until just beginning to color, about 20 minutes. Transfer the baking sheets to wire racks and let cool for 5 minutes. Transfer the cookies to the racks to cool completely. Store in an airtight container at room temperature for up to 1 week.

Makes about 2 dozen

Honey and Orange Madeleines

These classic, fancifully shaped sponge-cake cookies are baked in a special pan that has ridges like a seashell. Sifting the flour before measuring ensures that the cookies will have a light texture.

Preheat the oven to 400°F (200°C). Generously brush a 12-mold madeleine pan with melted butter; dust with flour.

In a heatproof bowl or the top pan of double boiler, combine the eggs, honey, sugar, orange zest, and allspice. Set over (but not touching) a pan of simmering water and whisk just until lukewarm.

Transfer the bowl to a work surface and, using an electric mixer set on high speed, beat until pale yellow, light, foamy, and tripled in volume, about 10 minutes. Beat in the vanilla. Reduce the speed to low and gradually mix in the flour.

Transfer one-third of the batter to another bowl and gradually fold the ³/₄ cup (6 fl oz/180 ml) melted butter into it. (Do not fold in any water that separated out at the bottom of the butter pan.) Gently fold the mixture into the remaining batter. Spoon into the prepared molds, filling each mold almost to the top and using about half the batter.

Bake until golden brown and springy to the touch, about 12 minutes, rotating the pan 180 degrees halfway through baking. Immediately invert the pan onto a wire rack. Using a knife, gently pry out the cookies. Sprinkle with Vanilla Sugar, if desired. Wipe out the pan, brush with melted butter, dust with flour, and repeat with the remaining batter. Let the cookies cool completely on the racks. Store in an airtight container at room temperature for up to 3 days.

Makes 2 dozen

Melted butter for brushing

2 eggs

¹/₂ cup (6 oz/185 g) honey

¹/₄ cup (2 oz/60 g) granulated sugar

1¹/₂ teaspoons grated orange zest (page 329)

¹/₈ teaspoon ground allspice

¹/₂ teaspoon vanilla extract (essence)

1 cup (4 oz/125 g) all-purpose (plain) flour, sifted before measuring, plus extra for dusting

³/₄ cup (6 oz/185 g) unsalted butter, melted and cooled to lukewarm

Vanilla Sugar (page 315) for sprinkling (optional)

Pine-Nut Tassies

You'll need miniature muffin tins to make these tiny, sweet, tartlike cookies, which are reminiscent of pecan pies. The sweet flavor of pine nuts makes these bite-sized treats an especially rich accompaniment to afternoon tea or coffee.

FOR THE PASTRY:

3 oz (90 g) cream cheese, at room temperature

1/2 cup (4 oz/125 g) unsalted butter, at room temperature

1 cup (5 oz/155 g) all-purpose (plain) flour

FOR THE FILLING:

1 egg, lightly beaten

3/4 cup (6 oz/185 g) firmly packed dark brown sugar

1 tablespoon unsalted butter, at room temperature

1 teaspoon vanilla extract (essence)

Pinch of salt

2/3 cup (3 1/2 oz/105 g) pine nuts

To make the pastry, combine the cream cheese and butter in a bowl. Using an electric mixer set on high speed, beat until well blended. Reduce the speed to low, add the flour, and mix just until incorporated.

Divide the dough between 2 large sheets of waxed paper. Using the paper as an aid, form each portion into a log 6 inches (15 cm) long. Wrap each log in the paper and refrigerate until firm, at least 1 hour or up to overnight.

Preheat the oven to 325°F (165°C). Unwrap the dough and cut each log into 12 rounds, each 1/2 inch (12 mm) thick. Press each round into the bottom and up the sides of a miniature muffin cup measuring 1 3/4 inches (4.5 cm) in diameter; build the edges up slightly beyond the rim.

To make the filling, combine the egg, brown sugar, butter, vanilla, and salt in a bowl and stir until smooth. Mix in half of the pine nuts. Spoon the mixture into the cups, filling almost to the tops. Use the remaining pine nuts to top the cookies.

Bake until the filling is set and the crusts begin to color, about 30 minutes. Let cool completely in the muffin tins on wire racks, then remove from the tins. Store in an airtight container in the refrigerator for up to 3 days.

Makes 2 dozen

Snickerdoodles

A cinnamon-and-sugar topping distinguishes these classic cookies. Served warm with a tall glass of cold milk, they make a favorite afternoon snack. Store cream of tartar, tightly covered, for up to 1 year.

2 tablespoons plus ³/₄ cup (6 oz/185 g) sugar

2 teaspoons ground cinnamon

1¹/₃ cups (5¹/₂ oz/170 g) all-purpose (plain) flour

1 teaspoon cream of tartar

¹/₂ teaspoon baking soda (bicarbonate of soda)

Pinch of salt

¹/₂ cup (4 oz/125 g) butter, softened

1 egg

¹/₂ teaspoon vanilla extract (essence)

Preheat the oven to 400°F (200°C).

In a bowl, stir together the 2 tablespoons sugar and the cinnamon. Set aside. In another bowl, whisk together the flour, cream of tartar, baking soda, and salt. Set aside.

In a large bowl, combine the butter, the ³/₄ cup (6 oz/185 g) sugar, egg, and vanilla. With an electric mixer set on medium-high speed, beat until the mixture is smooth and well blended. Reduce the speed to low, add the flour mixture, and continue to mix just until incorporated.

Roll 1 rounded teaspoonful of the dough between your palms into a ball. Roll the ball in the cinnamon-sugar mixture. Put the sugar-coated ball on an ungreased baking sheet, spacing the balls 2 inches (5 cm) apart on the baking sheet. Repeat with the remaining dough and a second baking sheet.

Bake until round, flat, and a light golden brown, 8–10 minutes. Transfer the baking sheets to wire racks and let cool for 1–2 minutes. Using a metal spatula, transfer the cookies to the racks to cool completely.

Makes about 2 dozen

Old-Fashioned Oatmeal Cookies

These tried-and-true cookies are a welcome treat anytime. But their sturdy shape also makes them ideally suited for toting to picnics or including in school lunches. Be sure to use quick-cooking rolled oats.

Preheat the oven on to 375°F (190°C).

In a bowl, whisk together the flour, oats, baking powder, baking soda, cinnamon, and salt. Set aside.

In another bowl, combine the butter, $^1/_2$ cup (4 oz/125 g) granulated sugar, the brown sugar, egg, and vanilla. With an electric mixer set on medium-high speed, beat until smooth and creamy. Reduce the speed to low, gradually add the flour mixture, and mix just until incorporated.

Put the 2 tablespoons granulated sugar in a small bowl. Roll 1 rounded tablespoon of dough into a ball. Dip the top of the ball in the sugar and place the ball, sugar side up, on an ungreased baking sheet, spacing the balls 2 inches (5 cm) apart on the baking sheets. Repeat with the remaining dough and a second baking sheet.

Bake until light golden brown, 10–12 minutes. Transfer the sheets to wire racks and let cool for 2 minutes. Using a metal spatula, transfer the cookies to the racks to cool completely.

Makes about 3 dozen

1 cup (5 oz/155 g) all-purpose (plain) flour

1 cup (3 oz/90 g) quick-cooking rolled oats

1/2 teaspoon baking powder

1/2 teaspoon baking soda (bicarbonate of soda)

1/4 teaspoon ground cinnamon

1/4 teaspoon salt

1/2 cup (4 oz/125 g) unsalted butter, at room temperature

1/2 cup (4 oz/125 g) plus 2 tablespoons granulated sugar

1/2 cup (3 1/2 oz/105 g) firmly packed light brown sugar

1 egg

1 teaspoon vanilla extract (essence)

Oatmeal, Date, and Walnut Cookies

This is a great recipe for a big batch of long-keeping, old-fashioned cookies. You can alter the baking time according to your preference for chewy or crisp cookies. Try serving with milk or warm spiced cider on a chilly day.

Preheat the oven to 375°F (190°C). Grease at least 2 baking sheets.

Sift together the flour, cinnamon, baking soda, and salt into a bowl; set aside. Place the butter in a large bowl. Using an electric mixer set on high speed, beat until light and fluffy. Beat in the granulated sugar and brown sugar. Add the whole eggs, egg yolk, milk, and vanilla and beat until light and fluffy, about 2 minutes. Reduce the speed to low, add the flour mixture, and mix just until incorporated. Mix in the oats, dates, and walnuts on low speed.

Drop the batter by rounded tablespoons onto the prepared baking sheets, spacing the mounds 2 inches (5 cm) apart. Bake until light brown, about 12 minutes for chewy cookies and about 15 minutes for crisp cookies. Repeat with the remaining dough. Transfer the baking sheets to wire racks and let cool for 1 minute. Transfer the cookies to the racks to cool completely. Store in an airtight container in the refrigerator for up to 1 week.

Makes about 4 dozen

2 cups (10 oz/315 g) all-purpose (plain) flour

1 tablespoon ground cinnamon

1 teaspoon baking soda (bicarbonate of soda)

1 teaspoon salt

3/4 cup (6 oz/185 g) unsalted butter, at room temperature, plus extra for greasing

1 cup (8 oz/250 g) granulated sugar

1 cup (7 oz/220 g) firmly packed dark brown sugar

2 whole eggs

1 egg yolk (page 324)

3 tablespoons milk

2 teaspoons vanilla extract (essence)

2 1/2 cups (7 1/2 oz/235 g) old-fashioned rolled oats or quick-cooking oats

1/2 lb (250 g) dates, chopped (about 1 1/2 cups)

2 cups (8 oz/250 g) walnuts, coarsely chopped

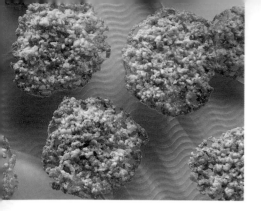

Lacy Oatmeal Crisps

Timing is important when making these delicate cookies: if the cookies don't cool long enough, they will lose their shape. If they cool too long, they will stick to the baking sheets. Follow the instructions closely.

3/4 cup (6 oz/185 g) firmly packed light brown sugar

1/2 cup (4 oz/125 g) unsalted butter, at room temperature

2 tablespoons milk

1 teaspoon vanilla extract (essence)

1/4 teaspoon salt

1 1/4 cups (3 1/2 oz/105 g) quick-cooking rolled oats

2 tablespoons all-purpose (plain) flour

Preheat the oven to 350°F (180°C).

In a bowl, combine the brown sugar, butter, milk, vanilla, and salt. With an electric mixer set on medium-high speed, beat until the mixture is well blended. Stir in the oats and flour.

Drop the dough by level teaspoonfuls onto the ungreased baking sheets, spacing the mounds 2 inches (5 cm) apart.

Bake until light golden brown around the edges, 8–12 minutes. Transfer the baking sheets to wire racks and let cool for about 2 minutes. Using a metal spatula, transfer the cookies to the racks to cool completely.

Makes about 40

Ginger Molasses Cookies

Keep a batch of these classic New England cookies in the cookie jar for the perfect anytime snack. Stored in an airtight container at room temperature, they will keep for up to one week.

Sift together the flour, baking soda, ginger, cinnamon, cloves, and salt into a bowl; set aside. In another bowl, combine the shortening, butter, and brown sugar. Using an electric mixer set on high speed, beat until fluffy. Add the egg, molasses, and orange zest and beat until blended. Reduce the speed to low, add the flour mixture, and mix until just incorporated. Cover and refrigerate for 1 hour or up to overnight.

Preheat the oven to 350°F (180°C). Lightly grease 2–3 baking sheets with butter.

Using wet hands, form the dough into 1¼-inch (3-cm) balls, then roll each ball in granulated sugar to coat evenly. Arrange on the prepared baking sheets, spacing about 2 inches (5 cm) apart.

Bake until pale golden and cracked on top but still soft, about 12 minutes. Transfer the baking sheets to wire racks and let cool for 1 minute. Transfer the cookies to wire racks to cool completely.

Makes about 2½ dozen

2 cups (10 oz/315 g) all-purpose (plain) flour

2 teaspoons baking soda (bicarbonate of soda)

2 teaspoons ground ginger

1½ teaspoons ground cinnamon

1 teaspoon ground cloves

1 teaspoon salt

½ cup (4 oz/125 g) vegetable shortening, at room temperature

¼ cup (2 oz/60 g) unsalted butter, at room temperature, plus extra for greasing

1 cup (7 oz/220 g) firmly packed dark brown sugar

1 egg

¼ cup (3 fl oz/80 ml) dark molasses

2 teaspoons grated orange zest (page 329)

Granulated sugar for coating

Cinnamon–Chocolate Chip Refrigerator Cookies

These cookies are a delicious variation on the traditional Mexican wedding cookie, flavored with cinnamon, chocolate, and orange zest. Their warming flavors go perfectly with cups of steaming hot chocolate on an especially cold day.

3/4 cup (6 oz/185 g) unsalted butter, at room temperature, plus extra for greasing

1 cup (8 oz/250 g) sugar

1½ teaspoons grated orange zest (page 329)

2¾ teaspoons ground cinnamon

¼ teaspoon salt

2 egg yolks

1¾ cups (9 oz/280 g) all-purpose (plain) flour

1 cup (6 oz/185 g) miniature semisweet (plain) chocolate chips

In a bowl, combine the butter, $^1/_2$ cup (4 oz/125 g) of the sugar, orange zest, $1^1/_4$ teaspoons of the cinnamon, and the salt. Using an electric mixer set on high speed, beat until light and fluffy. Add the egg yolks and beat until light and fluffy. Reduce the speed to low, gradually add the flour and chocolate chips, and mix just until incorporated.

Turn the dough out onto a lightly floured surface. Divide in half. Roll each piece between your palms and the work surface to form a log about $1^1/_2$ inches (4 cm) in diameter. Wrap the logs tightly in plastic wrap and refrigerate until firm, about 1 hour or up to overnight.

Preheat the oven to 350°F (180°C). Lightly grease baking sheets. Unwrap the dough and cut each log into rounds $^1/_4$ inch (6 mm) think. Transfer to the prepared baking sheets, spacing the slices $1^1/_2$ inches (4 cm) apart.

Bake until the edges are brown, about 15 minutes. Transfer the cookies to wire racks and let cool for 5 minutes.

Whisk together the remaining $^1/_2$ cup sugar and the remaining $1^1/_2$ teaspoons cinnamon in a bowl. Add several warm cookies and toss to coat with the sugar. Return the cookies to the racks to cool completely. Repeat with the remaining cookies. Store in an airtight container at room temperature for up to 5 days.

Makes about 4 dozen

Hazelnut Biscotti

These cookies can be made up to 5 days before serving and stored in an airtight container at room temperature. If they soften, recrisp them on a cookie sheet in a 250°F (120°C) oven for 5–10 minutes before serving.

2¹/₂ cups (12¹/₂ oz/390 g) all-purpose (plain) flour

1¹/₂ teaspoons baking powder

1 teaspoon ground cinnamon

¹/₂ teaspoon salt

¹/₂ cup (4 oz/125 g) unsalted butter, at room temperature

1 cup (8 oz/250 g) sugar

3 eggs

Juice and grated zest of 1 lemon (page 329)

1 tablespoon vanilla extract (essence)

¹/₂ teaspoon almond extract (essence)

2 cups (10 oz/315 g) hazelnuts (filberts) toasted and skinned (page 326), then coarsely chopped

Preheat the oven to 325°F (165°C).

In a bowl, whisk together the flour, baking powder, cinnamon, and salt. In another bowl, combine the butter and sugar. Using an electric mixer set on medium speed, beat the mixture until light and fluffy. Add the eggs, one at a time, beating well after each addition. Beat in the lemon juice and zest and vanilla and almond extracts. Reduce the speed to low and beat in the flour mixture, one-third at a time, mixing until incorporated. Fold in the nuts. The dough will be slightly granular.

Turn the dough out onto a floured work surface and divide it in half. Using your palms, roll each half into an oval log about 1¹/₂ inches (4 cm) in diameter. Place well spaced on an ungreased baking sheet.

Bake until golden brown, about 30 minutes. Remove from the oven and let rest until cool to the touch. Reduce the oven temperature to 250°F (120°C).

Cut each log on the diagonal into slices ¹/₃ inch (1 cm) thick. Arrange the slices, cut side down, on the ungreased baking sheet and return to the oven. Bake until lightly toasted and the edges are golden brown, about 10 minutes. Let cool either on the baking sheet or on a wire rack.

Makes 18–20

Hazelnut Amaretti

A recipe inspired by the outstanding almond amaretti in Carol Fields' *The Italian Baker*. For a special presentation or for gifts, wrap each cookie in tissue paper, twist the ends, and pack in cookie tins or boxes.

Preheat the oven to 300°F (150°C). Line a baking sheet with parchment (baking) paper or waxed paper.

In a food processor fitted with the metal blade, finely grind the hazelnuts (be careful not to grind to a paste). Add ¼ cup (1 oz/30 g) of the confectioners' sugar and the flour. Set aside.

In another bowl, beat the egg whites until soft peaks form. Gradually add the granulated sugar and beat until stiff, shiny peaks form. Fold in the almond extract and the nut mixture.

Spoon the batter into a pastry bag fitted with a ½-inch (12-mm) plain tip. Pipe the batter onto the prepared baking sheet in mounds 1½ inches (4 cm) in diameter, spacing them well apart. Using a wet finger, smooth the top of each cookie. Sprinkle with pearl sugar, if desired.

Bake until just beginning to brown, about 45 minutes. Turn off the oven, leave the oven door closed, and let the cookies dry for 30 minutes.

Transfer the cookies to wire racks to cool completely. Store in an airtight container at room temperature for up to 1 month.

Makes about 3 dozen

1¼ cups (6½ oz/200 g) hazelnuts (filberts)

¾ cup (3 oz/90 g) plus 3 tablespoons confectioners' (icing) sugar

1 teaspoon all-purpose (plain) flour

2 egg whites

⅓ cup (3 oz/90 g) granulated sugar

¾ teaspoon almond extract (essence)

Pearl sugar for sprinkling, optional

Chocolate-Chunk and Cherry Cookies

Use big hunks of premium chocolate to make these chocolate-rich cookies extra special. Dried cherries or cranberries provide sophisticated flavor; if they're unavailable, raisins or currants can be substituted with excellent results.

Preheat the oven to 350°F (180°C).

Sift together the flour, baking powder, baking soda, and salt into a bowl; set aside. In another bowl, combine the butter, brown sugar, and vanilla. Using an electric mixer set on high speed, beat until fluffy. Beat in the egg. Reduce the speed to low, add the flour mixture, and mix just until incorporated. Mix in the chocolate and cherries on low speed.

Drop the batter by slightly rounded tablespoons onto ungreased baking sheets, spacing the mounds 2 inches (5 cm) apart. Bake until golden brown, about 16 minutes. Transfer the cookies to wire racks to cool. Store in an airtight container at room temperature for up to 4 days.

Makes about 2 dozen

1 cup (5 oz/155 g) all-purpose (plain) flour

3/4 teaspoon baking powder

1/8 teaspoon baking soda (bicarbonate of soda)

1/8 teaspoon salt

1/2 cup (4 oz/125 g) plus 2 tablespoons unsalted butter, at room temperature

3/4 cup (6 oz/185 g) firmly packed dark brown sugar

1 teaspoon vanilla extract (essence)

1 egg

8 oz (250 g) semisweet (plain) chocolate, cut into 1/2-inch (12-mm) pieces (about 1 1/2 cups)

6 oz (185 g) dried pitted sour cherries, dried Bing cherries, or dried cranberries, chopped (about 1 1/2 cups)

Walnut-Cardamom Viennese Crescents

Using a food processor, it only takes minutes to get these Old World favorites into the oven. They can be made even faster if formed into 1-inch (2.5-cm) balls rather than crescent shapes.

1 cup (5 oz/155 g) all-purpose (plain) flour

3/4 cup (3 oz/90 g) walnuts

1/2 cup (4 oz/125 g) cold unsalted butter, cut into 1/2-inch (12-mm) pieces

1/4 cup (2 oz/60 g) granulated sugar

1 teaspoon vanilla extract (essence)

1/2 teaspoon ground cardamom

1/2 teaspoon grated orange zest (page 329)

Pinch of salt

Confectioners' (icing) sugar or Vanilla Sugar (page 315) for dusting

Preheat the oven to 325°F (165°C).

In a food processor fitted with the metal blade, combine the flour, walnuts, butter, granulated sugar, vanilla, cardamom, orange zest, and salt. Using rapid off-on pulses, process until the mixture resembles coarse meal. Continue to process until the dough begins to gather together.

Roll 2 teaspoons of the dough between your palms to form a rope 2 1/2 inches (6 cm) long, slightly tapering it at the ends. Arrange the rope on an ungreased baking sheet in a crescent shape. Repeat with the remaining dough, spacing the cookies 1 inch (2.5 cm) apart.

Bake until just firm to the touch, about 20 minutes. Let cool on the baking sheet for 5 minutes. Transfer the cookies to a wire rack. Dust confectioners' sugar over the cooled cookies (if using Vanilla Sugar, sprinkle it over the cookies while they are still warm). Store in an airtight container at room temperature for up to 5 days.

Makes about 2 dozen

Rugelach

The addition of cream cheese to the dough makes these cookies extra rich and flaky. With two different fillings, one batch should be enough to please everyone at the table.

In a bowl, combine the butter, cream cheese, and granulated sugar. With an electric mixer set on medium-high speed, beat until the mixture is well combined. Reduce the speed to low, add the flour, and beat until the mixture forms small crumbs. Using your hands, knead the crumbs in the bowl to form a smooth dough. Divide the dough into 4 pieces.

Roll each piece of dough into a ball. Place each ball on a separate sheet of plastic wrap. With your hands, flatten each ball into a thick circle, wrap, and refrigerate until firm, about 30 minutes. Preheat the oven to 350°F (180°C). Line 2 baking sheets with parchment (baking) paper.

Unwrap 1 piece of the dough and place it on a lightly floured work surface. With a rolling pin, roll out the dough into a circle 1/8 inch (3 mm) thick. If the dough is too firm to roll, let it sit at room temperature for about 10 minutes.

Either sprinkle one-fourth of the cinnamon-sugar mixture over the dough circle or spread 1 tablespoon apricot jam over the circle. Cut the circle into 8 wedges. Starting at the wide end of each wedge, roll up each piece of dough to the narrow pointed end. Place the cookies point side down on the prepared baking sheets. Repeat rolling out, filling, cutting, and rolling up until all of the dough and fillings have been used.

Bake until very light golden brown, 15–25 minutes. Transfer the baking sheets to wire racks and let cool for 5 minutes. Using a metal spatula, transfer the cookies to the racks and let cool completely. Dust with confectioners' sugar.

Makes 32

½ cup (4 oz/125 g) butter, at room temperature

3 oz (90g) cream cheese, at room temperature

1 teaspoon granulated sugar

1⅓ cups (7 oz/220 g) all-purpose (plain) flour

FOR CINNAMON FILLING:

2 tablespoons granulated sugar mixed with 2 teaspoons ground cinnamon

FOR APRICOT FILLING:

4 tablespoons (2½ oz/75 g) apricot jam

Confectioners' (icing) sugar for dusting

Othellos

Other chocolate cookies pale in comparison to these deeply rich, moist, loaded-with-flavor treats. If you find the bottoms are burning, try slipping a clean, unlined baking sheet under the first to create a double thickness.

8 oz (250 g) bittersweet chocolate, chopped (about 1²/₃ cups)

2 tablespoons unsalted butter

3 tablespoons all-purpose (plain) flour

¹/₄ teaspoon baking powder

2 extra-large eggs, at room temperature

²/₃ cup (5 oz/155 g) sugar

1 teaspoon vanilla extract (essence)

1²/₃ cups (10 oz/315 g) semisweet (plain) chocolate chips

2 cups (8 oz/250 g) whole macadamia nuts, pecan halves, or walnuts

Preheat the oven to 350°F (180°C). Line 2 baking sheets with aluminum foil, shiny side down, or with parchment (baking) paper.

Place the chocolate and butter in a heatproof bowl or the top pan of a double boiler. Set over (but not touching) a pan of gently simmering water. Stir until smooth. Let cool slightly.

Sift together the flour and baking powder into a small bowl. In another bowl, combine the eggs, sugar, and vanilla. Using an electric mixer set on high speed, beat until light and fluffy, 5–7 minutes. Fold in the cooled chocolate mixture, the flour mixture, and finally, the chocolate chips and nuts; do not overmix. Using a tablespoon, scoop up mounds of the batter about 1¹/₂ inches (4 cm) in diameter and place them about 1¹/₂ inches apart on the prepared baking sheets.

Bake one sheet at a time. Bake for 6 minutes, then turn the sheet 180 degrees and continue baking just until the tops appear dry, 3–4 minutes; they will still be very soft. Transfer the baking sheets to wire racks and let the cookies cool completely before lifting from the baking sheets.

Store in a covered container at room temperature for up to 2 weeks, or freeze for up to 2 months; defrost at room temperature in the container.

Makes about 3 dozen

Peanut Butter Cup Cookies

These thumbprint cookies taste just like peanut butter cup candies, only better. Serve them as an afternoon snack, accompanied by a tall glass of cold milk. Using creamy peanut butter will give you the best results.

$^3/_4$ cup (7 oz/220 g) creamy peanut butter

9 tablespoons (4$^1/_2$ oz/140 g) unsalted butter, at room temperature, plus extra for greasing

$^3/_4$ teaspoon vanilla extract (essence)

$^1/_2$ cup (2 oz/60 g) confectioners' (icing) sugar

1$^3/_4$ cups (9 oz/280 g) all-purpose (plain) flour

$^2/_3$ cup (2 oz/60 g) unsweetened cocoa powder

1 teaspoon baking soda (bicarbonate of soda)

$^1/_2$ teaspoon baking powder

$^1/_2$ teaspoon salt

$^1/_2$ cup (4 oz/125 g) vegetable shortening, at room temperature

1 cup (8 oz/250 g) granulated sugar, plus extra for coating

1 egg

2 tablespoons milk

$^1/_4$ teaspoon almond extract (essence)

Combine the peanut butter, 3 tablespoons of the butter, and the vanilla in a food processor fitted with the metal blade. Process until smooth. Add the confectioners' sugar and process until well blended. Set aside.

Preheat the oven to 350°F (180°C). Grease baking sheets with butter.

Sift together the flour, cocoa powder, baking soda, baking powder, and salt into a bowl; set aside.

In a bowl, combine the shortening, the remaining 6 tablespoons (3 oz/90 g) butter, and the 1 cup (8 oz/250 g) granulated sugar. Using an electric mixer set on high speed, beat until very fluffy, about 2 minutes. Reduce the speed to low and mix in the flour mixture just until incorporated.

Using damp hands, roll the dough between your palms to form 1-inch (2.5-cm) balls. Roll the balls in sugar to coat evenly. Place on the prepared baking sheets, spacing the balls 2 inches (5 cm) apart. Using your thumb or the back of a spoon, make a large indentation in the center of each.

Bake until puffed and slightly cracked, about 12 minutes. Remove from the oven and mound about 1 teaspoon of the peanut butter mixture in the center of each cookie. Let cool for 1 minute, then transfer to wire racks to cool completely. Store refrigerated in an airtight container for up to 3 days.

Makes about 4 dozen

Chocolate-Peppermint Cookie-Press Cookies

For an additional touch, finely chop peppermint candies or candy canes in a food processor, mix them with an equal amount of confectioners' (icing) sugar, and coat the warm cookies by tossing them in the mixture.

Preheat the oven to 375°F (190°C).

In a bowl, combine the butter and sugar. Using an electric mixer set on high speed, beat until light. Add the egg, vanilla and peppermint extracts, and salt and beat until light and fluffy. Reduce the speed to low and mix in the cocoa powder. Add the flour and mix just until incorporated.

Pack the dough into a cookie press. Fit with the desired design plate. Press the dough out onto ungreased baking sheets, spacing the cookies 1 inch (2.5 cm) apart.

Bake until firm to the touch, about 10 minutes. Transfer the cookies to wire racks to cool. Store in an airtight container at room temperature for up to 5 days.

Makes about 4 dozen

3/4 cup (6 oz/185 g) unsalted butter, at room temperature

3/4 cup (6 oz/185 g) sugar

1 egg

1½ teaspoons vanilla extract (essence)

1½ teaspoons peppermint extract (essence)

1/8 teaspoon salt

1/4 cup (3/4 oz/20 g) unsweetened cocoa powder, preferably Dutch process

1½ cups (7½ oz/235 g) all-purpose (plain) flour

Walnut, Chocolate, and Ginger Shortbread Fans

These picturesque cookies are the perfect accompaniment to fresh berries for a delightful dinner-party dessert. It is easy to make the pretty shape: Press the dough into a pie dish, then cut it into wedges before serving.

Preheat the oven to 350°F (180°C). Grease a 10-inch (25-cm) glass pie dish.

In a bowl, whisk together the flour, cornstarch, and salt; set aside.

In another bowl, combine the butter, granulated sugar, and vanilla. Using an electric mixer set on high speed, beat until light and fluffy. Reduce the speed to low, add the flour mixture, and mix just until beginning to gather together. Then mix in the walnuts, chocolate chips, and ginger.

Press the dough into the bottom of the prepared dish, building up the edges so they reach ½ inch (12 mm) up the sides. Using a fork, crimp the edges decoratively. Using a sharp knife and a ruler as a guide, cut into 12 wedges. Be sure to cut all the way through the dough. Pierce each wedge 3 times with a fork. Sprinkle with Vanilla Sugar, if desired.

Bake until barely firm to the touch and brown on the edges, about 30 minutes. Transfer the pie dish to a wire rack and recut the wedges. Let the cookies cool. Gently remove from the dish with a knife. Store in an airtight container at room temperature for up to 1 week.

Makes 1 dozen

1 cup (5 oz/155 g) all-purpose (plain) flour

2 tablespoons plus 2 teaspoons cornstarch (cornflour)

¼ teaspoon salt

½ cup (4 oz/125 g) unsalted butter, at room temperature, plus extra for greasing

⅓ cup (3 oz/90 g) granulated sugar

¾ teaspoon vanilla extract (essence)

½ cup (2 oz/60 g) walnuts, finely chopped

⅓ cup (2 oz/60 g) miniature semisweet (plain) chocolate chips

3 tablespoons firmly packed chopped crystallized ginger

Vanilla Sugar for sprinkling (page 315) (optional)

Lemon Squares

Fresh lemon zest and juice combine to give these gooey delights their tart citrusy flavor. Mixing the crust right in the cake pan makes them even easier to prepare.

7 tablespoons unsalted butter, at room temperature

1 cup (5 oz/155 g) plus 2 tablespoons all-purpose (plain) flour

1/4 cup (1 oz/30 g) plus 1 tablespoon confectioners' (icing) sugar

2 eggs

1 cup (8 oz/250 g) granulated sugar

Grated zest of 1 small lemon (page 329)

2 tablespoons fresh lemon juice

1/2 teaspoon baking powder

Pinch of salt

Preheat the oven to 350°F (180°C).

Place the butter in an 8-inch (20-cm) square cake pan. Put the pan in the oven until the butter melts, about 5 minutes. Let cool. Sprinkle the 1 cup flour and the 1/4 cup confectioners' sugar over the melted butter and mix the ingredients to form a dough. Press the dough evenly over the bottom of the pan. Return the pan to the oven and bake the crust for 15 minutes.

Meanwhile, in a bowl, combine the eggs and granulated sugar. With an electric mixer set on medium speed, beat until the mixture is well blended. Reduce the speed to low and beat in the remaining 2 tablespoons flour, the lemon zest and juice, the baking powder, and the salt until well combined.

Spread the lemon mixture over the hot crust. Return to the oven and bake until pale brown, 20–25 minutes. Transfer the pan to a wire rack and let cool.

When the cookies have cooled completely, dust the 1 tablespoon confectioners' sugar over the top. Cut into 2-inch (5-cm) squares.

Makes 16

Granola Bars

These delicious and sturdy treats pack well, and are a great snack for camping and hiking trips. They are so simple to make, you may never rely on store-bought granola bars again.

Preheat the oven to 350°F (180°C). Lightly grease an 8-inch (20-cm) square cake pan. Set aside.

In a bowl, whisk together the flour, baking soda, and cinnamon. In another bowl, combine the banana, brown sugar, oil, honey, egg white, and vanilla. With an electric mixer set on medium speed, beat just until blended. Reduce the speed to low, add the flour mixture, and mix just until incorporated. Stir in the granola.

Pour and scrape the batter into the prepared pan and spread evenly.

Bake until the top is a light golden brown and a toothpick inserted into the center comes out clean, about 15 minutes. Transfer to a wire rack and let cool completely. Cut into bars, each about 2 inches (5 cm) square.

Makes 16

1/3 cup (2 oz/60 g) all-purpose (plain) flour

1/2 teaspoon baking soda

1/2 teaspoon ground cinnamon

1 ripe banana, mashed

2 tablespoons firmly packed brown sugar

2 tablespoons canola oil, plus extra for greasing

2 tablespoons honey

1 egg white

1 teaspoon vanilla extract (essence)

1 1/3 cups (8 oz/250 g) granola

Fig and Walnut Hermits

Filled with fruit and nuts and glazed with a Confectioners' Sugar Icing, these cakey molasses bars are quite sturdy. Buy best-quality dried Calimyrna figs in bulk; they will keep for up to 6 months if refrigerated in an airtight containter.

2 cups (10 oz/315 g)
all-purpose (plain) flour

1 teaspoon ground cinnamon

3/4 teaspoon baking soda
(bicarbonate of soda)

3/4 teaspoon baking powder

1/2 teaspoon salt

1/2 teaspoon ground allspice

1/2 cup (4 oz/125 g) unsalted
butter, at room temperature,
plus extra for greasing

1/2 cup (3 1/2 oz/105 g) firmly
packed dark brown sugar

2 eggs

1/2 cup (5 1/2 fl oz/170 ml)
unsulfured light molasses

1 cup (5 oz/155 g) chopped
dried Calimyrna figs

1 cup (4 oz/125 g) coarsely
chopped walnuts

1/2 recipe Confectioners' Sugar
Icing (page 316)

Preheat the oven to 350°F (180°C). Grease a 9-by-13-inch (23-by-33-cm) baking dish with butter.

Sift together the flour, cinnamon, baking soda, baking powder, salt, and allspice into a bowl. Set aside. In another bowl, combine the butter and brown sugar. Using an electric mixer set on high speed, beat until fluffy. Beat in the eggs, one at a time, then continue beating until very fluffy, about 2 minutes. Mix in the molasses; do not worry if the mixture appears curdled. Reduce the speed to low, add the flour mixture, and mix just until incorporated. Fold in the figs and walnuts. Pour and scape the batter in the prepared dish and spread evenly.

Bake until the top is just springy to the touch, about 30 minutes. Transfer to a wire rack and let cool. Spread the icing evenly over the top and let stand until set, about 2 hours.

Cut into bars, each about 3 inches (7.5 cm) by 1 1/2 inches (4 cm). Wrap individually in plastic wrap and store at room temperature for up to 3 days.

Makes 2 dozen

White Chocolate–Cherry Bars

The tartness of dried cherries melds perfectly with white chocolate in these easy-to-make bars. Slivered almonds give them a delightful crunch. Dried cherries are available in specialty-food shops.

Preheat the oven to 350°F (180°C). Grease a 9-by-13-inch (23-by-33-cm) baking dish and dust with flour.

Sift together the sifted flour, baking powder, baking soda, and salt in a bowl.

In another bowl, combine the butter, brown sugar, and granulated sugar. Using an electric mixer set on medium speed, beat until light and fluffy, 2–3 minutes. Add the eggs one at a time, beating well after each addition. Beat in the almond extract. Reduce the speed to low, add the flour mixture, and beat just until incorporated. Stir in the cherries, white chocolate, and almonds. Pour and scrape the batter into the prepared dish and spread evenly.

Bake until the top is golden and the edges have just started to pull away from the sides, 35–45 minutes. Transfer to a wire rack and let cool completely, then cut into bars. Store in a covered container at room temperature for up to 1 week.

Makes 16–20

2¼ cup (9 oz/280 g) all-purpose (plain) flour, sifted before measuring, plus extra for dusting

1 teaspoon baking powder

½ teaspoon baking soda (bicarbonate of soda)

½ teaspoon salt

½ cup (4 oz/125 g) unsalted butter, at room temperature, plus extra for greasing

⅔ cup (5 oz/155 g) firmly packed light brown sugar

½ cup (4 oz/125 g) granulated sugar

2 eggs

1½ teaspoons almond extract (essence)

1 cup (4 oz/125 g) dried cherries or golden raisins (sultanas)

9 oz (280 g) white chocolate, coarsely chopped (scant 2 cups)

1 cup (4½ oz/140 g) slivered, blanched (page 326) almonds

White Chocolate and Macadamia Nut Blondies

This white-chocolate version of well-loved blondies are rich, gooey, and delicious treats that travel well on outdoor excursions such as picnics and bicycling trips. Drizzle them with Caramel Glaze (page 317) if you're feeling indulgent.

½ cup (4 oz/125 g) unsalted butter, at room temperature, plus extra for greasing

1¼ cups (9 oz/280 g) firmly packed golden brown sugar

2 teaspoons instant espresso powder

1 teaspoon vanilla extract (essence)

2 eggs

1 cup (5 oz/155 g) all-purpose (plain) flour

¾ cup (4 oz/125 g) macadamia nuts, coarsely chopped

3–4 oz (90–125 g) white chocolate, coarsely chopped

Caramel Glaze (page 317) for drizzling (optional)

Preheat the oven to 350°F (180°C). Grease an 8-inch (20-cm) square baking pan.

In a large bowl, combine the butter, brown sugar, espresso powder, and vanilla. Using an electric mixer set on high speed, beat until light and fluffy. Beat in the eggs, one at a time, beating well after each addition, then beat at high speed until very fluffy, about 2 minutes. Reduce the speed to low, add the flour, and mix just until incorporated. Fold in the nuts and white chocolate just until blended. Pour and scrape the batter in the prepared pan and spread evenly.

Bake until a toothpick inserted into the center comes out clean, about 40 minutes. Transfer to a wire rack and let cool. Drizzle with the Caramel Glaze, if desired. Cut into 24 bars. Wrap individually in plastic wrap and store at room temperature for up to 3 days.

Makes 2 dozen

Chocolate-Cranberry Bars

Dried cranberries add a touch of tartness to the gooey chocolate topping of these oatmeal-based bars. If you prefer, other tart dried fruits, such as chopped dried apricots or sour cherries, can be used instead.

Preheat the oven to 350°F (180°C). Line an 8-inch (20-cm) square baking pan with foil, leaving an overhang of about 2 inches (5 cm) on all sides to use for a handle. Grease the foil.

In a bowl, stir together the oats, brown sugar, $^1/_3$ cup flour, baking soda, and $^1/_8$ teaspoon salt. Add the melted butter and mix until crumbly. Transfer the mixture to the prepared pan and press firmly into the bottom to form a crust. Bake for 10 minutes.

Meanwhile, in a heavy saucepan over low heat, combine the room-temperature butter, chocolate, and espresso powder. Stir until melted and smooth. Remove from the heat.

Combine the eggs, granulated sugar, $^1/_4$ cup flour, vanilla, and remaining $^1/_8$ teaspoon salt in a bowl and whisk until well mixed. Whisk in the chocolate mixture and cranberries.

When the crust is ready, pour the chocolate mixture over the hot crust. Continue to bake until the edges are set but the center is still soft but not liquid, about 40 minutes. Transfer to a wire rack and let cool.

Using the foil, lift the cooled sheet from the pan and place on a work surface. Peel back the foil sides. Cut into bars, each about $2^1/_2$ inches (6 cm) by $1^1/_2$ inches (4 cm). Remove the bars from the foil. Wrap individually in plastic wrap and store at room temperature for up to 3 days.

Makes 15

1 cup (3 oz/90 g) old-fashioned rolled oats

1/2 cup (3 1/2 oz/105 g) firmly packed dark brown sugar

1/3 cup (2 oz/60 g) plus 1/4 cup (1 1/2 oz/45 g) all-purpose (plain) flour

1/4 teaspoon baking soda (bicarbonate of soda)

1/4 teaspoon salt

1/3 cup (3 oz/90 g) unsalted butter, melted

1/2 cup (1/4 lb/125 g) unsalted butter, at room temperature, plus extra for greasing

2 oz (60 g) unsweetened chocolate, chopped

1 teaspoon instant espresso powder

2 eggs

1 cup (8 oz/250 g) granulated sugar

2 teaspoons vanilla extract (essence)

1/2 cup (2 oz/60 g) dried cranberries

Chocolate Fudge Squares

These fudgy sweets have a texture and a taste akin to truffles but are made in a single pan and carved into small squares. Don't forget to cut them into squares while they are still hot.

5 oz (155 g) unsweetened chocolate, chopped (1 cup)

1/2 cup (4 oz/125 g) unsalted butter, plus extra for greasing

1/2 cup (4 oz/125 g) vegetable shortening

4 extra-large eggs

2 cups (1 lb/500g) sugar

2 cups (8 oz/250 g) all-purpose (plain) flour, sifted before measuring

Preheat the oven to 325°F (165°C). Grease a 9-inch (23-cm) square baking pan.

Place the chocolate, butter, and shortening in a heatproof bowl or the top pan of a double boiler. Set over (but not touching) a pan of gently simmering water. Stir until melted and smooth. Set aside to cool slightly.

In a bowl, combine the eggs and sugar. Using an electric mixer set on medium speed, beat until thick and light colored, 5–10 minutes. Fold in the cooled chocolate mixture and then the sifted flour, mixing only until the ingredients are incorporated.

Pour and scrape the batter into the prepared pan and bake until the top looks dry and feels firm to the touch, 45 minutes. Cut into 1 1/2-inch (4-cm) squares while still hot; cool before serving.

Makes 36

Chocolate-Mint Brownies

Here is the perfect example of the classic chocolate mint dessert: a rich chocolate base topped with a thin, creamy layer of mint icing. For a double treat, serve with mint chocolate-chip ice cream on the side.

Preheat the oven to 325°F (165°C). Line an 8-inch (20-cm) square baking pan with aluminum foil.

To make the brownies, combine the chocolate and butter in a large, heavy saucepan over low heat. Stir until melted and smooth. Let cool slightly.

Whisk the sugar, peppermint and vanilla extracts, and salt into the chocolate mixture. Whisk in the eggs, one at a time, whisking well after each addition, then continue to whisk until the mixture is velvety. Add the flour and whisk just until incorporated. Pour and scrape the batter into the prepared pan.

Bake until the top is just springy to the touch and a toothpick inserted into the center comes out with a few moist crumbs attached, about 40 minutes. Transfer to a wire rack and let cool.

To make the icing, combine the confectioners' sugar, butter, 1 tablespoon milk, and the peppermint extract in a food processor fitted with the metal blade. Process until smooth, thinning with more milk if necessary (the icing should be thick).

Using the foil, lift the sheet from the pan and place on a work surface. Peel back the foil from the sides. Spread the icing over the cooled brownies. Cut into 2-inch (5-cm) squares. Remove the brownies from the foil. Wrap individually in plastic wrap and store in the refrigerator for up to 3 days.

Makes 16

FOR THE BROWNIES:

4 oz (125 g) unsweetened chocolate, chopped

1/2 cup (4 oz/125 g) unsalted butter

1¼ cups (10 oz/315 g) granulated sugar

1½ teaspoons peppermint extract (essence)

3/4 teaspoon vanilla extract (essence)

1/4 teaspoon salt

3 eggs

3/4 cup (4 oz/125 g) all-purpose (plain) flour

FOR THE ICING:

1 cup (4 oz/125 g) confectioners' (icing) sugar

3 tablespoons unsalted butter, at room temperature

1 tablespoon milk, or as needed

2 teaspoons peppermint extract (essence)

Coconut, Almond, and Chocolate Bars

FOR THE CRUST:

1 cup (5 oz/155 g) all-purpose (plain) flour

1/4 cup (2 oz/60 g) firmly packed dark brown sugar

1/4 teaspoon salt

6 tablespoons (3 oz/90 g) cold unsalted butter, cut into 1/2-inch (12-mm) pieces, plus extra for greasing

3/4 cup (3 1/2 oz/105 g) slivered almonds, blanched and toasted (page 326), chopped

FOR THE FILLING:

1/2 cup (4 fl oz/125 ml) well-stirred canned cream of coconut

3 oz (90 g) white chocolate, chopped

1/4 cup (2 fl oz/60 ml) sour cream

1/4 cup (2 oz/60 g) unsalted butter, at room temperature

1 1/4 cups (5 oz/155 g) lightly packed, sweetened flaked coconut

FOR THE TOPPING:

3 tablespoons heavy (double) cream

3 tablespoons unsalted butter

3 1/2 oz (105 g) semisweet (plain) chocolate, chopped

Preheat the oven to 350°F (180°C). Line an 8-inch (20-cm) square baking pan with aluminum foil, leaving an overhang of about 2 inches (5 cm) on all sides to form a handle. Grease the foil.

To make the crust, in a food processor fitted with the metal blade, combine the flour, brown sugar, and salt. Process to mix well. Add the butter and almonds and process to the texture of a fine meal. Transfer the mixture to the prepared pan and press firmly into the bottom to form a crust.

Bake until the crust is barely firm to the touch, about 40 minutes. Transfer to a wire rack and let cool completely.

Meanwhile, make the filling: Place the cream of coconut in a small, heavy saucepan and bring to a simmer. Reduce the heat to low. Add the white chocolate and stir constantly until melted. Transfer to a bowl. Add the sour cream and butter and mix until melted and smooth. Stir in the coconut. Cover and refrigerate for 1 hour, stirring occasionally. Spoon the filling into the cooled crust; smooth the top. Refrigerate while preparing the topping.

To make the topping, in a small, heavy saucepan bring the cream and butter to a simmer, stirring frequently. Reduce the heat to low, add the chocolate, and stir to melt. Pour the hot topping over the filling. Using a small icing spatula or the back of a spoon, spread to cover evenly; shake the pan from side to side to smooth the surface. Cover and refrigerate overnight.

Using the foil, lift the sheet from the pan. Cut into bars, each about 1 1/2 inches (4 cm) by 3/4 inch (2 cm). Store refrigerated in an airtight container for up to 5 days.

Makes about 50

Cakes, Cupcakes & Cheesecakes

Buttermilk–Berry Crumble Coffee Cake

This coffee cake has a rich, moist crumb that contrasts pleasantly with its juicy pockets of berries and crisp topping. Try other berries such as whole blackberries or boysenberries or halved strawberries, and walnuts or pecans in place of almonds.

Unsalted butter at room temperature, for greasing

1/4 cup (2 oz/60 g) firmly packed dark brown sugar

2 tablespoons plus 1 1/2 cups (7 1/2 oz/235 g) all-purpose (plain) flour

Pinch of nutmeg

2 tablespoons plus 1/4 cup (2 oz/60 g) cold unsalted butter, cut into pieces

1/4 cup (1 1/4 oz/37 g) chopped blanched (page 326) almonds

1/4 cup (3/4 oz/20 g) old-fashioned rolled oats

1/2 cup (4 oz/125 g) granulated sugar

1/2 teaspoon baking powder

1/4 teaspoon baking soda (bicarbonate of soda)

1 egg, lightly beaten

1 cup (8 fl oz/250 ml) buttermilk

1/2 teaspoon vanilla extract (essence)

1 cup (4 oz/125 g) fresh or frozen raspberries or blueberries

Preheat the oven to 350°F (180°C). Grease an 8-inch (20-cm) square baking pan.

In a bowl, stir together the brown sugar, 2 tablespoons flour, and nutmeg. Using a pastry blender or 2 knives, cut in the 2 tablespoons cold butter until the mixture resembles coarse crumbs. Mix in the almonds and oats. Set aside.

In another bowl, stir together the 1 1/2 cups flour, the granulated sugar, the baking powder, and the baking soda. Using a pastry blender or 2 knives, cut in the 1/4 cup cold butter until the mixture resembles fine crumbs. Add the egg, buttermilk, and vanilla and stir just until blended.

Pour and scrape the batter into the prepared pan and spread evenly. Scatter the berries evenly over the surface, then sprinkle the crumble mixture evenly over the berries. Bake until the cake is well risen and golden and a toothpick inserted into the center comes out clean, about 50 minutes. Transfer to a wire rack and let cool for 15 minutes. Cut into squares and serve warm directly from the pan.

Makes one 8-inch (20-cm) square cake; serves 8–12

Cinnamon-Pecan Streusel Cake

This classic coffee cake is excellent with the day's first mug of coffee, as a midmorning snack, or cut into squares for a brunch buffet table. Substitute other nuts for the pecans, if you like.

Preheat the oven to 375°F (190°C). Grease an 8-inch (20-cm) square baking pan.

In a bowl, stir together the flour, 1 cup (8 oz/250 g) of the sugar, and the baking powder. Using a pastry blender or 2 knives, cut in the butter until the mixture resembles coarse crumbs. Add the egg, milk, and vanilla and stir just until combined. Pour and scrape the batter into the prepared pan.

In another bowl, stir together the remaining ¼ cup (2 oz/60 g) of the sugar, the cinnamon, and the pecans. Sprinkle the mixture evenly over the surface of the batter. Using a table knife, cut gently down through the batter at intervals of about 2 inches (5 cm) to spread a little of the topping into the batter.

Bake until the coffee cake is well risen and golden and a toothpick inserted into the center comes out clean, 25–30 minutes. Transfer to a wire rack and let cool for 15 minutes. Cut into squares and serve warm directly from the pan.

Makes one 8-inch (20-cm) square cake; serves 8–12

1¾ cups (9 oz/280 g) all-purpose (plain) flour

1¼ cups (10 oz/310 g) sugar

2 teaspoons baking powder

¼ cup (2 oz/60 g) unsalted butter, cut into pieces, plus extra for greasing

1 egg, lightly beaten

¾ cup (6 fl oz/180 ml) milk

1 teaspoon vanilla extract (essence)

2 teaspoons ground cinnamon

½ cup (2 oz/60 g) coarsely chopped pecans

Chocolate Pound Cake

For a pretty finish, dust this pound cake with confectioners' (icing) sugar, if you wish. Slice and serve plain, or top it with Whipped Cream (page 316), ice cream, or sliced fresh berries. If you prefer a less sugary cake, substitute the semisweet chocolate with bittersweet chocolate.

1½ cups (7½ oz/235 g) all-purpose (plain) flour

½ cup (1½ oz/45 g) unsweetened Dutch-process cocoa powder

¼ teaspoon salt

2 oz (60 g) semisweet (plain) chocolate

1 cup (8 oz/250 g) unsalted butter, at room temperature, plus extra for greasing

2 cups (14 oz/440 g) firmly packed light brown sugar

3 eggs

1 teaspoon vanilla extract (essence)

1 cup (8 fl oz/250 ml) sour cream

Preheat the oven to 350°F (180°C). Grease a 9-by-5-inch (23-by-13-cm) loaf pan. In a bowl, sift together the sifted flour, the sifted cocoa powder, and the salt. Set aside. Place the chocolate in the top pan of a double boiler or in a heatproof bowl. Place over (but not touching) a pan of simmering water and heat until melted, stirring until smooth.

Meanwhile, in a large bowl, using an electric mixer set on medium speed, beat together the butter and brown sugar until light and fluffy. Add in the eggs one at a time, beating well after each addition. Add the vanilla and the melted chocolate and mix well. Using a rubber spatula, fold the flour mixture into the butter mixture in 3 batches, alternating with the sour cream and beginning and ending with the flour mixture. Pour and scrape the batter into the prepared pan.

Bake until a toothpick inserted into the center comes out clean, about 1 hour. If the cake is browning too quickly, cover it loosely with aluminum foil. Transfer to a wire rack and let cool in the pan for 10 minutes. Invert the cake onto the rack, turn top side up, and let cool completely. Cut into slices and serve.

Makes 1 loaf; serves 6–8

Lemon-Clove Tea Cake

Offer this dense lemon cake with hot tea or coffee. It is best served the day it is made. To store until you are ready to serve it, wrap the cake in aluminum foil and keep it at room temperature for up to 8 hours.

Preheat the oven to 350°F (180°C). Grease an 8½-by-4½-by-2½-inch (21-by-11-by-6-cm) loaf pan (6-cup/48–fl oz/1.5-l) and dust with flour.

In a bowl, sift together the flour, baking powder, salt, and cloves. Set aside. In another bowl, using an electric mixer set on medium-high speed, beat the butter until light. Gradually add the granulated sugar, beating until fluffy and ivory colored, about 2 minutes.

In a small bowl, whisk together the eggs and lemon zest until blended. Using an electric mixer set on medium speed, gradually beat the egg mixture into the butter mixture. Reduce the speed to low and beat in the flour mixture just until combined. Pour and scrape the batter into the prepared pan, then smooth the top with a rubber spatula.

Bake until a toothpick inserted into the center comes out clean, about 1 hour. Transfer to a wire rack and let cool in the pan for 5 minutes. Invert the cake onto the rack and turn top side up.

In a small bowl, whisk together the confectioners' sugar and lemon juice until blended. Brush the mixture over the top and sides of the hot cake. Let cool completely before serving.

Makes 1 loaf; serves 8

1½ cups (6 oz/185 g) cake (soft-wheat) flour, plus extra for dusting

1 teaspoon baking powder

¼ teaspoon salt

¼ teaspoon cloves

¾ cup (6 oz/185 g) unsalted butter, at room temperature, plus extra for greasing

¾ cup (6 oz/185 g) granulated sugar

3 large eggs, at room temperature

1 tablespoon grated lemon zest (page 329)

½ cup (2 oz/60 g) confectioners' (icing) sugar

3 tablespoons fresh lemon juice

Peaches-and-Cream "Shortcake"

Pound cake is an excellent alternative to traditional shortcake biscuits. To peel peaches, cut an X in the stem ends, blanch for 1 minute in boiling water, remove with a slotted spoon, and drain. Let cool and slip off the skins.

1 vanilla bean, cut in half lengthwise

2 cans (12 fl oz/375 ml *each*) peach nectar

1/4 cup (2 oz/60 g) granulated sugar

1/4 cup (2 oz/60 g) cold unsalted butter, cut into small pieces

1 cup (8 fl oz/250 ml) cold heavy (double) cream

1/2 cup (4 fl oz/125 ml) sour cream

2 tablespoons firmly packed dark brown sugar

1 pound cake, purchased or homemade

3 large ripe peaches, peeled (see note), halved, pitted, and sliced

Using a small, sharp knife, scrape out the seeds from the vanilla bean into a large, deep, heavy saucepan. Add the peach nectar and granulated sugar and bring to a simmer over high heat. Reduce the heat to low and simmer, uncovered, until reduced to 1 1/2 cups (12 fl oz/375 ml), about 55 minutes. Remove from the heat and whisk in the butter until melted. Let cool completely.

In a large bowl, combine the heavy cream, sour cream, and brown sugar. Using an electric mixer set on medium-high speed, beat until soft peaks form. Cover and refrigerate until ready to use or for up to 8 hours.

Cut the cake into 12 slices, each about 1/2 inch (12 mm) thick. Overlap 2 slices on each individual plate. Top each serving with the peaches and then the cooled sauce, dividing it evenly. Spoon a dollop of the whipped cream mixture atop each serving. Serve immediately.

Serves 6

CAKES, CUPCAKES & CHEESECAKES | 225

Walnut Cake

This light and delicate Greek nut torte is ideal to serve with a fruit dessert such as compote, baked figs, or poached pears, or with a little sweetened plain yogurt, or homemade Whipped Cream (page 316).

To make the syrup, in a heavy saucepan over medium heat, combine the sugar, honey, and 1 cup (8 fl oz/250 ml) water. Bring to a simmer, stirring to dissolve the sugar, then add the cloves, cinnamon stick, and lemon zest and juice. Reduce the heat to medium-low and simmer until the syrup is slightly thickened, about 10 minutes. Remove from the heat and set aside to cool.

To make the cake, preheat the oven to 350°F (180°C). Lightly grease a 9-by-12-by-3-inch (23-by-30-by-7.5-cm) cake pan, then dust with flour.

In a bowl, using an electric mixer set on high speed, beat together the butter and sugar until light and fluffy, 5–8 minutes. Add the egg yolks one at a time, beating well after each addition. In another bowl, sift together the flour, baking powder, cinnamon, cloves, and salt. Slowly fold the flour mixture into the butter mixture, then fold in the nuts and orange zest.

In a large bowl, using and electric mixer fitted with clean, dry beaters and set on high speed, beat the egg whites until stiff peaks form. Stir one-third of the beaten whites into the batter to lighten it, then, using a rubber spatula, gently fold in the remaining whites just until no white streaks remain. Pour and scrape the batter into the prepared pan.

Bake until golden brown and the top springs back when lightly touched, about 45 minutes. Remove from the oven and pour the cooked syrup evenly over the top. Transfer to a wire rack and let cool in the pan.

To serve, cut into diamonds or squares.

Makes one 9-by-12-inch (23-by-30-cm) cake; serves 12–16

FOR THE SYRUP:

3/4 cup (6 oz/185 g) sugar

1/2 cup (6 oz/185 g) honey

4 whole cloves

1 cinnamon stick, about 2 inches (5 cm) long

1 lemon zest strip, 2 inches (5 cm) long and 1/2 inch (12 mm) wide (page 329)

2 tablespoons fresh lemon juice

FOR THE CAKE:

1/2 cup (4 oz/125 g) unsalted butter, at room temperature, plus extra for greasing

1/2 cup (4 oz/125 g) sugar

8 eggs, separated

1/2 cup (2 1/2 oz/75 g) all-purpose (plain) flour, plus extra for dusting

2 teaspoons baking powder

2 teaspoons ground cinnamon

1/4 teaspoon ground cloves

Pinch of salt

2 1/2 cups (10 oz/315 g) ground walnuts

1 tablespoon finely grated orange zest (page 329)

Cranberry-Cherry Cake

Add this festive cake to your breakfast or brunch menu for Christmas morning—or any morning of the year. Chopped dried apricots or golden raisins (sultanas) can be substituted for the dried cherries.

3 cups (12 oz/375 g) cake (soft-wheat) flour

1½ teaspoons baking soda (bicarbonate of soda)

½ teaspoon salt

1½ cups (12 oz/375 g) granulated sugar

½ cup (4 oz/125 g) unsalted butter, melted and cooled, plus extra for greasing

2 large eggs, at room temperature

1 teaspoon grated lemon zest (page 329)

1¼ cups (10 fl oz/310 ml) buttermilk

1½ cups (6 oz/185 g) fresh or frozen cranberries

1 cup (4 oz/125 g) dried pitted cherries

Confectioners' Sugar Icing (page 316) mixed with ⅛ teaspoon ground cloves

Preheat the oven to 350°F (180°C). Grease a 2½-qt (2½-l) nonstick Bundt pan 10 inches (25 cm) in diameter and 3 inches (7.5 cm) deep.

In a bowl, sift together the flour, baking soda, and salt. In another bowl, whisk together the sugar, melted butter, eggs, and lemon zest until well blended. Dividing the flour mixture into 3 batches, whisk the flour mixture into the sugar mixture alternately with the buttermilk, beginning and ending with the flour mixture. Fold in the cranberries and cherries. Pour and scrape the batter into the prepared pan.

Bake until toothpick inserted near the center comes out clean, about 50 minutes. Transfer to a wire rack and let cool in the pan for 10 minutes. Invert the cake onto the rack and let cool completely.

Transfer the cake to a plate and drizzle the icing evenly over the top, allowing it to run over the sides slightly. Let stand until the icing sets, about 1 hour. Serve right away, or cover with a cake dome and store at room temperature for up to 1 day.

Makes one 10-inch (25-cm) cake; serves 12

Applesauce Spice Cake

Applesauce gives this cake a marvelously moist texture. Use any good-quality, plain, smooth unsweetened applesauce. For added spice, serve with Whipped Cream (page 316) sprinkled with cinnamon

Preheat the oven to 350°F (180°C). Grease a 2¹/₂-qt (2¹/₂-l) nonstick Bundt pan 10 inches (25 cm) in diameter and 3 inches (7.5 cm) deep.

In a bowl, sift together the flour, cinnamon, baking soda, allspice, nutmeg, and salt. Set aside. In another bowl, using an electric mixer set on medium speed, beat together the butter and brown sugar until well blended. Add the eggs, one at a time, beating well after each addition. Beat in the vanilla extract. Divide the flour mixture into 3 batches and whisk into the sugar mixture alternately with the applesauce, beginning and ending with the flour mixture. Stir in the 1 cup (4 oz/125 g) toasted pecans. Pour and scrape the batter into the prepared pan.

Bake until a toothpick inserted near the center comes out clean, about 55 minutes. Transfer to a wire rack and let cool in the pan for 10 minutes. Invert the cake onto the rack and let cool completely.

Transfer the cake to a plate and drizzle the icing evenly over the top, allowing it to run over the sides slightly. Sprinkle on the 2 tablespoons toasted pecans, then let stand until the icing sets, about 1 hour. Serve immediately, or cover with a cake dome and store at room temperature for up to 1 day.

Makes one 10-inch (25-cm) cake; serve 12

3¹/₃ cups (13¹/₂ oz/420 g) cake (soft-wheat) flour

1 tablespoon ground cinnamon

1¹/₂ teaspoons baking soda (bicarbonate of soda)

1¹/₄ teaspoons ground allspice

1¹/₄ teaspoons ground nutmeg

¹/₄ teaspoon salt

1 cup (8 oz/250 g) unsalted butter, at room temperature, plus extra for greasing

1²/₃ cups (12 oz/375 g) firmly packed dark brown sugar

3 large eggs, at room temperature

2 teaspoons vanilla extract (essence)

2 cups (18 oz/560 g) unsweetened applesauce

1 cup (4 oz/125 g) plus 2 tablespoons pecan pieces, toasted (page 326)

Confectioners' Sugar Icing flavored with brown sugar (page 316)

Gingerbread with Crystallized Ginger

The optional confectioners' sugar topping can also be stenciled on the cake:
Cut out paper into the desired designs, place on the cake, and sift the sugar over
the cutouts until they are evenly coated, then carefully lift off the paper.

1¹/₂ cups (7¹/₂ oz/235 g) all–
purpose (plain) flour, plus
extra for dusting

1 teaspoon ground cinnamon

³/₄ teaspoon ground ginger

¹/₂ teaspoon baking powder

¹/₂ teaspoon baking soda
(bicarbonate of soda)

¹/₂ teaspoon salt

¹/₂ cup (4 oz/125 g) unsalted
butter, at room temperature,
plus extra for greasing

¹/₂ cup (3¹/₂ oz/105 g) firmly
packed brown sugar

1 large egg

¹/₂ cup (5¹/₂ fl oz/170 ml) light
(unsulfured) molasses

¹/₂ cup (4 fl oz/125 ml) apple
juice

¹/₄ cup (1¹/₂ oz/45 g) chopped
crystallized ginger

Confectioners' (icing) sugar for
dusting (optional)

Preheat the oven to 350°F (180°C). Grease an 8-inch (20-cm) square baking pan with 2-inch (5-cm) sides and dust with flour.

In a bowl, sift together the flour, cinnamon, ground ginger, baking powder, baking soda, and salt. In another bowl, using an electric mixer set on medium-high speed, beat the butter until light. Add the brown sugar and beat until fluffy, about 3 minutes. Add the egg and molasses and beat until well blended. Reduce the speed to low. Divide the flour mixture into 3 batches, then beat into the butter mixture alternately with the apple juice, beginning and ending with the flour mixture. Stir in the crystallized ginger. Pour and scrape the batter into the prepared pan.

Bake until a toothpick inserted into the center comes out clean, about 35 minutes. Transfer to a wire rack and let cool in the pan for 20 minutes. Invert the cake onto the rack, turn top side up, and transfer to a serving plate.

Using a fine-mesh sieve, dust confectioners' sugar over the cake just before serving, if desired. Serve warm or at room temperature, cut into squares. Alternatively, let the cake cool, wrap it in aluminum foil, and let stand at room temperature for up to 1 day before serving. Dust with confectioners' sugar just before serving, if desired.

Makes one 8-inch (20-cm) cake; serves 9

Chocolate Chiffon Cake

Position a rack in the lower third of the oven and preheat to 325°F (165°C).

In a bowl, combine the boiling water and cocoa powder and stir to dissolve; set aside. Sift together the sifted flour, sugar, baking powder, and salt into another bowl. Add the cocoa mixture, egg yolks, oil, and vanilla. Using a whisk or an electric mixer set on low speed, beat until thoroughly combined.

In a large bowl using an electric mixer fitted with clean, dry beaters and set on high speed, beat together the egg whites and cream of tartar until stiff and glossy but not dry. Stir one-fourth of the whites into the batter to lighten it, then, using a rubber spatula, gently fold in the remaining whites just until no white streaks remain. Pour and scrape the batter into an ungreased 10-inch (25-cm) tube pan with a removable bottom, and smooth the top with a rubber spatula.

Bake for 55 minutes. Raise the oven temperature to 350°F (180°C) and continue baking until a toothpick inserted in the center comes out clean, 10–15 minutes longer. Remove from the oven. Invert the pan; if it does not have legs around the top rim, place the tube over an inverted metal funnel or the neck of a bottle for support. Cool upside down for at least 2 hours.

To remove the cake from the pan, run a long metal icing spatula between the cake and the pan. Gently ease the cake out of the pan and place top side up, on a serving plate. Top with the fruit and serve.

Makes one 10-inch (25-cm) cake; serves 8–10

3/4 cup (6 fl oz/180 ml) boiling water

1/2 cup (1 1/2 oz/45 g) unsweetened cocoa powder (not Dutch-process type)

1 3/4 cups (7 oz/220 g) all-purpose (plain) flour, sifted before measuring

1 3/4 cups (14 oz/440 g) sugar

1 tablespoon baking powder

1/2 teaspoon salt

7 eggs, separated (page 324), at room temperature

1/2 cup (4 fl oz/125 ml) canola oil

2 teaspoons vanilla extract (essence)

1/2 teaspoon cream of tartar

Strawberries, oranges, or kiwi fruit slices for garnish

Chocolate Angel Food Cake

Preheat the oven to 350°F (180°C). Sift together the flour, the cocoa powder, and ³/₄ cups (6 oz/185 g) of the granulated sugar into a large bowl. Repeat the sifting 2 more times. Set aside.

In another large bowl, using an electric mixer set on low speed, beat the egg whites just until foamy on top, about 30 seconds. Add the cream of tartar, salt, and vanilla; raise the speed to medium and beat until the whites have increased in size to about 5 times their original volume, have formed a foamy white mass that is still quite soft, and flatten out when you stop beating.

Continuing to beat, gradually add the remaining ³/₄ cup granulated sugar, taking about 15 seconds to incorporate it. Then beat until the whites form a shiny, high-volume mass of very tiny bubbles. They should barely hold their shape when the beater is lifted, and slide when the bowl is tilted.

Sift the flour mixture over the whites, then, using a rubber spatula, gently and quickly fold it in, just until there are no unblended drifts of the flour mixture. Pour the batter into an ungreased 10-inch (25-cm) angel food or tube pan and tap the pan firmly but gently on the counter once or twice to settle the batter.

Bake until the cake has risen to the top of the pan, or higher, and a thin wooden skewer inserted into the center comes out clean, 45–55 minutes. Remove from the oven. Invert the pan; if it doesn't have legs around the top rim, place the tube over an inverted metal funnel or the neck of a bottle for support. Cool upside down for at least 2 hours, or longer.

To remove the cake from the pan, run a long metal icing spatula between the cake and the pan. Gently ease the cake out of the pan and place top side up, on a serving plate. Top with confectioners' sugar, garnish with fruit, if desired, and serve.

Makes one 10-inch (25-cm) cake; serves 10

³/₄ cup (3 oz/90 g) cake (soft-wheat) flour

¹/₄ cup (³/₄ oz/20 g) unsweetened cocoa powder

1¹/₂ cups (12 oz/370 g) granulated sugar

2 cups (16 fl oz/500 ml) egg whites (about 13) (page 324)

1¹/₂ teaspoons cream of tartar

¹/₂ teaspoon salt

2 teaspoons vanilla extract (essence)

Confectioners' (icing) sugar for dusting (optional)

Strawberry or peach slices for garnish (optional)

Orange Layer Cake

For a pretty garnish, press thin half-slices of orange, curved side up, firmly against the bottom edge of the cake. To add a more intense orange flavor, brush each cake layer with 2 tablespoons Grand Marnier before frosting.

Preheat the oven to 350°F (180°C). Grease 2 round cake pans each 9 inches (23 cm) in diameter and 1 1/2 inches (4 cm) deep and dust with flour.

In a small bowl, sift together the flour, baking powder, and baking soda. In another bowl, using an electric mixer set on medium-high speed, beat together the butter and sugar until fluffy and light, about 2 minutes. Beat in the orange zest and vanilla extract. Add the eggs, one at a time, beating well after each addition. Reduce the speed to low and, dividing the flour mixture into 3 batches, beat the flour mixture into the butter mixture alternately with the milk and orange juice concentrate, beginning and ending with the flour mixture. Divide the batter evenly between the prepared pans.

Bake until a toothpick inserted into the centers comes out clean, about 25 minutes. Transfer to wire racks and let cool in the pans for 10 minutes. Invert the cakes onto the racks, turn top side up, and let cool completely.

Place 1 cake layer, top side down, on a plate. Spread 1 1/4 cups (10 fl oz/310 ml) of the frosting over the top. Place the second cake layer, top side down, on top of the first. Spread the remaining frosting over the top and sides of the cake. Serve immediately, or cover with a cake dome and refrigerate for up to 1 day. Bring to room temperature before serving.

Makes one 9-inch (23-cm) cake; serves 12

2 1/2 cups (10 oz/315 g) cake (soft-wheat) flour, plus extra for dusting

3/4 teaspoon baking powder

1/4 teaspoon baking soda (bicarbonate of soda)

3/4 cup (6 oz/185 g) unsalted butter, at room temperature, plus extra for greasing

1 1/3 cups (11 oz/330 g) sugar

2 teaspoons grated orange zest (page 329)

1 teaspoon vanilla extract (essence)

4 large eggs, at room temperature

1/2 cup (4 fl oz/125 ml) milk

1/4 cup (2 fl oz/60 ml) undiluted, thawed frozen orange juice concentrate

Cream Cheese Frosting flavored with orange (page 316)

Fresh Strawberry–Vanilla Layer Cake

This gorgeous cake is perfect for a bridal shower or garden party and can be quick to make if a purchased pound cake is used. Select large, richly colored, blemish-free strawberries for decorating the top.

1/4 cup (1 oz/30 g) confectioners' (icing) sugar

2 tablespoons strawberry preserves

1 tablespoon fresh lemon juice

2 cups (8 oz/250 g) thinly sliced hulled strawberries, plus 12–15 large strawberries with green leaves and hulls intact, cut in half lengthwise through the hulls

3/4 cup (3 oz/90 g) sliced (flaked) almonds, toasted (page 326)

1 pound cake, purchased or homemade

Vanilla Buttercream flavored with vanilla bean (page 316)

In a bowl, stir together the confectioners' sugar, preserves, and lemon juice. Add the sliced strawberries and toss gently. Let stand for 30 minutes.

Using a long serrated knife, trim the ends of the cake to make even surfaces. Turn the cake onto a long side and cut lengthwise into 6 long slices. Place 2 slices side by side on a platter to form a square. Drain the sliced berries, reserving the juices. Brush the slices with half of the berry juices. Spread 1/2 cup (4 fl oz/125 ml) of the buttercream over the juice-soaked slices. Top with half of the sliced berries, arranged in a single layer. Cover with 2 more cake slices, side by side. Brush these cake slices with the remaining berry juices and then spread another 1/2 cup of the buttercream over them. Top with the remaining sliced berries, arranging them in a single layer. Top with the remaining cake slices, side by side.

Spread the remaining buttercream over the top and sides of the cake. Press the toasted almonds onto the sides of the cake. Arrange the halved berries in slightly overlapping rows atop the cake. Serve immediately or cover with a cake dome and refrigerate for up to 1 day. Bring to room temperature before serving.

Makes one 8-inch (20-cm) square cake; serves 9

Almond-Scented White Cake

Preheat the oven to 350°F (180°C). Grease 2 round cake pans each 9 inches (23 cm) in diameter and 1 1/2 inches (4 cm) deep and dust with flour.

In a bowl, sift together the flour, baking powder, and salt. In another bowl, using an electric mixer set on medium speed, beat the butter until light. Gradually add the sugar, beating until well blended. Beat in the vanilla and almond extracts. Reduce the speed to low and, dividing the flour mixture into 3 batches, beat the flour mixture into the butter mixture alternately with the milk just until combined.

In a large bowl, using an electric mixer fitted with clean, dry beaters and set on high speed, beat the egg whites until stiff peaks form. Using a rubber spatula, gently fold the beaten whites into the batter just until no white streaks remain. Divide the batter between the prepared pans; smooth with the spatula.

Bake until a toothpick inserted into the centers comes out clean, about 30 minutes. Transfer to wire racks and let cool in the pans for 10 minutes. Run a sharp knife around the pan sides to loosen the cakes. Invert onto racks and let cool completely.

Using a long serrated knife, cut each cake in half horizontally. Place 1 layer on a plate. Spread 1/2 cup (4 fl oz/125 ml) of the frosting over the top, then drizzle on 1/4 cup (2 fl oz/60 ml) of the melted preserves. Top with another layer and repeat with the same amounts of frosting and preserves. Top with a third layer and again repeat with the same amounts of frosting and preserves. Top with the fourth cake layer, cut side down. Spread the remaining frosting over the top and sides. Press the toasted almonds onto the sides, and ring the top with raspberries, if desired.

Serve immediately or cover with a cake dome and refrigerate for up to 1 day. Bring to room temperature before serving.

Makes one 9-inch (230cm) cake; serves 10–12

2 cups (10 oz/315 g) all-purpose (plain) flour, plus extra for dusting

1 tablespoon baking powder

1/2 teaspoon salt

3/4 cup (6 oz/185 g) unsalted butter, at room temperature, plus extra for greasing

1 1/2 cups (12 oz/375 g) sugar

2 teaspoons vanilla extract (essence)

1 teaspoon almond extract (essence)

1 cup (8 fl oz/250 ml) milk

5 large egg whites, at room temperature

Cream Cheese Frosting (page 316) with 1 1/2 teaspoons almond extract (essence) stirred in

3/4 cup (7 1/2 oz/235 g) raspberry preserves, melted

1 1/4 cups (5 oz/155 g) sliced (flaked) almonds, lightly toasted (page 326) and cooled

Raspberries for garnish (optional)

Carrot Cake

This cake is also good flavored with coconut: Spread with coconut-flavored Cream Cheese Frosting (page 316), then press 1 cup (3 oz/90 g) toasted sweetened shredded coconut evenly onto the sides of the cake for a decorative finish.

Unsalted butter for greasing

2 cups (10 oz/315 g) all-purpose (plain) flour. plus extra for dusting

2 teaspoons baking soda (bicarbonate of soda)

2 teaspoons baking powder

2 teaspoons ground cinnamon

1/2 teaspoon salt

1/2 teaspoon ground allspice

4 large eggs

3/4 cup (6 fl oz/180 ml) canola oil

3/4 cup (6 oz/185 g) granulated sugar

1 cup (7 oz/220 g) firmly packed brown sugar

1/2 cup (4 fl oz/125 ml) buttermilk

3 cups (12 oz/375 g) lightly packed peeled, shredded carrots

Cream Cheese Frosting (page 316)

Preheat the oven to 350°F (180°C). Grease 2 round cake pans each 9 inches (23 cm) in diameter and 2 inches (5 cm) deep and dust with flour.

In a bowl, sift together the flour, baking soda, baking powder, cinnamon, salt, and allspice. In another bowl, whisk together the eggs, oil, granulated and brown sugars, and buttermilk until blended.

Stir the flour mixture into the egg mixture just until combined. Fold in the carrots. Divide the batter evenly between the prepared pans.

Bake until a toothpick inserted into the centers comes out clean, about 40 minutes. Transfer to wire racks and let cool in the pans for 15 minutes. Invert the cakes onto the racks and let cool completely.

Place 1 cake layer, top side down, on a plate. Spread 1 1/4 cups (10 fl oz/310 ml) of the frosting over the top. Place the second cake layer, top side down, on top. Spread the remaining frosting decoratively over the top and sides of the cake. Serve right away or cover with a cake dome and refrigerate for up to 2 days. Bring to room temperature before serving.

Makes one 9-inch (23-cm) cake; serves 12

Chocolate Layer Cake

This splendid confection makes the perfect birthday celebration cake. This recipe calls for using a half recipe of Chocolate Whipped Cream (page 317) between the layers If you like, cover the top with lukewarm Chocolate Ganache (page 317).

Preheat the oven to 350°F (180°C). Grease two 9-inch (23-cm) round cake pans. Line the bottoms with parchment (baking) paper or waxed paper cut to fit precisely. Butter the paper and dust with flour.

Sift together the sifted flour, baking soda, and baking powder into a bowl. Set aside.

In a small saucepan set over medium heat, warm the milk until small bubbles appear at the edges. Remove from the heat and whisk in the chocolate until it melts and the mixture is smooth. Let cool completely. Stir in the sour cream.

In a bowl, combine the granulated and brown sugars and the butter. Using an electric mixer set on high speed, beat until fluffy, 3–5 minutes. Reduce the speed to medium and beat in the vanilla. Add the eggs, one at a time, beating well after each addition. On low speed, beat in the flour mixture alternately with the chocolate mixture; mix only until the ingredients are incorporated.

Pour and scrape the batter into the prepared pans and smooth the tops. Bake until the edges start to pull away from the pan and a toothpick inserted in the center comes out clean, 30–40 minutes. Transfer to wire racks and let cool in the pans for 15 minutes. Invert the cakes onto the racks to cool completely. Peel off the paper.

Place 1 cake layer, top side down, on a serving plate. Spread with half of the chocolate whipped cream. Top with the remaining cake layer, top side down, and spread with the remaining whipped cream.

Makes one 9-inch (23-cm) layer cake; serves 8–10

1³/₄ cups (6 oz/185 g) cake (soft-wheat) flour, sifted before measuring, plus extra for dusting

1 teaspoon baking soda (bicarbonate of soda)

1¹/₂ teaspoons baking powder

¹/₂ cup (4 fl oz/125 ml) milk

3 oz (90 g) unsweetened chocolate, coarsely chopped (scant ²/₃ cup)

1 cup (8 fl oz/250 ml) sour cream

1 cup (8 oz/250 g) granulated sugar

²/₃ cup (5 oz/155 g) firmly packed dark brown sugar

³/₄ cup (6 oz/185 g) unsalted butter, at room temperature, plus extra for greasing

2 teaspoons vanilla extract (essence)

3 extra-large eggs

Chocolate Whipped Cream (page 317)

Flourless Chocolate Cake

As this cake bakes, it rises like a soufflé and then falls as it cools. For a nice finishing touch, press 1 cup (5 oz/155 g) chopped toasted hazelnuts (filberts) or macadamia nuts onto the sides of the freshly glazed cake.

10 oz (315 g) bittersweet chocolate, chopped

3/4 cup (6 oz/185 g) unsalted butter, cut into pieces, plus extra for greasing

2 teaspoons vanilla extract (essence)

5 large eggs, at room temperature

1 cup (8 oz/250 g) sugar

Bittersweet Chocolate Glaze (page 317)

Preheat the oven to 350°F (180°C). Grease a springform pan 9 inches (23 cm) in diameter and 3 inches (7.5 cm) deep. Line the bottom of the pan with a piece of parchment (baking) paper cut to fit precisely. Grease the paper then dust with flour.

In a heavy saucepan over medium-low heat, combine the chocolate and butter. Heat, stirring, until the mixture is smooth. Remove from the heat and let cool. Whisk in the vanilla.

In a large bowl, combine the eggs and sugar. Using an electric mixer set on medium-high speed, beat until the mixture lightens and triples in volume, about 6 minutes. Pour the chocolate mixture over the egg mixture. Using a rubber spatula, gently fold them together. Pour and scrape the batter into the prepared pan.

Bake until the top forms a crust and cracks and a toothpick inserted into the center comes out with some wet batter attached, about 45 minutes. Transfer to a wire rack. Immediately run a knife around the pan sides to loosen the cake; it will fall in the center. Press down on the edges to even the top. Let cool.

Release the pan sides and remove them. Trim off any crumbly edges. Invert a flat plate over the cake and then invert them together. Lift off the pan bottom and peel off the parchment paper. Tuck strips of waxed or parchment paper under the edges of the cake and pour the lukewarm glaze over the cake top; use an icing spatula to coax it down the sides. When the glaze stops dripping, remove the paper strips.

Refrigerate until the glaze sets, about 1 hour. Serve immediately, cold or at room temperature, or cover with a cake dome and refrigerate for up to 1 week.

Makes one 9-inch (23-cm) cake; serves 12–14

Reine de Saba

This is truly the Queen of Tortes. The difference between a cake and a torte is that the former is made with flour and the latter with ground nuts and only rarely a small amount of flour. Use ground almonds, walnuts, or toasted hazelnuts (filberts).

Position a rack in the lower third of the oven and preheat the oven to 350°F (180°C). Grease a 10-inch (25-cm) layer cake pan or springform pan with 3-inch (7.5-cm) sides. Line the pan bottom with a circle of parchment (baking) paper or waxed paper cut to fit precisely. Grease the paper, then dust with flour.

Place the chocolate in the top pan of a double boiler. Set over (but not touching) a pan of simmering water. Stir until melted and smooth. Remove from the heat and let cool slightly.

Separate the eggs (page 324) and set aside the whites. In a bowl, combine the butter and sugar. Using an electric mixer set on high speed, beat until light and fluffy, 8–10 minutes. Add the egg yolks, one at a time, beating well after each addition. Beat in the cooled chocolate and the nuts.

In a large bowl, with an electric mixer fitted with clean, dry beaters, beat the egg whites until they are stiff and glossy by not dry. Using a rubber spatula, gently but thoroughly fold the egg whites into the chocolate mixture. Pour into the prepared pan; smooth the top.

Bake until the top puffs and forms a thin crust, about 50 minutes. Be careful not to overbake. Transfer to a wire rack and cool in the pan for 15 minutes. Invert the cake onto the rack and let cool completely. Peel off the paper. Transfer to a plate and spread the warm chocolate ganache over the top and sides. Allow the topping to set, then cut into slices and serve.

Makes one 10-inch (25-cm) cake; serves 10

All-purpose (plain) flour for dusting

8 oz (250 g) bittersweet chocolate, chopped (1²/₃ cups)

3/4 cup (6 oz/185 g) unsalted butter, at room temperature, plus extra for greasing

3/4 cup (6 oz/185 g) sugar

6 extra-large eggs, at room temperature

1¹/₂ cups (6 oz/185 g) ground nuts (see note)

3 cups (24 fl oz/750 ml) Chocolate Ganache (page 317), warmed

Bête Noire

This is the world's easiest chocolate cake — and with a double dose of chocolate, probably the richest. It is delicious served hot from the oven with a dollop of Whipped Cream (page 316) over the top.

1¹/₃ cups (11 oz/340 g) granulated sugar

8 oz (250 g) unsweetened chocolate, chopped (1²/₃ cups)

4 oz (125 g) semisweet (plain) chocolate, coarsely chopped (scant 1 cup)

1 cup (8 oz/250 g) unsalted butter, at room temperature, cut into pieces, plus extra for greasing

5 extra-large eggs, at room temperature

Confectioners' (icing) sugar for dusting

Orange zest strips for garnish (page 329)

Preheat the oven to 350°F (180°C). Grease a 9-inch (23-cm) round cake pan. Line the bottom with a circle of parchment (baking) paper or waxed paper cut to fit. Grease the paper. Place the pan inside a baking pan large enough so the sides of the pans do not touch.

In a saucepan, combine ¹/₂ cup (4 fl oz/125 ml) water and 1 cup (8 oz/250 g) of the sugar. Bring to a boil, stirring until the sugar dissolves completely. Remove from the heat, add the chocolates, and stir until completely melted. Add the butter, piece by piece, stirring until melted and thoroughly incorporated.

In a bowl, combine the eggs and the remaining ¹/₃ cup (3 oz/90 g) sugar. Using an electric mixer set on medium speed, beat until slightly thickened, about 3 minutes. Using a rubber spatula, fold the chocolate mixture into the egg mixture until well combined. Pour and scrape the batter into the prepared pan and smooth the top. Place in the oven and pour hot water into the outer pan to reach ¹/₂ inch (12 mm) up the sides of the cake pan.

Bake until the cake looks dry but is not firm, 30 minutes. Remove the cake pan from the oven, let cool briefly, and cover the top of the cake with a sheet of plastic wrap. Invert onto a flat plate. Peel off the paper. Invert a flat plate on top and invert the plate and cake. Remove the plastic wrap. Let cool to room temperature. Dust with confectioners' sugar and decorate with orange zest strips.

Makes one 9-inch (23-cm) cake; serves 8

Raspberry Surprise Cupcakes

These light cupcakes each carry a pocket of sweet raspberry preserves that is revealed when you bite into them. You can use lime or orange for flavoring the icing, or try your own favorite citrus-flavored icing.

1½ cups (7½ oz/235 g) all-purpose (plain) flour

2 teaspoons baking powder

¼ teaspoon salt

1 cup (8 oz/250 g) granulated sugar

¾ cup (6 fl oz/180 ml) milk

6 tablespoons (3 oz/90 g) unsalted butter, melted

3 large egg whites (page 324), at room temperature

1 teaspoon vanilla extract (essence)

3 tablespoons raspberry preserves

Double recipe Confectioners' Sugar Icing flavored with lemon (page 316)

Preheat the oven to 350°F (180°C). Line 11 cups of a standard 12-cup muffin pan with paper liners; fill the unused cup with water to prevent warping.

In a bowl, sift together the flour, baking powder, and salt. Stir in the granulated sugar. Add the milk, melted butter, egg whites, and vanilla; whisk until smooth. Spoon an equal amount of the batter into each prepared muffin cup.

Bake until a toothpick inserted into the center of a cupcake comes out clean, about 20 minutes. Immediately invert onto a wire rack. Turn the cupcakes top side up and let cool completely. (To store the cupcakes, pack in a single layer in an airtight container and keep at room temperature for up to 2 days before filling and icing.)

Using the small end of a melon baller, scoop out a pocket in the top center of each cupcake. Spoon ¾ teaspoon raspberry preserves into each pocket. Spread the icing over the cupcakes and serve.

Makes 11 cupcakes

Chocolate Cupcakes with Sour Cream–Fudge Frosting

For a nice topping, use 2 tablespoons of peppermint candies processed in a food processor, or placed in a lock-top plastic bag and crushed with a frying pan. Make sure to crush the candies just before sprinkling.

Preheat the oven to 350°F (180°C). Line 10 cups of a standard 12-cup muffin pan with paper liners; fill the unused cups with water to prevent warping.

Sift the flour into a large bowl. Stir in the sugar, baking soda, and salt. In a heavy saucepan over medium-high heat, combine the milk, butter, and cocoa powder. Bring to a boil, whisking constantly. Remove from the heat and add to the flour mixture, whisking until well combined. Whisk in the egg and vanilla extract until blended. Spoon an equal amount of the batter into each prepared muffin cup.

Bake until a toothpick inserted into the center of a cupcake comes out clean, about 25 minutes. (The cupcakes will be flat on top when fully baked.) Immediately invert onto a wire rack. Turn the cupcakes top side up and let cool completely.

To make the frosting, chop the chocolate. In a medium saucepan over low heat, combine the butter and cream and stir frequently until the butter melts. Add the chocolate and whisk until smooth, about 2 minutes. Remove from the heat and let cool to barely lukewarm, about 8 minutes. Whisk in the sour cream, add the peppermint extract if using, and the confectioners' sugar. Let stand until thick enough to spread. If it is too thick, heat briefly over low heat and whisk again.

If you wish to store the unfrosted cupcakes, pack in a single layer in an airtight container and refrigerate for up to 2 days. Bring to room temperature and spread about 2 tablespoons frosting over each cupcake. Sprinkle with the crushed peppermint candies before serving, if desired.

Makes 10 cupcakes

1 cup (5 oz/155 g) all-purpose (plain) flour

1 cup (8 oz/250 g) plus 2 tablespoons sugar

1/2 teaspoon baking soda (bicarbonate of soda)

1/4 teaspoon salt

3/4 cup (6 fl oz/180 ml) milk

1/2 cup (4 oz/125 g) unsalted butter

1/3 cup (1 1/3 oz/40 g) unsweetened cocoa powder

1 large egg

1 teaspoon vanilla extract (essence)

FOR THE FROSTING:

1/4 cup (2 oz/60 g) butter

1/4 cup (2 fl oz/60 ml) heavy (double) cream

10 oz (315 g) bittersweet chocolate

3/4 cup (6 fl oz/180 ml) sour cream

1/2 teaspoon peppermint extract (essence) (optional)

1 cup (4 oz/125 g) confectioners' (icing) sugar

Chocolate Chip–Banana Cupcakes

These moist little cakes marry two complementary flavors, banana and chocolate. For a double-chocolate treat, use Sour Cream–Fudge frosting (page 251), without the addition of peppermint extract, to top some of the cupcakes.

Preheat the oven to 350°F (180°C). Line 14 standard muffin-pan cups with paper liners; fill any unused cups with water to prevent warping.

In a bowl, sift together the flour, sugar, baking soda, and salt. In another bowl, whisk together the mashed banana, melted butter, egg, and buttermilk until well blended. Add the flour mixture and whisk just until combined. Stir in the chocolate chips. Spoon an equal amount of the batter into each prepared muffin cup.

Bake until a toothpick inserted into the center of a cupcake comes out clean, about 25 minutes. Immediately invert onto a wire rack. Turn the cupcakes top side up and let cool completely.

If you wish to store the unfrosted cupcakes, pack in a single layer in an airtight container and refrigerate for up to 2 days. Bring to room temperature spread about 1 tablespoon buttercream over each cupcake before serving.

Makes 14 cupcakes

1½ cups (7½ oz/235 g) all-purpose (plain) flour

¾ cup (6 oz/185 g) sugar

1½ teaspoons baking soda (bicarbonate of soda)

¼ teaspoon salt

1¼ cups (10 oz/315 g) mashed very ripe banana (about 3 bananas)

½ cup (4 oz/125 g) unsalted butter, melted

1 large egg, at room temperature

3 tablespoons buttermilk

½ cup (3 oz/90 g) semisweet (plain) chocolate chips

About 1 cup (8 fl oz/250 ml) Vanilla Buttercream (page 316)

Boysenberry–Vanilla Bean Cheesecake Tartlets

FOR THE CRUST:

2¹/₄ cups (7 oz/220 g) graham cracker crumbs

¹/₃ cup (2¹/₂ oz/75 g) firmly packed brown sugar

¹/₂ cup (4 oz/125 g) plus 1 tablespoon unsalted butter, melted and cooled

FOR THE FILLING:

1 lb (500 g) cream cheese, at room temperature

¹/₂ cup (4 oz/125 g) granulated sugar

1 teaspoon vanilla extract (essence)

1 vanilla bean (page 329), cut in half lengthwise

¹/₂ cup (4 fl oz/125 ml) heavy (double) cream

¹/₂ teaspoon unflavored gelatin

¹/₃ cup (4 oz/125 g) seedless boysenberry or blackberry preserves

3 cups (12 oz/375 g) boysenberries

Preheat the oven to 350°F (180°C).

To make the crust, in a food processor fitted with the metal blade, combine the graham cracker crumbs, brown sugar, and melted butter. Process until the crumbs begin to stick together. With your hand draped with plastic wrap to form a glove, firmly press about ¹/₃ cup (1¹/₂ oz/45 g) of the crumbs onto the bottom and up the sides of 8 tartlet pans with removable bottoms 4¹/₂ inches (11.5 cm) in diameter. Bake the crusts until set, about 8 minutes. Let cool, then refrigerate until cold.

To make the filling, in a bowl, combine the cream cheese, granulated sugar, and vanilla. Using an electric mixer set on medium speed, beat until well blended. Using a small, sharp knife, scrape the seeds from the vanilla bean directly into the cream-cheese mixture. Add the cream and continue to beat on medium speed until fluffy, about 1 minute.

Place 1 tablespoon water in a small saucepan. Sprinkle the gelatin over the top and let soften for 5 minutes. Place the saucepan over low heat and stir until the gelatin dissolves. Add the gelatin mixture to the cream-cheese mixture and beat until fluffy, about 1 minute.

Spoon about ¹/₃ cup (3 fl oz/80 ml) of the filling into each crust and smooth the tops. Cover with aluminum foil and keep refrigerated for at least 2 hours or for up to overnight.

Remove the pan sides from the tartlets. In a small, heavy saucepan over medium heat, stir the preserves until melted. Remove from the heat and let cool slightly. Arrange the berries atop the tartlets. Using a pastry brush, brush the melted preserves over the berries. Refrigerate for at least 10 minutes, then serve.

Makes 8 tartlets

Classic Lemon Cheesecake

For a fancier dessert, top the cake with your favorite tropical fruits. Sliced peeled mango, papaya, and pineapple are a winning trio. Once the cheesecake has been topped with fruit, it should be stored in the refrigerator for no more than 4 hours.

Preheat the oven to 350°F (180°C).

To make the crust, in a food processor fitted with the metal blade, combine the graham cracker crumbs, brown sugar, and lemon zest. Process to mix well. Add the melted butter and process just until the crumbs being to stick together. With your hand draped with plastic wrap to form a glove, press the crumbs firmly onto the bottom and 2 inches (5 cm) up the sides of a springform pan 9 inches (23 cm) in diameter and 2 1/2 inches (6 cm) deep. Bake the crust until set, about 10 minutes. Let cool.

To make the filling, in a bowl, combine the cream cheese and granulated sugar. Using an electric mixer set on medium speed, beat until well blended. Beat in 1/2 cup (4 fl oz/125 ml) of the cream and the lemon juice and zest.

Place 1 tablespoon water in a small saucepan. Sprinkle the gelatin over the top and let soften for 5 minutes. Place the saucepan over low heat and stir until the gelatin dissolves. Gradually whisk in the remaining 1/2 cup cream into the gelatin mixture, then add the gelatin mixture to the cream-cheese mixture and beat until fluffy, about 1 minute. Pour and scrape the filling into the cooled crust and smooth the top. Cover with aluminum foil and refrigerate overnight or for up to 2 days.

To serve, run a knife around the pan sides to loosen the cake. Release the pan sides and place the cake on a plate. Overlap the lemon slices atop the center of the cake, cut into wedges, and serve.

Makes one 9-inch (23-cm) cake; serves 12

FOR THE CRUST:

1 3/4 cups (5 1/2 oz/170 g) graham cracker crumbs

1/4 cup (2 oz/60 g) firmly packed light brown sugar

1 teaspoon grated lemon zest (page 329)

1/2 cup (4 oz/125 g) unsalted butter, melted and cooled

FOR THE FILLING:

2 lb (1 kg) cream cheese, at room temperature

1 cup (8 oz/250 g) granulated sugar

1 cup (8 oz/250 ml) heavy (double) cream

3 tablespoons fresh lemon juice

2 teaspoons grated lemon zest (page 329)

1 teaspoon unflavored gelatin

3 thin lemon slices

Triple-Berry Cheesecake

FOR THE CRUST:

2 cups (6 oz/185 g) graham cracker crumbs

1/4 cup (2 oz/60 g) sugar

1/2 cup (4 oz/125 g) unsalted butter, melted and cooled

FOR THE FILLING:

2 lb (1 kg) cream cheese, at room temperature

1 cup (8 oz/250 g) sugar

2 tablespoons fresh lemon juice

2 teaspoons vanilla extract (essence)

4 large eggs, at room temperature

FOR THE TOPPING:

1 1/2 cups (12 fl oz/375 ml) sour cream

3 tablespoons sugar

1/3 cup (3 1/2 oz/105 g) seedless raspberry preserves

1 cup (4 oz/125 g) strawberries, hulled and sliced

1/2 cup (2 oz/60 g) raspberries

1/2 cup (2 oz/60 g) blueberries

Preheat the oven to 350°F (180°C).

To make the crust, in a food processor fitted with the metal blade, combine the graham cracker crumbs, sugar, and melted butter. Process until the crumbs begin to stick together. With your hand draped with plastic wrap to form a glove, press the crumbs firmly onto the bottom and 2 1/4 inches (5.5 cm) up the sides of a springform pan 9 inches (23 cm) in diameter and 2 1/2 inches (6 cm) deep. Wrap aluminum foil around the outside of the pan. Bake the crust until set, about 10 minutes. Let cool. Leave the oven set at 350°F (180°C).

To make the filling, in a bowl, combine the cream cheese, sugar, lemon juice, and vanilla. Using an electric mixer set on medium speed, beat until well blended. Add the eggs, one at a time, beating after each addition just until combined. Pour and scrape the filling into the cooled crust.

Bake until the edges are set but the center still quivers slightly when the pan is shaken, about 1 hour and 10 minutes.

Meanwhile, to make the topping, in a bowl, stir together the sour cream and sugar. When the cheesecake is done, spoon the sour-cream mixture over the top. Return the cake to the oven for 5 minutes longer to set. Transfer to a wire rack and let cool. Cover with aluminum foil and refrigerate overnight or for up to 2 days.

On the day the cake is to be served, run a knife around the pan sides to loosen the cake. In a large, heavy frying pan over medium heat, stir the preserves until melted. Remove from the heat, add all the berries, and toss to coat. Mound the berries atop the cake. Refrigerate for 30 minutes or for up to 2 hours.

To serve, remove the foil from the pan and release the pan sides. Place the cheese-cake on a plate, cut into wedges, and serve.

Makes one 9-inch (23-cm) cake; serves 12

Citrus and Honey Cheesecake with Nut Crust

Use dark honey for a fuller-bodied, more intense flavor. The cheesecake is best served slightly warm or at room temperature. Surround the base with 2 cups (8 oz/250 g) hulled strawberries, if desired.

FOR THE CRUST:

2¹/₃ cups (12 oz/375 g) hazelnuts (filberts), toasted (page 326) and skinned

¹/₃ cup (3 oz/90 g) sugar

¹/₂ teaspoon ground cinnamon

4–5 tablespoons (2–2¹/₂ oz/ 60–75 g) unsalted butter, melted

FOR THE FILLING:

1¹/₂ lb (750 g) cream cheese, at room temperature

¹/₂ cup (4 fl oz/125 ml) sour cream, at room temperature

³/₄ cup (9 oz/280 g) honey

6 eggs, separated (page 324), at room temperature

2 tablespoons grated orange zest (page 329)

1 teaspoon vanilla extract (essence)

3 tablespoons chopped Candied Orange Peel (optional) (page 314)

¹/₄ cup (2 oz/60 g) sugar

To make the crust, in a food processor, combine 2 cups (10 oz/315 g) of the hazelnuts, the sugar, and the cinnamon. Chop the mixture finely, without processing to a paste. Transfer to a small bowl and stir in enough of the melted butter for the mixture to hold together in clumps. Press the mixture into the bottom and partially up the sides of a 9-inch (23-cm) springform pan. Set aside.

Preheat the oven to 350°F (180°C).

To make the filling, in a bowl, using an electric mixer set on high speed, beat together the cream cheese and sour cream until smooth. Add the honey and beat until no lumps remain. Add the egg yolks, orange zest, vanilla, and the candied orange peel, if using; mix well.

In a large bowl, using an electric mixer fitted with clean, dry beaters and set on high speed, beat the egg whites until frothy. Gradually beat in the sugar until the peaks are almost stiff. Stir one-third of the egg whites into the cheese mixture to lighten it, then fold in the remaining egg whites just until no white streaks remain. Pour and scrape the filling into the crust.

Bake until the edges are set but the center still quivers slightly when the pan is shaken, 45–50 minutes. Turn off the oven, prop the door open, and leave the cheesecake inside for an additional 2 hours. Release and remove the sides from the pan and slide the cheesecake onto a serving plate. Chop the remaining ¹/₃ cup (2 oz/60 g) hazelnuts, scatter over the top, cut the cake into wedges, and serve.

Serves 8–10

Pumpkin-Hazelnut Cheesecake

Preheat the oven to 350°F (180°C). In a food processor fitted with the metal blade, combine the gingersnap crumbs and $^{1}/_{4}$ cup (2 oz/60 g) of the brown sugar. Process to mix well. Add the melted butter and process until the crumbs stick together. With your hand draped with plastic wrap to form a glove, press the crumbs firmly onto the bottom and 2 inches (5 cm) up the sides of a springform pan 9 inches (23 cm) in diameter and $2^{1}/_{2}$ inches (6 cm) deep. Wrap aluminum foil around the outside of the pan. Bake the crust until set, 9–10 minutes. Let cool. Leave the oven set at 350°F (180°C).

In a large bowl, combine the cream cheese and the $1^{1}/_{3}$ cups brown sugar. Using an electric mixer set on medium speed, beat until well blended. Beat in the pumpkin, vanilla, cinnamon, and allspice. Add the eggs, one at a time, beating after each addition just until combined. Pour and scrape the filling into the cooled crust, spreading it to the edges of the pan.

Bake until the edges are set but the center still quivers slightly when the pan is shaken, about $1^{1}/_{2}$ hours. Transfer to a wire rack and let cool for 1 hour.

In a small, heavy pan over medium heat, combine the remaining $^{1}/_{4}$ cup (2 oz/60 g) brown sugar, the room-temperature butter, and the cream and stir until the sugar dissolves. Bring to a boil. Add the hazelnuts and boil, stirring occasionally, until the mixture thinly coats the nuts, about 2 minutes. Spoon evenly over the cooled cake and let cool. Cover the cake with aluminum foil and refrigerate overnight or for up to 4 days.

To serve, run a knife around the pan sides to loosen the cake. Remove the foil from the pan and release the pan sides. Place the cheesecake on a plate, cut into wedges, and serve.

Makes one 9-inch (23-cm) cake; serves 12

2 cups (6 oz/185 g) gingersnap cookie crumbs

$^{1}/_{2}$ cup (4 oz/120 g) plus $1^{1}/_{3}$ cups ($9^{1}/_{2}$ oz/295 g) firmly packed brown sugar

5 tablespoons ($2^{1}/_{2}$ oz/75 g) unsalted butter, melted and cooled, plus $^{1}/_{4}$ cup (2 oz/60 g) unsalted butter at room temperature

2 lb (1 kg) cream cheese, at room temperature

$1^{1}/_{3}$ cups ($10^{1}/_{2}$ oz/330 g) canned pumpkin purée

1 tablespoon vanilla extract (essence)

$1^{1}/_{2}$ teaspoons ground cinnamon

$^{1}/_{4}$ teaspoon ground allspice

5 large eggs, at room temperature

$^{1}/_{4}$ cup (2 fl oz/60 ml) heavy (double) cream

1 cup (5 oz/155 g) hazelnuts (filberts), toasted (page 326) and skinned

Eggnog Cheesecake

For an elegant finish to this special holiday cheesecake, ring the cake top with rosettes of sweet Whipped Cream (page 316) and then sprinkle the whipped cream with freshly grated nutmeg.

Preheat the oven to 350°F (180°C).

To make the crust, in a food processor fitted with the metal blade, combine the toasted pecans, the graham cracker crumbs, and brown sugar and process to form fine crumbs. Add the melted butter and process until the crumbs being to stick together. With your hand draped with plastic wrap to form a glove, press the crumbs firmly onto the bottom and 2 inches (5 cm) up the sides of a springform pan 9 inches (23 cm) in diameter and 2 1/2 inches (6 cm) deep. Wrap aluminum foil around the outside of the pan. Bake the crust until set, about 10 minutes. Let cool. Leave the oven set at 350°F (180°C).

To make the filling, in a bowl, combine the cream cheese and granulated sugar. Using an electric mixer set on medium speed, beat until well blended. Beat in the Cognac, vanilla, and nutmeg. Add the eggs, one at a time, beating well after each addition just until combined. Pour and scrape the filling into the cooled crust and smooth the top.

Bake until the edges are set but the center still quivers slightly when the pan is shaken, about 1 hour. Transfer to a wire rack and let cool. Cover with aluminum foil and refrigerate overnight or for up to 3 days.

To serve, run a knife around the pan sides to loosen the cake. Remove the foil from the pan and release the pan sides. Place the cheesecake on a plate. Using a fine-mesh sieve, dust the confectioners' sugar over the top just before serving, if desired. Cut into wedges and serve.

Makes one 9-inch (23 cm) cake; serves 12

FOR THE CRUST:

1 cup (4 oz/125 g) pecan halves toasted (page 326)

1 cup (3 oz/90 g) graham cracker crumbs

1/4 cup (2 oz/60 g) firmly packed brown sugar

5 tablespoons (2 1/2 oz/75 g) unsalted butter, melted and cooled

FOR THE FILLING:

2 lb (1 kg) cream cheese, at room temperature

1 cup (8 oz/250 g) granulated sugar

3 tablespoons Cognac or dark rum

2 teaspoons vanilla extract (essence)

3/4 teaspoon ground nutmeg

4 large eggs, at room temperature

2 tablespoons confectioners' (icing) sugar (optional)

Espresso-Spice Cheesecake

This rich, spiced cheesecake is for coffee lovers only! If you like, offer freshly brewed espresso or cappuccino to go along with this sophisticated dessert for a deliciously strong finish.

FOR THE CHOCOLATE CRUMB CRUST:

1 package (9 oz/280 g) chocolate wafer cookies, broken

¼ cup (2 oz/60 g) sugar

½ cup (4 oz/125 g) unsalted butter, melted and cooled

FOR THE FILLING:

2 tablespoons instant espresso powder

1 tablespoon boiling water

2 lb (1 kg) cream cheese, at room temperature

1⅓ cups (11 oz/345 g) sugar

¼ cup (2 fl oz/60 ml) heavy (double) cream

1½ teaspoons ground cinnamon

½ teaspoon ground allspice

4 large eggs, at room temperature

2 teaspoons unsweetened cocoa powder

To make the crust, in a food processor fitted with the metal blade, combine the cookies and sugar. Process to form fine crumbs. Add the melted butter and process until the crumbs begin to stick together. With your hand draped with plastic wrap to form a glove, press the crumbs firmly onto the bottom and all the way up the sides of a springform pan 9 inches (23 cm) in diameter and 2½ inches (6 cm) deep. Wrap aluminum foil around the outside of the pan. Set aside.

Preheat the oven to 350°F (180°C).

To make the filling, in a bowl, dissolve the espresso powder in the boiling water. In another bowl, combine the cream cheese and sugar. Using an electric mixer set on medium speed, beat until well blended and smooth. Beat in the dissolved espresso, the cream, cinnamon, and allspice. Add the eggs, one at a time, beating after each addition just until combined and stopping occasionally to scrape down the sides of the bowl. Pour and scrape the filling into the crust and smooth the top.

Bake until the edges are set but the center still quivers slightly when the pan is shaken, about 1 hour. Transfer to a wire rack and let cool. Cover with aluminum foil and refrigerate overnight or for up to 3 days.

To serve, run a knife around the pan sides to loosen the cake. Remove the foil from the pan and release the pan sides. Place the cheesecake on a plate and, using a fine-mesh sieve, dust the cocoa powder over the top just before serving. Cut into wedges and serve.

Makes one 9-inch (23-cm) cake; serves 12

Chocolate-Mint Cheesecake

The cool flavor and velvety texture of this cake are elegant on their own, but for a pretty decoration, pipe Whipped Cream (page 316) around the top edge of the cake, then garnish with fresh mint leaves.

FOR THE CRUST:

1 package (9 oz/280 g) chocolate wafer cookies, broken

1/4 cup (2 oz/60 g) sugar

1/2 cup (4 oz/125 g) unsalted butter, melted and cooled

FOR THE FILLING:

10 oz (315 g) bittersweet chocolate, chopped

2 lb (1 kg) cream cheese, at room temperature

1 1/4 cups (10 oz/315 g) sugar

1/3 cup (1 oz/30 g) unsweetened cocoa powder

1 teaspoon peppermint extract (essence)

4 large eggs, at room temperature

Fresh mint leaves for garnish

To make the crust, in a food processor fitted with the metal blade, combine the cookies and sugar. Process to form fine crumbs. Add the melted butter and process until the crumbs begin to stick together. With your hand draped in plastic wrap to form a glove, press the crumbs firmly onto the bottom and all the way up the sides of a springform pan 9 inches (23 cm) in diameter and 2 1/2 inches (6 cm) deep. Wrap aluminum foil around the outside of the pan. Set aside.

Preheat the oven to 350°F (180°C).

To make the filling, in a heavy saucepan over very low heat, melt the chocolate, stirring constantly, until smooth. Remove from the heat and set aside. In a bowl, combine the cream cheese and sugar. Using an electric mixer set on medium speed, beat until well blended. Beat in the cocoa powder and peppermint extract. Add the eggs, one at a time, beating after each addition just until combined. Add the melted chocolate and beat just until smooth, stopping occasionally to scrape down the sides of the bowl. Pour and scrape the filling into the crust and smooth the top.

Bake until the the edges are set but the center still quivers slightly when the pan is shaken, about 50 minutes. Transfer to a wire rack and let cool. Cover with aluminum foil and refrigerate overnight or for up to 4 days.

To serve, run a knife around the pan sides to loosen the cake. Remove the foil from the pan and release the pan sides. Place the cheesecake on a plate and garnish with mint leaves. Cut into wedges and serve.

Makes one 9-inch (23-cm) cake; serves 12

White Chocolate Cheesecake

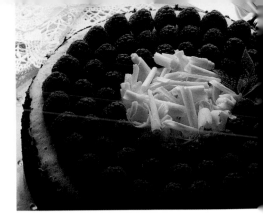

This cheesecake is the height of decadent elegance. Crown it with some white chocolate shavings and you have a showstopping dessert. Use only cream cheese that has been packaged in bars.

Preheat the oven to 350°F (180°C). Prepare the crust in a 9-inch (23-cm) springform pan with 2¹/₂-inch (6-cm) sides. Prebake the crust like a pie crust, following the directions on page 321, and let cool.

Turn the oven heat to 325°F (165°C).

Place the white chocolate in a heatproof bowl or the top pan of a double boiler. Set over (but not touching) a pan of simmering water. Stir until melted and smooth. Remove from the heat and gradually whisk in the cream, stirring until smooth.

In a food processor fitted with the metal blade, combine the cream cheese, sugar, and egg yolks. Process until smooth. Add the chocolate mixture and vanilla; process until smooth.

In a bowl using an electric mixer set on high speed, beat the egg whites until stiff peaks form. Using a rubber spatula, fold half of the egg whites into the chocolate mixture to lighten it. Then fold in the remaining egg whites just until no white streaks remain. Pour and scrape the batter into the cooled crust and smooth the top.

Bake until the top rises slightly and is light golden brown, 50–55 minutes. Turn off the oven but leave the cake in with the door closed for 1 hour. Transfer to a wire rack to cool completely, then transfer to a serving plate. Do not refrigerate.

Serve with the fresh berries or with the raspberry sauce. To cut the cake, use a knife dipped in very hot water and dried.

Makes one 9-inch (23-cm) cake; serves 10–12

Chocolate Crumb Crust
(page 266)

10 oz (315 g) white chocolate, chopped (2 cups)

¹/₂ cup (4 fl oz/125 g) heavy (double) cream, at room temperature

1 lb (500 g) best-quality cream cheese, at room temperature

¹/₂ cup (4 oz/125 g) sugar

4 large eggs, at room temperature, separated

1 tablespoon vanilla extract (essence)

2 cups (8 oz/250 g) fresh blueberries or raspberries, or 3 cups (24 fl oz/750 ml) Raspberry Sauce (page 315)

Pies, Tarts & Fruit Desserts

Apple-Pear Pie

Pears and apples are an especially good combination, and a blend of sherry and cinnamon brings out the flavor of the fruits. This pie is a nice finish to a full meal, served with a wedge of good blue cheese.

Basic Pie Pastry for a 9-inch (23-cm) double-crust pie (page 313)

3 large, firm but ripe pears, peeled, cored, and sliced

3 large apples, peeled, cored, and sliced

2 tablespoons fresh lemon juice

1/2 cup (3 1/2 oz/105 g) firmly packed brown sugar

3 tablespoons all-purpose (plain) flour

1/2 teaspoon ground cinnamon

1/4 teaspoon salt

3 tablespoons dry or sweet sherry

2 tablespoons unsalted butter

1 tablespoon heavy (double) cream

1 tablespoon raw sugar or granulated sugar

Preheat the oven to 425°F (220°C). Roll out the pastry for the bottom crust and use to line a 9-inch (23-cm) pie pan. Roll out the pastry for the top crust and set it aside.

In a bowl, combine the pears and apples. Add the lemon juice and toss to coat. In another bowl, stir together the brown sugar, flour, cinnamon, and salt. Add to the fruit and toss to combine. Add the sherry and toss until mixed. Pile the fruit into the pastry-lined pan and dot with bits of the butter. Cover with the top crust and trim and flute the edges (page 321). Cut a few vents in the top for steam to escape. Brush the top crust with the cream and sprinkle with the granulated sugar.

Bake for 30 minutes, then reduce the heat to 350°F (180°C) and bake until the crust is browned and the fruit is tender when pierced with a knife inserted through a vent, about 35 minutes longer. Cut into wedges and serve warm.

Makes one 9-inch (23-cm) pie; serves 8–10

Rhubarb-Raspberry Pie

Select a different berry if you wish, depending on what is available. Blackberries, loganberries, and boysenberries would all be a good choice, although you may need to increase the sugar if they are very tart.

Basic Pie Pastry for a 9-inch (23-cm) double-crust pie (page 313)

1 cup (8 oz/250 g) sugar

3 tablespoons (1 oz/30 g) cornstarch (cornflour)

1/4 teaspoon salt

1 1/2 lb (625 g) rhubarb stalks (page 328), peeled and sliced into 1/2-inch (12-mm) pieces

2 cups (8 oz/350 g) raspberries

2 tablespoons unsalted butter

Preheat the oven to 425°F (220°C). Roll out the pastry for the bottom crust and use to line a 9-inch (23-cm) pie pan. Roll out the pastry for the top crust and set it aside.

In a bowl, stir together the sugar, cornstarch, and salt. Add the rhubarb and raspberries and toss to mix well. Pile the fruit mixture into the pastry-lined pan and dot with bits of the butter. Cover with the top crust and trim and flute the edges (page 321). Cut a few vents in the top for steam to escape.

Bake for 20 minutes, then reduce the oven temperature to 350°F (180°C) and bake until the juices are bubbling and the top is browned, 30–40 minutes longer. Cut into wedges and serve warm.

Makes one 9-inch (23-cm) pie; serves 8–10

Fresh Peach Pie

This pie showcasing summer's sweet peaches is one of the best pies you'll ever make, with a lattice top to show off the beautiful filling. For some reason, peaches taste even better when baked.

Preheat the oven to 425°F (220°C). Roll out the pastry for the bottom crust and use to line a 9-inch (23-cm) pie pan. Roll out the pastry for the top crust and cut it into strips about ¾ inch (2 cm) wide; set aside.

Place the peaches in a large bowl. Sprinkle with the lemon juice and toss to coat well; set aside. In another bowl, stir together the flour, sugar, salt, and nutmeg. Add to the peaches and toss to combine. Pile the fruit mixture into the pastry-lined pan and dot with bits of the butter.

Use the strips to make a lattice top, then trim and flute the edges (page 321).

Bake for 25 minutes, then reduce the oven temperature to 350°F (180°C) and bake until the juices are bubbling and the top is browned, about 25 minutes longer. Cut into wedges and serve warm.

Makes one 9-inch (23-cm) pie; serves 8–10

Basic Pie Pastry for a 9-inch (23-cm) double-crust pie (page 313)

6 cups (1¼ lb/625 g) peeled (page 224), pitted, and sliced peaches

2 tablespoons fresh lemon juice

¼ cup (1½ oz/45 g) all-purpose (plain) flour

⅔ cup (5 oz/155 g) sugar

¼ teaspoon salt

Pinch of ground nutmeg

2 tablespoons unsalted butter

Cherry-Almond Pie

Sour cherries make a great pie, but they can be difficult to find. If you are able to use them, increase the amount of sugar to 1⅓ cups (11 oz/345 g). Almonds give the filling added texture and they complement the cherry flavor.

Preheat the oven to 425°F (220°C). Roll out the pastry for the bottom crust and use to line a 9-inch (23-cm) pie pan. Roll out the pastry for the top crust and cut it into strips about ³/₄ inch (2 cm) wide; set aside.

In a food processor or blender, combine the almonds, sugar, and cornstarch. Process until the nuts are finely ground; be sure not to grind to a paste. In a large bowl, combine the cherries, the sugar mixture, and the salt and toss to mix well. Pile the cherry mixture into the pastry-lined pan and dot with bits of the butter.

Use the strips to make a lattice top, then trim and flute the edges (page 321).

Bake for 25 minutes, then reduce the oven temperature to 350°F (180°C) and bake until the juices are bubbling and the top is browned, about 35 minutes longer. Cut into wedges and serve warm.

Makes one 9-inch (23-cm) pie; serves 8–10

Basic Pie Pastry for a 9-inch (23-cm) double-crust pie (page 313)

¹/₃ cup (2 oz/60 g) almonds, toasted (page 326)

²/₃ cup (5 oz/155 g) sugar, if using sweet cherries, or 1¹/₃ cups (11 oz/345 g), if using sour cherries

3 tablespoons (1 oz/30 g) cornstarch (cornflour)

5 cups (1¹/₄ lb/625 g) pitted sweet or sour cherries

¹/₄ teaspoon salt

2 tablespoons unsalted butter

Ginger-Molasses Pumpkin Pie

The whipped topping for this pie is studded with bits of crystallized ginger, which adds a sweet-spicy twist to the traditional holiday dessert. If you like, you can increase the amount of ground ginger to 1 teaspoon, for added flavor.

Basic Pie Pastry for a 9-inch (23-cm) pie shell (page 313)

FOR THE FILLING:

1 can (16 oz/500 g) unsweetened pumpkin purée

1/2 cup (3 1/2 oz/105 g) plus 2 tablespoons brown sugar

1 tablespoon all-purpose (plain) flour

1/2 teaspoon *each* ground ginger, ground cinnamon, ground nutmeg, and salt

3 eggs

1 cup (8 fl oz/250 ml) heavy (double) cream

1/4 cup (2 fl oz/60 ml) milk

1/4 cup (3 oz/90 g) molasses

1 1/2 teaspoons vanilla extract (essence)

FOR THE TOPPING:

1 cup (8 fl oz/250 ml) heavy (double) cream, chilled

3 tablespoons brown sugar

1 tablespoon vanilla extract (essence)

1/2 cup (2 1/2 oz/75 g) crystallized ginger, minced

Preheat the oven to 450°F (230°C). Roll out the pastry and use to line a 10-in (25-cm) pie pan. Trim and flute the edges (page 321). Brush with water and press on shapes cut from leftover dough, if desired. Bake the crust partially (page 321) and let cool completely. Reduce the oven temperature to 375°F (190°C).

To make the filling, in a bowl, combine the pumpkin purée, brown sugar, flour, ginger, cinnamon, nutmeg, and salt and whisk until smooth. Whisk in the eggs, cream, milk, molasses, and vanilla. Pour into the cooled crust. Bake for 20 minutes. Reduce the oven temperature to 325°F (165°C) and bake until the filling no longer jiggles in the center when the pan is shaken, about 30 minutes longer. Transfer to a wire rack and let cool.

To make the topping, in a bowl, combine the cream, brown sugar, and vanilla. Using an electric mixer set on high speed, beat until soft peaks form. Fold in the crystallized ginger. Cover and refrigerate if not using immediately.

Cut into wedges and serve warm with the topping.

Makes one 10-inch (25-cm) pie; serves 8–10

Maple-Pecan Pie

Here pecans are a perfect foil for the subtle taste of maple syrup, and although a simple pie pastry will work, the buttery flavor of tart pastry is especially good with this filling. Accompany it with unsweetened whipped heavy cream, if you wish.

Preheat the oven to 425°F (220°C). Roll out the pastry and use to line a 9-inch (23-cm) pie pan. Set aside.

In a bowl, beat the eggs until blended. Add the maple syrup, corn syrup, sugar, melted butter, vanilla, and salt; beat until combined. Stir in the pecan halves.

Pour the pecan mixture into the pastry-lined pan. Bake for 15 minutes, then reduce the oven temperature to 350°F (180°C) and bake until the filling has puffed and set around the edges but the center is slightly soft, about 25 minutes longer. Cut into wedges and serve warm or at room temperature.

Makes one 9-inch (23-cm) pie; serves 8–10

Basic Tart Pastry for a 9-inch (23-cm) tart shell (page 314)

3 eggs

1 cup (11 fl oz/345 ml) maple syrup

1/4 cup (2 1/2 fl oz/70 ml) dark corn syrup

1/4 cup (2 oz/60 g) sugar

1/4 cup (2 oz/60 g) unsalted butter, melted

1 teaspoon vanilla extract (essence)

1/4 teaspoon salt

1 1/2 cups (6 oz/185 g) pecan halves

Chocolate-Pecan Pie

Chocolate seems a natural addition to gooey, sweet, nutty pecan pie. Here it is added in semisweet (plain) chocolate chips, which remain whole, adding taste and texture to the filling.

Basic Pie Pastry for a 9-inch (23-cm) pie shell (page 313)

1½ cups (6 oz/185 g) pecans, coarsely chopped

6 oz (185 g) semisweet (plain) chocolate chips (scant 1¼ cups)

¼ cup (2 oz/60 g) unsalted butter, at room temperature

½ cup (5 fl oz/155 ml) light corn syrup

½ cup (3½ oz/105 g) firmly packed dark brown sugar

2 extra-large eggs

2 teaspoons vanilla extract (essence)

Preheat the oven to 350°F (180°C). Roll out the pastry and use to line a 9-inch (23-cm) pie pan. Trim and flute the edges (page 321). Bake the crust partially (page 321) and let cool completely. Prick the bottom of the pie crust in several places with a fork. Reduce the oven temperature to 325°F (165°C).

Sprinkle the pecans and chocolate chips evenly over the cooled crust. In a bowl, beat together the butter, corn syrup, brown sugar, eggs, and vanilla until smooth. Pour slowly and evenly over the nuts and chips so as not to disturb them. Bake until set and slightly firm, about 50 minutes. Transfer to a wire rack and let cool completely. Cut into wedges and serve at room temperature.

Makes one 9-inch (23-cm) pie; serves 8–10

Black-and-White Fudge Pie

Preheat the oven to 425°F (220°C).

To make the crust, grind the walnuts in a food processor; be sure not to grind them to a paste. Combine the flour, walnuts, cocoa, sugar, and salt in a mixing bowl and toss to combine. Add the butter and blend it into the dry ingredients with your fingertips. Stir in the milk and the vanilla until the dough is a cohesive mass.

Press the pastry into a 9-inch (23-cm) pie pan (or roll it out after chilling the dough for 1 hour). Use a fork to poke holes in the bottom of the crust. Bake the crust partially (page 321) and let cool completely.

Reduce the oven temperature to 325°F (180°C). Put the cream cheese on a plate and let reach room temperature.

To make the chocolate batter, in a heatproof bowl or the top bowl of a double boiler set over (but not touching) a pan of simmering water, stir the chocolate and butter together until melted and smooth, about 5 minutes; set aside. In a bowl, beat the eggs until blended. Add the sugar, flour, and salt and beat until well mixed. Stir in the melted chocolate and the walnuts. Set aside $^1/_2$ cup (4 fl oz/125 ml) of the batter; spread the remainder in the cooled pie shell.

To make the cream-cheese batter, in another bowl, beat the cream cheese until smooth. Beat in the sugar, egg, and vanilla until well blended. Spread the cheese batter over the chocolate batter in the pie shell—do not worry about getting it perfectly even—then spoon the reserved chocolate batter randomly over the top. With a knife, swirl the batters together to form a marbled effect.

Bake until the filling is set, about 40 minutes. Cut into wedges and serve at room temperature or refrigerate and serve chilled.

Makes one 9-inch (23-cm) pie; serves 8–10

FOR THE CRUST:

1 cup (4 oz/125 g) all-purpose (plain) flour

1/2 cup (2 oz/60 g) walnuts

1/3 cup (1 oz/45 g) unsweetened cocoa

1/4 cup (1 oz/60 g) sugar

1/4 teaspoon salt

1/2 cup (4 oz/125 g) unsalted butter, chilled

1/4 cup (2 fl oz/60 ml) milk

1 teaspoon vanilla extract (essence)

FOR CHOCOLATE BATTER:

4 oz (125 g) bittersweet chocolate, broken into pieces

1/2 cup (4 oz/125 g) unsalted butter

2 eggs

2/3 cup (5 oz/155 g) sugar

1/4 cup (1¹/2 oz/35 g) all-purpose (plain) flour

1/4 teaspoon salt

1/2 cup (2 oz/60 g) chopped walnuts

FOR CREAM-CHEESE BATTER:

8 oz (250 g) cream cheese

1/3 cup (3 oz/90 g) sugar

1 egg

1 teaspoon vanilla extract (essence)

Sweet Chocolate Pie

This new take on chocolate cheesecake yields a divine combination of chocolate textures and tastes, between the dark chocolate cookie crumb crust, the smooth baked cream cheese filling, and the ethereally light chocolate cream topping.

FOR THE CHOCOLATE CRUMB CRUST:

1 package (9 oz/280 g) chocolate wafer cookies, broken

¹/₄ cup (2 oz/60 g) sugar

¹/₂ cup (4 oz/125 g) unsalted butter, melted and cooled

¹/₃ cup (3 fl oz/80 ml) heavy (double) cream

3 tablespoons instant-coffee granules

4 oz (125 g) semisweet (plain) chocolate, chopped (scant 1 cup)

1 lb (500 g) cream cheese, at room temperature

2 extra-large eggs

³/₄ cup (6 oz/185 g) sugar

1 teaspoon vanilla extract (essence)

1¹/₂ cups (12 fl oz/375 ml) Chocolate Whipped Cream (page 317)

Strawberries, raspberries, or chocolate coffee beans for garnish

Preheat the oven to 425°F (220°C).

To make the crust, in a food processor fitted with the metal blade, combine the cookies and sugar. Process to form fine crumbs. Add the melted butter and process until the crumbs begin to stick together. With your hand draped with plastic wrap to form a glove, press the crumbs firmly onto the bottom and all the way up the sides of a 10-inch (25-cm) pie pan. Use a fork to poke holes in the bottom of the crust. Bake the crust partially (page 321) and let cool completely.

Reduce the oven temperature to 325°F (165°C).

In a small saucepan over medium heat, gently warm the cream until bubbles form at the edges. Add the coffee and stir to dissolve. Set aside.

Place the chocolate in a heatproof bowl or the top pan of a double boiler. Set over (but not touching) a pan of simmering water. Stir until smooth. Let cool slightly.

In a bowl, combine the cream cheese, eggs, sugar, and vanilla. Using an electric mixer set on low speed, beat until very smooth. Stir in the coffee mixture, then the cooled chocolate. Pour the batter into the cooled crust and smooth the top.

Bake until the top is dry to the touch and slightly firm, 35–45 minutes. Transfer to a wire rack and let cool completely. Top with the chocolate whipped cream and garnish with berries or chocolate coffee beans. Cut into wedges and serve warm.

Makes one 10-inch (25-cm) pie; serves 8–10

2 cups (8 oz/250 g) cherries

2 tablespoons amaretto

FOR THE TART SHELL PASTRY:

1¼ cups (6½ oz/200 g)
all-purpose (plain) flour

¼ cup (2 oz/60 g) sugar

½ cup (4 oz/125 g) cold
unsalted butter, cut into
½-inch (12-mm) pieces

1 egg yolk

2 tablespoons heavy (double)
cream

1 tablespoon amaretto

1 teaspoon grated lemon zest
(page 329)

FOR THE CHEESE FILLING:

½ lb (250 g) cream cheese, at
room temperature

⅓ cup (3 oz/90 g) sugar

2 whole eggs or 1 whole egg
and 2 egg yolks (page 324)

2 tablespoons amaretto

½ teaspoon almond extract
(essence)

Bing Cherry–Cheese Tart

Stem and pit the cherries. In a bowl, toss together the cherries and liqueur. Cover and let stand for 4 hours to blend the flavors.

To make the pastry, in a bowl, whisk together the flour and sugar. Using 2 knives or a pastry blender, cut in the butter until the mixture resembles cornmeal. In a small bowl, whisk together the egg yolk, cream, liqueur, and lemon zest. Add to the flour mixture and, using a fork, stir together until the dough forms a rough mass. Gather the dough into a ball, flatten it, and wrap in plastic wrap. Chill for at least 1 hour or for up to 1 day.

Preheat the oven to 400°F (200°C).

On a well-floured surface, roll out the pastry into a round about 11 inches (28 cm) in diameter. Carefully transfer the round to a 9-inch (23-cm) tart pan with a removable bottom. If the dough is difficult to roll out, press by hand into the tart pan. Do not fit the dough too snugly to the pan, as the crust will shrink as it bakes. Make the sides slightly higher than the pan rim, then trim off any excess overhang. Using a fork, prick a few holes in the bottom of the crust. Line with aluminum foil and fill with pie weights. Bake for 15 minutes, then remove the weights and foil. Reduce the oven temperature to 350°F (180°C) and bake until lightly colored, about 15 minutes longer. Transfer to a wire rack and cool completely. Leave the oven set at 350°F (180°C).

Meanwhile, to make the cheese filling, in a bowl, combine the cream cheese, sugar, eggs, liqueur, and almond extract. Using an electric mixer set on medium speed, beat until well combined.

Distribute the cherries evenly on the bottom of the cooled tart shell. Pour the cheese mixture over the cherries. Bake until the custard is set, about 15 minutes. Let cool on a wire rack, then cut into wedges and serve.

Makes one 9-inch (23-cm) tart; serves 8–10

Blue Plum Tart

Preheat the oven to 400°F (200°C). Roll out the pastry on a lightly floured surface. Use to line an 8-by-11-inch (20-by-28 cm) rectangular tart pan or a 10-inch (25-cm) round tart pan. Set aside in the freezer while you make the filling.

Finely chop the ¹/₂ cup (2 oz/60 g) hazelnuts and place in a bowl or the bowl of a food processor fitted with the metal blade, along with the ¹/₂ cup (4 oz/125 g) sugar, cinnamon, ginger, and butter. Pulse or cut in the butter with a pastry cutter or 2 knives until blended into a paste. Press onto the bottom of the pastry-lined tart pan. Top with the plums. Sprinkle the remaining 2 tablespoons sugar over the top and bake for 10 minutes. Reduce the oven temperature to 350°F (180°C) and bake until the plums are bubbling and the crust is golden, 20–30 minutes longer.

Meanwhile, melt the orange marmalade in a small saucepan; strain and keep warm. Coarsely chop the remaining 2 tablespoons hazelnuts. When the tart is done, brush the marmalade over the plums and sprinkle with the nuts. If desired, serve each piece with a dollop of citrus-flavored whipped cream.

Makes one 8-by-11-inch (20-by-28-cm) rectangular tart or one 10-inch (25-cm) round tart

Basic Pie Pastry for a 9-inch (23-cm) pie shell (page 313)

¹/₂ cup (2¹/₂ oz/75 g) plus 2 tablespoons skinned hazelnuts, toasted (page 326)

¹/₂ cup (4 oz/125 g) plus 2 tablespoons sugar

¹/₂ teaspoon ground cinnamon

¹/₂ teaspoon ground ginger

3 tablespoons unsalted butter, at room temperature

16–20 Italian prune plums, halved and pitted

³/₄ cup (7¹/₂ fl oz/230 ml) orange marmalade

Whipped Cream (page 316) flavored with about 1 teaspoon grated orange zest (page 329) (optional)

Banbury Tart

Here is a full-sized version of the individual raisin tartlets from Banbury, England. This tart calls for a beautiful streusel topping, and the dark filling looks and tastes remarkably like mincemeat. It is perfect for afternoon tea with guests.

Preheat the oven to 400°F (200°C). Roll out the pastry and use to line a 9-inch (23-cm) square or round tart pan. Use a fork to poke holes in the bottom of the crust, and bake the crust partially (page 321). Let cool completely before filling.

In a heavy-bottomed saucepan, combine the raisins, 1 cup (8 fl oz/250 ml) water, the sugar, crackers, and lemon zest. Bring to a boil over high heat. Reduce the oven temperature to low and simmer until slightly thickened, about 10 minutes. Remove from the heat and stir in the lemon juice and egg; set aside.

To make the topping, combine the flour, butter, sugar, and salt in a small bowl. Using your fingertips, blend together the ingredients until the mixture resembles fine crumbs.

Pour the raisin mixture into the cooled tart shell and sprinkle the crumb mixture over the top. Bake until lightly browned on top, about 35 minutes. Serve warm.

Makes one 9-inch (23-cm) tart

Basic Tart Pastry for a 9-inch (23-cm) tart shell (page 314)

1½ cups (9 oz/280 g) raisins

⅔ cup (5 oz/155 g) sugar

4 soda crackers, finely crushed

2 teaspoons freshly grated lemon zest (page 329)

2 tablespoons fresh lemon juice

1 egg, beaten

FOR THE TOPPING:

½ cup (2½ oz/75 g) all-purpose (plain) flour

3 tablespoons unsalted butter

2 tablespoons sugar

¼ teaspoon salt

Apple-Walnut Custard Tart

This tart of caramelized apples in a sweet walnut custard is a little more work than some of the others, but well worth the effort for a special occasion. It may also be made with firm pears, such as Boscs.

Basic Tart Pastry for a 9-inch (23-cm) tart shell (page 314)

¼ cup (2 oz/60 g) unsalted butter

⅓ cup (3 oz/90g) sugar

3 large apples, preferably Golden Delicious, peeled, cored, and cut into ½-inch (12-mm) dice

FOR THE WALNUT CUSTARD:

¼ cup (scant 1 oz/30 g) walnuts, ground (page 326), plus ½ cup (2 oz/60 g) chopped walnuts

1 egg

2 tablespoons sugar

½ cup (4 fl oz/125 ml) heavy (double) cream

1 teaspoon vanilla extract (essence) or 1 tablespoon Calvados

¼ teaspoon salt

FOR THE APRICOT GLAZE:

½ cup (8 oz/250 g) apricot jam

Preheat the oven to 425°F (220°C). Roll out the pastry and use to line a 9-inch (23-cm) tart pan. Bake the crust fully, until browned and crisp (page 321). Let cool completely before filling. Reduce the oven temperature to 350°F (180°C).

In a frying pan over medium heat, combine the butter and sugar and cook, stirring constantly, until melted and bubbling, then cook for 2 minutes longer, continuing to stir constantly. Add the apples and cook, stirring and tossing frequently, until they are slightly golden and any juices have evaporated, about 8 minutes. Spread the apple mixture in the cooled tart shell.

To make the custard, in a bowl, whisk together the ground walnuts, egg, sugar, cream, vanilla, and salt. Pour over the apples. Sprinkle the chopped walnuts on top and bake until the custard is set, about 25 minutes.

To make the apricot glaze, bring the jam to a boil in a small saucepan, stirring frequently. Place a strainer over a bowl and pour the jam into the strainer. Using the back of a spoon, press the jam through the strainer to remove the pulp. Discard the pulp and return the strained jam to the saucepan.

Transfer to a wire rack and let cool for 30 minutes. Bring the apricot glaze to a boil, then carefully brush the top of the tart with the warm glaze before serving. Store any unused glaze in an airtight container in the refrigerator.

Makes one 9-inch (23-cm) tart; serves 8–10

Tart Tatin

This version of the famous upside-down apple tart Tatin uses puff pastry. Look for puff pastry in the freezer section of well-stocked food stores or in food-specialty markets, or buy fresh puff pastry at a bakery.

Preheat the oven to 350°F (180°C).

In a 10-inch (25-cm) cast-iron or other heavy ovenproof frying pan over medium-high heat, melt together the butter and sugar, stirring constantly. Heat until the syrup is a rich caramel color, about 8 minutes.

Reduce the heat to low. Add the apple slices, arranging them in a decorative swirl starting from the outside edges of the pan. Place the apple slices rounded sides down, because the tart will be turned upside down when it is served. Simmer, uncovered, until the apples are slightly tender yet firm, about 10 minutes. Shake the pan occasionally to prevent scorching. Remove from the heat.

Trim the corners of the puff pastry to form a rough 10-inch (25-cm) circle. Place the pastry over the apples and, using the tip of a knife, push it down between the apples and the edge of the pan. Bake until the pastry is golden and puffed, about 20 minutes. Let cool for 10 minutes.

Using a knife, loosen the edges of the tart from the pan. Invert a serving plate over the pan and then, holding the pan and plate together firmly, invert them together. Lift off the pan. Cut into wedges and serve warm or at room temperature.

Makes one 10-inch (23-cm) tart; serves 6

3 tablespoons unsalted butter

½ cup (4 oz/125 g) sugar

6 Granny Smith or other firm tart apples, peeled, cored, and thickly sliced

1 square puff pastry, 10 inches (25 cm), thawed if frozen

Lemon Tart

Basic Tart Pastry for a 9-inch (23-cm) tart shell (page 314)

6 lemons

2 cups (1 lb/500 g) sugar

2 eggs

1/2 cup (4 fl oz/125 ml) heavy (double) cream

Pinch of salt

1/2 cup (5 oz/155 g) apricot preserves

Preheat the oven to 425°F (220°C). Line a 9-inch (23-cm) tart pan with the pastry. Bake the crust fully until browned and crisp (page 321). Let cool completely.

Grate the zest from 2 lemons (page 329) and juice them. Set the juice and zest aside. With a small, sharp knife, peel the remaining 4 lemons, cutting deeply enough to remove all the white pith and expose the flesh all around. Slice crosswise 1/4 inch (6 mm) thick. Pick out any seeds.

In a saucepan, combine 1 1/2 cups (12 oz/375 g) sugar with 1/2 cup (4 fl oz/125ml) water. Stir over low heat until the sugar dissolves. Raise the heat to medium-high and clip a candy thermometer onto the side of the pan. Boil until the thermometer registers 238°F (114°C), 10–15 minutes. Add the lemon slices and return to a simmer. Remove from the heat; set aside for at least 1 hour.

Preheat the oven to 350°F (180°C). In a bowl, whisk together the reserved lemon juice and zest, the remaining 1/2 cup (4 oz/125 g) sugar, and the eggs. Stir in the cream and salt. Pour into the cooled tart shell and bake until just set, about 20 minutes. Let cool to room temperature.

Carefully lift the lemon slices from the syrup and lay them on the filling—two forks are useful for this. In a small saucepan over medium-high heat, combine 1/4 cup (2 fl oz/60 ml) of the cooking syrup with the preserves. Bring to a boil and cook until thickened, about 3 minutes. Strain through a fine-mesh sieve. Brush the glaze over the lemon slices. Serve immediately.

Makes one 9-inch (23-cm) tart; serves 8–10

Sugar Tart

This is a very delicate tart that tastes of butter, sugar, and cream. The spicy, crunchy topping is a good contrast to the smooth custard underneath. Cider vinegar, a traditional American ingredient, adds sweet apple flavor to the dessert.

Preheat the oven to 425°F (220°C). Roll out the pastry and use to line a 9-inch (23-cm) tart pan. Bake the crust fully, until browned and crisp (page 321). Let cool completely before filling. Reduce the oven temperature to 325°F (165°C).

In a bowl, combine the eggs, sugar, cornmeal, vinegar, salt, and melted butter. Beat until smooth. Pour the egg mixture into the tart shell. Bake until the custard is barely set and the center still quivers when the pan is shaken, about 30 minutes.

Meanwhile, make the topping. In a small bowl, combine the sugar, butter, and cinnamon. Using your fingertips, rapidly work the ingredients together until fully blended; the mixture should be light and dry. When the tart has baked for 30 minutes and is barely set, carefully remove it from the oven and sprinkle it with the topping. Return the tart to the oven and bake until the filling is set and the topping has melted a little, about 10 minutes longer. Serve warm.

Makes one 9-inch (23-cm) tart; serves 8–10

Basic Tart Pastry for a 9-inch (23-cm) tart shell (page 314)

3 eggs

3/4 cup (6 oz/185 g) sugar

2 tablespoons cornmeal

1 tablespoon cider vinegar

1/4 teaspoon salt

7 tablespoons (3 1/2 oz/110 g) unsalted butter, melted

FOR THE TOPPING:

1/3 cup (3 oz/90 g) sugar

1 tablespoon cold unsalted butter

1/2 teaspoon ground cinnamon or nutmeg

Quince Tart

Uncooked quinces are harsh tasting, but simmering them in sugar syrup transforms them, turning the flavor sweet and delicate. Only a bit of cinnamon and lemon zest is needed to bring out their unique flavor.

Basic Tart Pastry for a 9-inch (23-cm) tart shell (page 314)

1½ cups (12 oz/375 g) sugar

1 cinnamon stick, about 2 inches (5 cm)

1 teaspoon freshly grated lemon zest (page 329)

3 quinces

½ cup (5 oz/155 g) apricot preserves

Preheat the oven to 425°F (220°C). Roll out the pastry and use to line a 9-inch (23-cm) tart pan. Bake the crust fully, until browned and crisp (page 321). Let cool completely before filling.

In a saucepan, combine 2½ cups (20 fl oz/625 ml) water, the sugar, cinnamon stick, and lemon zest. Bring to a boil over medium heat, stirring until the sugar dissolves. Reduce the heat to low.

Peel, halve, and core the quinces. Cut each half into 4 wedges. Drop the wedges into the simmering sugar syrup and cook, partially covered, until tender but not mushy, 15–20 minutes. Remove from the heat and let cool completely. Drain the quinces well, reserving the liquid. Pat them dry on paper towels.

Cut each wedge lengthwise into 2 or 3 slices; set aside. In a small, heavy-bottomed saucepan over high heat, combine the preserves with ¼ cup (2 fl oz/60 ml) of the reserved quince liquid and bring to a boil. Cook until thick and syrupy, about 3 minutes. Strain the syrup through a fine-mesh sieve to remove the pulp. Brush a thin coating of the warm glaze over the bottom of the cooled tart shell. Arrange the quince attractively in the tart shell, overlapping the slices. Carefully brush with the remaining glaze and serve immediately.

Makes one 9-inch (23-cm) tart; serves 8–10

Strawberry-Rhubarb Brown Betty

Preheat the oven to 375°F (190°C). Grease a 2¹/₂-qt (2.5-l) shallow baking dish.

In a bowl, using a fork, stir together the bread crumbs and brown sugar. Add the nutmeg and melted butter and stir until all the ingredients are evenly distributed. In another bowl, combine the rhubarb and strawberries and toss to mix. Sprinkle half of the crumb mixture in the bottom of the prepared dish. Spread the fruit mixture evenly over the top, then sprinkle with the remaining crumb mixture.

Bake until the top is golden and the fruit is bubbling, about 45 minutes. Let cool for 15 minutes before serving, or serve at room temperature.

Serves 8

2 cups (4 oz/125 g) fine fresh bread crumbs

1 cup (7 oz/220 g) firmly packed light brown sugar

¹/₂ teaspoon ground nutmeg

¹/₂ cup (4 oz/125 g) unsalted butter, melted, plus extra for greasing

2¹/₂ cups (12 oz/375 g) thinly sliced rhubarb (page 328)

6 cups (1¹/₂ lb/750 g) hulled, sliced strawberries

Apple Crumble

Preheat the oven to 350°F (180°C). Butter a 2¹/₂-qt (2¹/₂-l) baking dish.

Arrange the apple slices in the prepared dish. Pour the apple juice over and then sprinkle with the lemon juice, cinnamon, and allspice. Gently toss to combine. Set aside.

In a bowl, stir together the sugar and flour. Add the butter pieces. Using your fingertips, a pastry blender, or 2 knives, cut in the butter until the mixture resembles fine crumbs. Sprinkle the crumbs evenly over the apples in the dish.

Bake until the apples are tender, the juices are bubbling, and the topping is light golden brown, about 1 hour. Transfer to a wire rack and let cool. Serve immediately, or let cool on a wire rack to room temperature.

Serves 6

5 large apples, peeled, cored, and thickly sliced

¹/₂ cup (4 fl oz/15 ml) apple juice

Juice of ¹/₂ lemon

¹/₂ teaspoon ground cinnamon

¹/₄ teaspoon ground allspice

³/₄ cup (6 oz/185 g) sugar

³/₄ cup (4 oz/125 g) all-purpose (plain) flour

¹/₂ cup (4 oz/125 g) unsalted butter, cut into small pieces, plus extra for greasing

Blueberry Crisp

Tart blueberries and a slightly crunchy, sweet topping come together in this easy-to-make dessert. For maximum taste, try to find wild berries (fresh or frozen), rather than the cultivated ones. This crisp is terrific served with vanilla ice cream.

Preheat the oven to 375°F (190°C). Grease a shallow 1½-qt (1.5-l) baking dish.

Spread the blueberries evenly over the bottom of the prepared baking dish and sprinkle with the lemon juice.

In a bowl, using a fork, toss and stir together the brown sugar, flour, cinnamon, butter, and oats until well combined. Sprinkle evenly over the blueberries.

Bake until the top is golden and the blueberries are bubbling, about 30 minutes. Transfer to a wire rack to cool. Serve hot or warm.

Serves 6

4 cups (1 lb/500 g) fresh or frozen thawed blueberries

1 tablespoon fresh lemon juice

3/4 cup (6 oz/185 g) firmly packed light brown sugar

1/2 cup (2½ oz/75 g) all-purpose (plain) flour

1/2 teaspoon ground cinnamon

1/4 cup (2 oz/60 g) unsalted butter, at room temperature, cut into pieces, plus extra for greasing

3/4 cup (2½ oz/75 g) rolled oats

Warm Blueberry Shortcakes

1³/₄ cups (9 oz/280 g) all-purpose (plain) flour, plus extra for dusting

¹/₂ teaspoon salt

1 tablespoon baking powder

2 teaspoons sugar

6 tablespoons (3 oz/90 g) cold unsalted butter, cut into ¹/₂-inch (12-mm) pieces

1 cup (8 fl oz/250 ml) milk

Grated zest of 1 orange or 2 lemons (page 329)

About 3 tablespoons unsalted butter, melted, or heavy (double) cream

FOR THE BLUEBERRY COMPOTE:

6 cups (1¹/₂ lb/750 g) fresh or thawed frozen blueberries

2 tablespoons lemon juice

1 teaspoon ground cinnamon

1¹/₂ cups (12 oz/375 g) sugar

Grated zest of 1 orange or 1 lemon (page 329)

FOR THE MAPLE WHIPPED CREAM:

1 cup (8 fl oz/250 ml) heavy (double) cream

2 tablespoons pure maple syrup

¹/₄ teaspoon vanilla extract (essence)

Preheat the oven to 450°F (230°C).

To make the shortcakes, in a bowl, stir together the flour, salt, baking powder, and sugar. Add the butter and, using 2 knives, cut it in until the mixture resembles a coarse meal. Make a well in the center and add the milk and zest.

Stir vigorously until the dough pulls away from the sides of the bowl, about 1 minute. Turn out the dough onto a lightly floured work surface and knead gently and quickly for about 12 turns, or until the dough is no longer sticky. Pat into a disk about ¹/₂ inch (12 mm) thick.

Using a round biscuit cutter 2¹/₄ inches (5.5 cm) in diameter and dipping it into flour each time, cut out 12 biscuits. Place on an ungreased baking sheet and brush the tops with the melted butter. Bake until pale gold, 12–15 minutes.

Meanwhile, make the compote: In a heavy saucepan over medium heat, combine 4 cups (1 lb/500 g) of the blueberries with the lemon juice, cinnamon, sugar, and zest. Bring to a simmer and cook, stirring occasionally, until thickened, about 5 minutes. Stir in the remaining blueberries, remove from the heat, and set aside.

To make the whipped cream, in a large bowl, combine the cream, maple syrup, and vanilla. Using an electric mixer set on medium-high speed, beat until soft peaks form.

When the shortcakes are ready, remove from the oven, let cool slightly, then split the warm biscuits in half horizontally. Place 2 bottoms on each of 6 individual plates. Spoon half of the blueberry compote on the biscuit bottoms, add a dollop of the whipped cream, and then add a little more compote to each. Top with the remaining biscuit halves. Spoon on the remaining compote and serve at once.

Serves 6

Cranberry-Apple Slump

Apples and cranberries have wonderfully complementary flavors. In this cobbler-like dessert, they are baked with a biscuit topping. The juices from the fruit bubble up through the nooks and crannies and are absorbed by the flaky topping.

Preheat the oven to 375°F (190°C).

In a large bowl, combine the apple slices and cranberries. Add the sugar and toss to mix. Scatter the fruit mixture evenly over the bottom of a large ovenproof frying pan. Place over medium heat and cook, uncovered, until the juices are bubbling, about 10 minutes.

Meanwhile, make the topping: Sift together the flour, baking powder, and salt into a bowl. Add the butter and, using a pastry blender or 2 knives, cut it into the flour mixture until it is the consistency of coarse meal. Gradually add the milk, stirring with a fork just until the flour is incorporated. Do not overmix.

For cut biscuits, roll out the dough 3/4 inch (2 cm) thick on a lightly floured work surface. Using a biscuit cutter or a glass 2 inches (5 cm) in diameter, cut out the biscuits. Place atop the apples and cranberries, arranging them evenly on the surface. Alternatively, if you prefer dropped biscuits, drop the flour mixture by heaping tablespoons onto the fruit.

Bake until the biscuits are golden and the fruit is bubbling, about 35 minutes. Serve immediately, or let cool on a wire rack and serve at room temperature.

Serves 6

1½ lb (750 g) Granny Smith or other firm tart green apples, peeled, cored, and sliced (about 4 cups)

2 cups (8 oz/250 g) fresh or thawed frozen cranberries

1 cup (8 oz/250 g) sugar

FOR THE BISCUIT TOPPING:

1¼ cups (6½ oz/200 g) all-purpose (plain) flour

2 teaspoons baking powder

½ teaspoon salt

⅓ cup (3 oz/90 g) unsalted butter, at room temperature

½ cup (4 fl oz/125 ml) milk

Grated zest of 1 orange (page 329)

Three-Berry Cobbler

Cobblers, a tradition in Southern America, conjure up memories of irresistible aromas filling warm, friendly kitchens. This recipe combines fresh blackberries, raspberries, and strawberries under a sweet biscuit crust.

Unsalted butter for greasing

FOR THE FILLING:

1¹/₂ cups (6 oz/185 g) hulled, sliced strawberries

1¹/₂ cups (6 oz/185 g) raspberries

1¹/₂ cups (6 oz/185 g) blackberries

¹/₂ cup (4 oz/125 g) sugar

FOR THE BISCUIT TOPPING:

¹/₃ cup (3 oz/90 g) unsalted butter, at room temperature

¹/₃ cup (3 oz/90 g) sugar, plus extra for sprinkling (optional)

2 cups (10 oz/315 g) all-purpose (plain) flour

¹/₂ teaspoon salt

1 teaspoon baking powder

¹/₂ cup (4 fl oz/125 ml) milk

Preheat the oven to 375°F (190°C). Grease a deep 2-qt (2-l) baking dish.

To make the filling, in the prepared dish, combine the strawberries, raspberries, and blackberries. Sprinkle the sugar over the berries and toss to mix. Set aside.

To make the topping, in a bowl, combine the butter and sugar. Using a wooden spoon or an electric mixer set on medium-high speed, beat until fluffy, about 3 minutes. In another bowl, sift together the flour, salt, and baking powder. Add the flour mixture alternately with the milk to the butter mixture, stirring with a fork just until the flour is completely incorporated. Do not overmix.

Turn out the dough onto a lightly floured work surface and roll out or pat into the shape and size of the baking dish. Lift the dough onto the dish to cover the fruit; it should reach just slightly short of the dish sides. Crimp or flute the edges of the dough to form an attractive rim. Cut several slits in the top for steam to escape. Sprinkle with sugar, if desired.

Bake until the top is golden and the berries are bubbling, about 50 minutes. Transfer to a wire rack to cool. Serve hot, warm, or at room temperature.

Serves 6–8

Pear Clafouti

A clafouti is a rustic raised fruit "pancake" from the Limousin region of France. It is traditionally prepared with unpitted cherries, but pears are a delicious, and easier to eat, alternative. Be sure to let it cool before dusting with confectioners' sugar.

Preheat the oven to 375°F (190°C).

Peel, halve, and core the pears, and cut into 1-inch (2.5-cm) pieces. In a small saucepan over medium heat, combine the pears, brandy, and crystallized ginger, if using. Cook gently, stirring occasionally, until the pears are tender but not mushy, about 10 minutes.

Meanwhile, grease a 10-inch (25-cm) pie pan or other shallow round baking dish with the butter. When the pears are ready, distribute them and their juices evenly on the bottom of the prepared pan.

In a bowl, whisk together the eggs, flour, granulated sugar, cinnamon (if using), milk, cream, zest, vanilla, and salt until well mixed. To eliminate any lumps, scrape down the sides of the bowl and whisk the batter again. Let rest for about 5 minutes.

Pour the batter evenly over the pears. Bake until puffed and set, 35–40 minutes. Transfer to a wire rack and let cool for 10–15 minutes. Dust confectioners' sugar over the top and serve warm.

Makes one 10-inch (25-cm) pancake; serves 6

1½–2 lb (750 g–1 kg) firm but ripe Bosc or Anjou pears

⅓ (3 fl oz/80 ml) pear brandy or ½ cup (4 fl oz/125 ml) sweet white wine

3 tablespoons minced crystallized ginger (optional)

2 tablespoons unsalted butter

3 eggs

½ cup (2½ oz/75 g) all-purpose (plain) flour

½ cup (4 oz/125 g) granulated sugar

½ teaspoon ground cinnamon (optional)

1 cup (8 fl oz/250 ml) milk

½ cup (4 fl oz/125 ml) heavy (double) cream

Grated zest of 1 lemon or ½ orange (page 329)

1 teaspoon vanilla extract (essence)

Pinch of salt

Confectioners' (icing) sugar for dusting

Basic Recipes & Techniques

These basic recipes and techniques are used throughout *Baking*. Once mastered, you'll find that you turn to them again and again to create delicious baked goods.

Basic Pizza Dough

Here is an all-purpose dough that will complement almost any pizza.

1 tablespoon active dry yeast

3/4 cup plus 2 tablespoons (7 fl oz/210 ml) lukewarm water (110°F/43°C)

2 3/4 cups (14 oz/440 g) all-purpose (plain) flour, plus 1/2 cup (2 oz/60 g) for kneading, plus extra for dusting

1 teaspoon salt

1 tablespoon extra-virgin olive oil

In a small bowl, dissolve the yeast in the water and let stand until slightly foamy on top, about 10 minutes.

In a bowl, stir together the 2 3/4 cups flour and salt, forming a mound. Make a well in the center and add the yeast mixture to the well. Using a fork and stirring with a circular motion, slowly pull the flour into the yeast mixture. Continue stirring until a dough forms.

Transfer the dough to a lightly floured work surface. Using the heel of your hand, knead the dough until it is smooth and elastic, about 10 minutes. As you work, sprinkle additional flour on the work surface, 1 tablespoon at a time, only if needed to prevent the dough from sticking to the surface.

Form the dough into a ball. Brush the inside of a large bowl with the olive oil and place the dough in it, coating the dough with the oil. Cover with plastic wrap and let rise at room temperature until doubled in size, 1–2 hours.

Turn the dough out onto a lightly floured work surface. Punch the dough down and, using your hands, begin to press it out gently into the desired shape. Then place one hand in the center of the dough and, with the other hand, pull, lift, and stretch the dough, gradually working your way all around the edge, until it reaches the desired thickness, about 1/4 inch (6 mm) thick for a crusty pizza base, and 1/2 inch (12 mm) thick for a softer one. Flip the dough over from time to time as you work with it. Alternatively, roll out the dough with a rolling pin. The dough should be slightly thinner in the middle than at the edge. Lift the edge of the pizza to form a slight rim.

Transfer the dough to a baker's peel or baking sheet, cover with a clean kitchen towel, and let it rise again until almost doubled in size, about 20 minutes. Top and bake as directed in the recipe.

Makes a 12-inch (30-cm) thin-crust pizza or a 9-inch (24-cm) thick-crust pizza

Sourdough Starter

If your starter ever develops a foul odor or pinkish color, it has gone bad and should be thrown away.

1 package (2 1/4 teaspoons) active dry yeast

2 1/2 cups (20 fl oz/625 ml) lukewarm water (110°F/43°C), plus more as needed for feeding starter

2 1/2 cups (12 1/2 fl oz/390 g) unbleached bread flour, plus flour as needed for feeding starter

In a glass bowl, combine the yeast and 1/2 cup (4 fl oz/125 ml) of the lukewarm water and let stand until bubbles start to rise, 5 minutes. Stir in the 2 1/2 cups flour and then add the remaining 2 cups (16 fl oz/500 ml) water and mix well. Pour into a 4-qt (4-l) glass crock and cover with cheesecloth (muslin). Let stand for 4 days in a warm place (70–75°F/21–24°C). It will bubble and ferment, increase 4–6 times in volume, and then return to its original size.

Transfer to a tightly covered glass container and keep refrigerated. Feed the starter every 10 days by stirring in 1/2 cup (2 1/2 oz/75 g) flour and 1/2 cup (4 fl oz/125 ml) lukewarm water. Each time the starter is used, reserve at least 1 cup (8 fl oz/250 ml) of the original mixture and replace the amount taken with equal amounts of flour and lukewarm water.

Bring to room temperature and stir gently before using.

Makes about 4 cups (32 fl oz/1 l)

Tapenade

To store this spread, pour a thin layer of olive oil over the top, cover, and refrigerate for up to 2 months.

1/2 lb (250 g) oil-cured black olives, pitted

2 tablespoons olive oil

2 cloves garlic, chopped

1 tablespoon well-drained capers

1/2 teaspoon herbes de Provence

Freshly ground pepper

In a food processor or blender, combine the olives, olive oil, garlic, capers, herbs, and pepper to taste. Pulse until the mixture is evenly chopped. Cover tightly and chill in the refrigerator. Serve cold.

Makes about 3/4 cup (4 1/2 oz/140 g)

Savory Butters

This Tomato-Basil blend is fragrant and summery while the Caper-Mustard mixture has a strong, piquant taste.

FOR TOMATO-BASIL BUTTER:

1/2 cup (4 oz/125 g) unsalted butter, at room temperature

3 tablespoons tomato paste

2 tablespoons chopped fresh basil

1/2 teaspoon salt

FOR CAPER-MUSTARD BUTTER:

1/2 cup (4 oz/125 g) unsalted butter, at room temperature

2 tablespoons well-drained capers, chopped

2 tablespoons Dijon mustard

1/4 teaspoon *each* salt and freshly ground pepper

For either butter, combine the ingredients in a food processor. Process until smooth and well mixed. Scrape into a small bowl. Alternatively, use a spoon to beat together all the ingredients in a small bowl until completely mixed. Cover and refrigerate for up to 1 week; serve at room temperature.

Makes about 3/4 cup (6 oz/185 g)

Basic Pie Pastry

Follow three rules to avoid a tough crust: Don't overblend; add enough water so the dough is rolled out easily; and handle it no more than necessary.

FOR A 9-INCH (23-CM) CRUST:

1 1/2 cups (7 1/2 oz/235 g) all-purpose (plain) flour

1/2 teaspoon salt

1/2 cup (4 oz/125 g) vegetable shortening

3–4 tablespoons cold water, more or less, as needed

FOR A 9-INCH (23-CM) DOUBLE-CRUST:

2 1/4 cups (11 1/2 oz/360 g) all-purpose (plain) flour

3/4 teaspoon salt

3/4 cup (6 oz/185 g) vegetable shortening

6–7 tablespoons cold water

Hand method: In a bowl, combine the flour and salt. Add the shortening. With two knives or a pastry blender, blend the ingredients together, working quickly, until you have a mixture of tiny, irregular flakes about the size of coarse bread crumbs.

Sprinkle in the water 1 tablespoon at a time, stirring gently with a fork after each addition. Add just enough water for the dough to form a rough mass.

With floured hands, pat the dough into a smooth disk—for a double-crust pie, make 2 disks, one slightly larger than the other. The dough is now ready to use. There is no need to chill the dough, although it may be wrapped in plastic wrap and refrigerated for up to 2 days.

Food-processor method: The food processor works very quickly, so be careful not to overblend. Put the flour, salt, and shortening (in one lump) in the work bowl of a food processor. Process with 15 rapid off-on pulses; the mixture should be light and dry and resemble tiny flakes. Add 2 tablespoons water (4 tablespoons for a double-crust pie) and process in 5 rapid pulses. Add 1 more tablespoon water (2 tablespoons for a double-crust pie) and process in 3 rapid pulses.

Stop and feel the dough, without touching the blade; it should be just damp enough to mass together. If necessary, add water by teaspoonfuls, processing for an instant after each addition. The total mixing time is less than 1 minute; the dough should not form a ball, it should be a rough, shaggy mass. Use it immediately or chill it as described in the hand method (above).

Rolling out the dough: On a lightly floured surface, roll the dough out (using the larger piece if it is the bottom of a double-crust pie) until it is about 1/8 inch (3 mm) thick and 12 inches (30 cm) in diameter, or 2 inches (5 cm) larger than the top of the pan. Keep the dough as round as possible.

Transfer the rolled-out pastry to the pie pan. Pat the pastry in around the edges to fit the pan's shape. If you are making a single crust pie, the pie shell may now be filled unbaked, partially baked, or fully baked, depending on the recipe (see page 321 for detailed instructions). If you are making a double-crust pie, roll out the remaining pastry for the top crust and set it aside on waxed paper.

Makes one 9-inch (23-cm) pie crust

Basic Tart Pastry

Because it is made with more butter, tart pastry is firmer and more crumbly than the lighter, more flaky pie pastry.

1¼ cups (6½ oz/200 g) all-purpose (plain) flour

1 tablespoon sugar

¼ teaspoon salt

½ cup (4 oz/125 g) unsalted butter, chilled

2–3 tablespoons cold water

Hand method: Combine the flour, sugar, and salt in a bowl and toss together. Cut the butter into bits, drop them into the bowl, and, with two knives or a pastry blender, blend until the mixture looks like particles about the size of oatmeal flakes. Sprinkle 1 tablespoon water over the flour mixture, then stir gently with a fork. Sprinkle on another tablespoon of water and stir again. Feel the dough; it should be damp enough to form a rough, but not wet, mass. Add a few more drops of water if necessary to

achieve the correct consistency. Dump the dough onto a work surface, gather it together, and pat it into a disk. The dough is ready to use right away, though it may be easier to roll out if it is wrapped and chilled for 30 minutes.

Food-processor method: Put the flour, sugar, and salt in a food processor. Cut the butter into bits, drop them into the bowl, and process, using rapid on-off pulses, until the mixture resembles small particles about the size of oatmeal flakes. Add 1 tablespoon of the water and process for a couple of seconds. Add another tablespoon of the water and process with 3 or 4 pulses.

Feel the dough; it should be damp enough to form a rough, but not wet, mass. Add more water by teaspoonfuls, if needed to achieve the correct consistency. Dump the dough onto a work surface, gather it together, and pat it into a disk. Use it right away or chill the dough as described in the hand method (above).

Rolling out the dough: Roll the dough out on a floured surface to ⅛ inch (3 mm) thick and 11 inches (28 cm) in diameter. Keep the shape as round as possible.

Transfer the rolled-out pastry to the tart pan. Pat some of the overhang back in around the edge to make the sides of the tart shell a little thicker than the bottom. Trim any remaining overhang.

The tart shell may now be filled unbaked, partially baked, or fully baked, depending upon the recipe (see page 321 for detailed instructions).

Makes one 9-inch (23-cm) tart shell

Candied Citrus Peel

This recipe is simple but it takes several days. Store the peels in lock-top plastic bags, in the refrigerator for 1 month or in the freezer for 6 months.

8 large lemons or 6 medium oranges

3 qt (3 l) water

1 tablespoon salt

3¼ cups (26 oz/815 g) sugar

Scrub the fruits under running water. Cut crosswise into halves. Use a citrus reamer to extract all the juice. Pull out the membranes, leaving just the colored outer shells and white pith.

In a large bowl, combine the water and salt and stir to dissolve the salt. Add the citrus peels and let soak for 1 hour to draw out the bitterness from the pith. Drain and rinse well.

In a saucepan over high heat, combine the peels with water to cover. Bring to a boil, reduce the heat to low, and simmer until tender when pierced with a knife, about 1 hour. Remove from the heat and drain, reserving the cooking liquid. Measure the cooking liquid, then add enough water to total 4 cups (32 fl oz/1 l). Place in a nonaluminum saucepan and add 2 cups (1 lb/500 g) sugar. Bring to a boil over high heat, stirring to dissolve the sugar, 4–5 minutes. Add the peels, reduce the heat to low, and simmer for 5 minutes. Remove from the heat and transfer the peels and syrup to a bowl. Cover and chill for 2 days.

Drain the syrup into a nonaluminum saucepan. Add 1 cup (8 oz/250 g) sugar and bring to a boil. Add the peels, reduce the heat to low, and simmer until semitransparent, 35–40 minutes.

Remove from the heat, pour the peels and syrup into a bowl, and allow to cool. Cover and let stand at room temperature for 4–6 hours.

Drain the syrup, measure it, and add enough water to total 2 cups (16 fl oz/ 500 ml). Place in a nonaluminum saucepan and add 1/4 cup (2 oz/60 g) sugar. Bring to a boil over high heat, add the peels, and boil for 5 minutes.

Using a slotted spoon, remove the peels and place, colored sides up, onto a wire rack set over a large plate to catch drips. Let dry at room temperature for at least 12 hours. Chop just before using.

Makes about 1 lb (500 g)

Vanilla Sugar

This mixture will keep for months in an airtight container and can be substituted for vanilla extract (essence) and sugar in almost any recipe.

1 1/2 vanilla beans

2 cups (1 lb/500 g) granulated sugar

Cut the vanilla beans into 1 1/2-inch (4-cm) lengths. Place in a food processor or blender and process until coarsely chopped. Add 1/2 cup (4 oz/125 g) of the sugar and process until the vanilla beans are finely chopped. Add the remaining 1 1/2 cups (12 oz/375 g) sugar and process until thoroughly mixed.

Strain through a fine-mesh sieve and use as directed in the recipe.

Makes about 2 cups (1 lb/500 g)

Strawberry Jam Butter

The powdered milk in this spread helps absorb moisture, keeping the mixture from forming rivulets of separation.

1/2 cup (4 oz/125 g) unsalted butter, at room temperature

2 tablespoons nonfat dry milk (milk powder)

1/3 cup (4 oz/125 g) strawberry jam

1/2 cup (2 oz/60 g) confectioners' (icing) sugar

Pinch of salt

In a food processor, process the butter until smooth, scraping down the work bowl once or twice. Add half of the dry milk, the jam, and sugar and process until blended. Add the remaining dry milk and the salt and process until smooth. Store tightly covered in the refrigerator for up to 1 week; bring to room temperature before serving.

Makes about 1 cup (8 oz/250 g)

Strawberry Jam

It only takes minutes to make this delicious uncooked jam, but it will keep in the refrigerator for up to 5 days.

6 cups strawberries (1 1/2 lb/ 750 g total weight), stemmed

1/3–1/2 cup (3–4 oz/90–125 g) sugar

1–2 tablespoons fresh lemon juice

In a bowl, mash the berries to a pulp. Add the sugar and lemon juice to taste (more ripe fruit will need the smaller amounts of sugar and lemon juice). Let sit for 1 hour, stirring occasionally.

Makes about 2 cups (22 oz/680 g)

Pear-Ginger Jam

This spicy, fresh jam is great on breads and muffins, especially those made with whole grains, nuts, and seeds.

3 ripe pears (about 1 1/2 lb/750 g total weight), peeled, cored, and cut into chunks

1/2 cup (4 oz/125 g) sugar

3 tablespoons fresh lemon juice

1 tablespoon finely grated fresh ginger

In a food processor, purée the pears until smooth. Add the sugar, lemon juice, and ginger, and process briefly. Serve at room temperature. To store, place the jam in a jar, press plastic wrap directly onto the surface of the jam, cover with a tight cap, and refrigerate for up to 3 days. Stir before serving.

Makes about 1 1/2 cups (1 lb/500 g)

Raspberry Sauce

For a stronger flavor, add a few drops of fresh lemon juice. This sauce will keep for up to 2 weeks in the refrigerator or for up to 6 week frozen.

2 1/2 cups (10 oz/315 g) fresh raspberries or thawed, frozen unsweetened raspberries

1/2 cup (3 1/2 oz/105 g) superfine (caster) sugar

1/4 cup (2 fl oz/60 ml) framboise or other raspberry-flavored liqueur (optional)

Put the raspberries, sugar, and liqueur, if using, in a blender or a food processor and purée. For a seedless sauce, pass the purée through a fine-mesh sieve.

Makes about 3 cups (24 fl oz/750 ml)

Vanilla Buttercream

Buttercream is a classic French frosting used to frost a wide variety of cakes.

2/3 cup (5 oz/155 g) sugar

4 large egg yolks (page 324), at room temperature

1 cup (8 oz/250 g) unsalted butter, at room temperature, cut into tablespoon-sized pieces

1 1/2 teaspoons vanilla extract (essence)

In a metal bowl, whisk together the sugar, egg yolks, and 1 tablespoon water. Set over (but not touching) a saucepan of simmering water. Whisk constantly until the mixture registers 170°F (77°C) on a candy thermometer, 3–4 minutes.

Remove the bowl from over the water. Using an electric mixer set on high speed, beat the egg mixture until cool and thick, 4–5 minutes. Add the butter, 1 tablespoon at a time, beating after each addition. Beat in the vanilla extract. If the buttercream seems lumpy, set the bowl over simmering water for a few seconds, and beat again.

To store, cover and refrigerate for up to 2 days. Before using, let stand at room temperature until softened. If necessary, rewarm over a saucepan of simmering water for a few seconds, until smooth.
Makes about 2 1/3 cups (19 fl oz/580 ml)

For vanilla bean flavor: Cut 1 vanilla bean in half lengthwise and, using the tip of a small, sharp knife, scrape the seeds from the bean into the finished buttercream; beat in evenly.

Confectioners' Sugar Icing

Drizzle or spread this simple icing and try the variations for extra flavor.

1/4 cup (2 oz/60 g) unsalted butter

1 tablespoon water

1/2 cup (2 oz/60 g) confectioners' (icing) sugar

In a small saucepan over medium heat, stir together the butter and water until the butter melts. Remove from the heat and let stand until cool, about 5 minutes.

Add the sugar to the butter and whisk vigorously until thickened, about 1 minute. Use it quickly, or the icing may become to thick to drizzle. If necessary, rewarm it for 2 or 3 seconds over low heat, whisking constantly.
Makes a scant 1/2 cup (4 fl oz/125 ml)

For brown sugar flavor: Add 1/4 cup (2 oz/60 g) firmly packed brown sugar to the warm butter mixture and stir until the sugar dissolves; let cool, then whisk in the confectioners' sugar.

For lemon flavor: Use 1 tablespoon fresh lemon juice instead of water and add 1/2 teaspoon grated lemon zest (page 329) with the sugar.

Cream Cheese Frosting

Spread this frosting on any dessert for a rich, tangy topping. It will keep for 1 week, covered, in the refrigerator.

1 lb (500 g) cream cheese

6 tablespoons (3 oz/90 g) unsalted butter, at room temperature

1 1/4 cups (5 oz/155 g) confectioners' (icing) sugar

1 1/2 teaspoons vanilla extract (essence)

Bring the cream cheese to room temperature (page 323). In a large bowl, combine the cream cheese and butter. Using an electric mixer set on medium-high speed, beat until smooth. Reduce the speed to low, add the sugar, and beat until smooth. Beat in the vanilla. Bring to room temperature before using.
Makes about 2 3/4 cups (22 fl oz/680 ml)

For orange flavor: Add 2 tablespoons undiluted, thawed frozen orange juice concentrate and 1 1/2 teaspoons grated orange zest with the vanilla extract.

For coconut flavor: Beat 1 1/2 teaspoons coconut extract (essence) and 1 cup (3 oz/90 g) toasted coconut into the finished cream cheese frosting.

Whipped Cream

To store, spoon the whipped cream into a fine-mesh sieve over a bowl, cover with plastic wrap, and chill for up to 4 hours. It won't be as light after storage, but any liquid it releases will drain so the topping won't be runny.

FOR WHIPPED CREAM:

1 cup (8 fl oz/250 ml) heavy (double) cream, chilled

4 teaspoons sugar

1 tablespoon nonfat dry milk (milk powder)

1 teaspoon vanilla extract (essence)

In a chilled metal bowl, combine the cream, sugar, dry milk, and vanilla and beat with chilled beaters until the cream stands in soft peaks.

To pipe the cream through a pastry bag, beat it until it has stiff peaks.

Makes about 2 cups (16 fl oz/500 ml)

FOR CHOCOLATE WHIPPED CREAM:

2 cups (16 fl oz/500 ml) heavy (double) cream, chilled

1 cup (3–4 oz/90–125 g) confectioners' (icing) sugar, sifted before measuring

1/2 cup (1 1/2 oz/45 g) unsweetened cocoa, sifted before measuring

Using a chilled metal bowl and chilled beaters, whip the cream for 2 minutes until it just starts to thicken. Add the sugar and cocoa and continue beating until thick enough to hold firm peaks.

Makes about 4 cups (32 fl oz/1 l)

Basic Glaze

A thick coat of one of these glazes will add flair to muffins and quick breads.

FOR ORANGE GLAZE:

1 cup (4 oz/125 g) confectioners' (icing) sugar, sifted

2 tablespoons fresh orange juice, or more if needed

2 teaspoons orange zest (page 329)

Pinch of salt

FOR LEMON GLAZE:

1 cup (4 oz/125 g) confectioners' (icing) sugar, sifted

2 tablespoons fresh lemon juice, or more if needed

2 teaspoons lemon zest (page 329)

Pinch of salt

For either glaze, combine all of the ingredients in a small bowl and whisk briskly until smooth and well blended. If the glaze is too stiff, beat in a few drops more juice. Drizzle or spread the glaze over bread or muffins while they are still warm.

Makes about 1/4 cup (2 fl oz/60 ml), enough for 12 muffins or 1 loaf of bread

Caramel Glaze

For this simple glaze, caramel candies are melted in water for a tasty result.

8 oz (250 g) caramel candies (about 1 cup packed)

1/4 cup (2 fl oz/60 ml) water

In a small saucepan over low heat, combine the caramels and water. Stir until the caramels are melted and smooth. Remove from the heat.

To use, drizzle the hot glaze with a fork or use a spatula to spread it, as directed in the recipe. Let stand until the glaze cools, 25–30 minutes.

Makes about 3/4 cup (6 fl oz/180 ml)

Bittersweet Chocolate Glaze

Use this simple glaze whenever you desire a thin, shiny coating for a cake.

6 tablespoons (3 fl oz/90 ml) heavy (double) cream

6 tablespoons (3 fl oz/90 ml) dark corn syrup

8 oz (250 g) bittersweet chocolate, chopped

In a heavy saucepan over medium heat, combine the cream and corn syrup. Bring to a simmer, then reduce the heat to low. Add the chocolate and whisk until smooth, about 1 minute.

Remove from the heat and let stand until lukewarm, about 10 minutes. The glaze should be thick but still pourable.

Makes about 1 1/3 cups (11 fl oz/330 ml)

Chocolate Ganache

Keep ganache tightly covered in the refrigerator for up to 1 month, or frozen for up to 6 months. Reheat before using.

1 cup (8 fl oz/250 ml) heavy (double) cream

10 oz (315 g) semisweet (plain) or bittersweet chocolate, chopped (about 2 cups)

In a small saucepan over medium heat, gently warm the cream until bubbles appear at the edges. Remove from the heat. Stir in the chocolate until it has melted and the mixture is smooth. Do not stir so vigorously that bubbles form.

Alternatively, place the chocolate in a food processor. Pour the hot cream over the chocolate and let sit for 15 seconds. With the lid in place to prevent splattering, process until smooth.

If there are any visible lumps, strain the mixture through a fine-mesh sieve.

Makes about 3 cups (24 fl oz/750 ml)

Making Yeast Breads

Yeast breads take about 3 hours when you include the time it takes for rising and baking; however, the hands-on work takes only about 20 minutes. Here are a few tips to keep in mind.

Recipes often use quick-rise yeast instead of active dry yeast, which must be proofed separately. In either case, liquids should be at about 110°F (43°C) to successfully activate the yeast.

Dough rises best in a warm, draft-free environment and should be baked on the middle rack of your oven.

Note that home-baked breads lack the preservatives in commercial breads, so extra loaves should be wrapped airtight and frozen for up to 3 months.

1. Dissolve the yeast in lukewarm (110°F/43°C) liquid and let stand for 5 minutes, until the yeast bubbles slightly. Add seasonings and two-thirds of the flour and mix gently. Add more flour to form the right consistency.

2. Turn out the dough onto a floured surface and knead. To knead bread dough by hand, fold the dough, press down and away with the heel of your hand, turn the dough, and repeat, adding flour until smooth and elastic.

3. Put the dough in a lightly greased bowl and turn it to coat all sides evenly. Cover the bowl loosely with greased plastic wrap and leave it at warm room temperature to rise as directed in the recipe, most often until doubled in bulk.

4. Turn out the risen dough onto a floured work surface and press out any pockets of air. Shape the dough as instructed, place on a greased baking sheet, cover, and let rise as directed. When it rises, preheat the oven.

5. Before baking, slash and glaze the dough if instructed. Bake the loaf as directed, until it has darkened, and sounds hollow when tapped on the bottom or a wooden skewer inserted into the center comes out clean.

Shaping Techniques

There are several different dough shapes throughout this book, including braided and twisted loaves. Here are some general instructions for the others. Specific recipes will give you more details as needed for the best results

HARVEST WHEAT SHEAF

Following the recipe on page 142, divide the dough into three balls and use the first ball to form the sheaf base. Follow the steps below to complete this elaborate edible centerpiece.

1. Cut the second ball of dough in half. Set aside half to use for the "tie" and roll out the other half into a rectangle ¼ inch (6 mm) thick. Cut into thin strands and roll them into thin ropes. Brush the lower third of the sheaf's prepared dough base with egg glaze and arrange the dough strands on top like stalks of wheat.

2. Roll out the third ball of dough into a rectangle about ¼ inch (6 mm) thick and cut out 1-inch (2.5-cm) diamonds. With a small knife, make two cuts on each of two adjacent edges to resemble ears of wheat. Brush the upper section of the base with egg glaze and arrange the ears in rows starting at the top, overlapping the edges of the base slightly.

3. Cut the reserved ball of dough into 3 equal pieces. Roll each piece into a rope about 10 inches (25 cm) long and braid tightly (page 111). Place the braid across the stalks at the narrowest part of the base. Tuck the ends underneath the base to secure.

ROUND LOAVES

1. Press the risen dough flat and form it into a ball. Stretch the sides down and under, rotating the ball to form a tight, compact shape. Pinch the seam closed.

2. To provide a controlled, decorative place to release gas during baking, many round loaves are slashed on the surface. Use a small, sharp knife to cut slashes as directed, usually ½ inch (12 mm) deep.

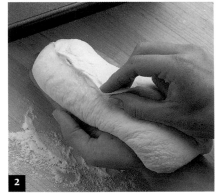

RECTANGULAR LOAVES

1. With a rolling pin, roll out the ball of dough into a flat, even rectangle of the size specified. Starting at a short side, roll up the rectangle like a jelly roll.

2. With slightly dampened fingers, pinch together the long seam and the spiral seams on both ends to seal them closed. Place the dough in a greased loaf pan with its long seam down.

Cake-Baking Basics

However a cake is leavened, flavored, or shaped, these principles apply to most cake recipes. For the best results, unless otherwise noted, all ingredients should be at room temperature for easy blending. Use an oven thermometer to gauge the accuracy of your oven and ensure that your cake is baking at the precise temperature required.

PREPARING THE PAN

A cake pan is often prepared with butter and flour to prevent sticking. Using your fingers or a paper towel, smear a thin, even coating of softened butter on the bottom and sides of the pan. Add a spoonful of flour to the pan, then tilt and shake the pan in all directions to coat the butter evenly with the flour. Carefully tap out any excess flour. Cake pans are also sometimes lined with parchment (baking) paper .

Only very delicate cake batters that must cling to the sides of the pan to help them rise will skip these steps.

MIXING THE INGREDIENTS

Recipes will give specific instructions, but for the lightest, moistest, most finely textured cakes, use the basic mixing methods listed below. Also, be sure to alternately add the liquid and dry ingredients for even blending.

1. Using an electric mixer set on medium-high speed, beat the room temperature butter and sugar until the mixture looks fluffy and pale yellow to ivory in color, about 2 minutes.

2. Using an electric mixer set on low speed or a wooden spoon, add dry and liquid ingredients in alternating batches, beating until blended after each addition.

3. Beaten egg whites contribute a light consistency to some cakes. To beat them to maximum volume, start with room-temperature eggs and separate them carefully, keeping the egg whites free of any trace of yolk.

4. Be sure your bowl and utensils are clean and dry. Put the egg whites in a large bowl (adding cream of tartar, if the recipe calls for it). Using an electric mixer, beat the whites until they form stiff peaks. Sugar is sometimes added as the egg whites mount.

5. Some batters require that the dry ingredients be folded into the beaten egg whites. Use a rubber spatula to gently add the dry ingredients in batches, cutting down into the center of the bowl and scooping the whites up and over them. Continue to add and fold, preserving as much of the volume as possible.

UNMOLDING A CAKE

Some cakes cool in their pans before unmolding; others are unmolded while hot and left to cool on wire racks. This technique can be used to remove any cake from its pan without damaging it.

1. If the pan is hot, put it on folded towels to protect the work surface. Invert a wire rack on top of the pan. Firmly grasp the rack and pan together and invert both (use oven mitts to protect your hands, if necessary).

2. Still inverted, set down the rack and pan. Gently lift the pan (using oven mitts, if necessary). If the cake does not unmold, invert again, loosen the edges with a knife, and repeat from step 1.

Pie Basics

SINGLE-CRUST PIES

Single-crust pies, sometimes called open-face pies, have no top crust. The bottom crust, called a pie shell, can be filled unbaked, partially baked, or fully baked, depending upon the recipe.

Unbaked Pie Shells There should be about 1 inch (2.5 cm) of pastry hanging over the side of the pan. Fold it under to make an upstanding rim around the edge of the pan, then decoratively flute the edges with your thumb and fingertips by applying pressure to the dough at regular intervals. The pie shell is now ready to be filled and baked according to the recipe instructions.

Partially or Fully Baked Pie Shells For a partially baked pie shell, prick the the shell all over with the tines of a fork. Poke holes in a double-thick 12-inch (30-cm) square of aluminum foil, then press it snugly into the pastry-lined pan. Bake in a preheated 425°F (220°C) oven for 8 minutes. Remove the foil and bake for about 4 minutes more, until the pastry is dry but not brown. If it puffs up while baking, poke it gently with a fork. Remove from the oven and set on a wire rack to cool completely.

For a fully baked pie shell, proceed as directed, but after removing the foil, bake for 8–10 minutes more, or until the pastry is light brown and crisp. Cool completely on a wire rack before filling.

DOUBLE-CRUST PIES

After filling, brush the rim of the bottom crust with water. Lay the top crust over it and trim the pastry, leaving $^1/_2$ inch (12 mm) of overhang. Press the rim to seal the crusts, then fold the overhang under to make an edge. Flute the edge. With a small knife, cut 4 or 5 slits in the top crust so steam can escape during baking. Bake as directed.

Fruit pies may boil over during baking. To catch drips, place a large sheet of aluminum foil on a rack under the pie.

If, during baking, the edges of the crust brown too much, remove the pie from the oven, mold aluminum foil around the edges, then continue baking.

LATTICE TOP

1. Roll out the pastry for the top crust, cut into 12 strips, about $^3/_4$ inch (2 cm) wide, of varying lengths. Use the long strips near the center of the pie and the short ones near the edges. Cross two long strips over the center of the filled pie. Place the second strip over the first.

2. Now you can make the lattice top: Fold back every other strip and lay a cross strip in place, then return the folded-back strips to their original position. Continue weaving the strips in this fashion, working from the center of pie toward the edges, until all of the pastry strips are used.

3. When all the pastry strips are in place, trim off any overhanging pastry with clean scissors or kitchen shears. Brush the edges of the pastry lightly with water and press gently on the strips all around to seal them to bottom crust. Finally, flute around the rim with your thumb and fingers.

Glossary

Amaretto This is a sweet, almond-flavored Italian liqueur that gets its nutty taste from apricot kernels. It has a strong flavor, so be careful not to overuse it.

Baking Powder A commercial product, baking powder combines the following three ingredients: baking soda, the source of the carbon-dioxide gas that causes some cakes to rise; an acid such as cream of tartar, calcium acid phosphate, or sodium aluminum sulphate, which causes the baking soda to release its gas when combined with a liquid; and a starch such as cornstarch or flour, to keep the powder from absorbing moisture.

Baking Soda Also known as sodium bicarbonate or bicarbonate of soda; the active component of baking powder and the source of carbon-dioxide gas often used as a leavener in recipes that include acidic ingredients.

Baking Stone Also called a baking tile, pizza stone, or baker's peel, this is a flat, rectangular, square, or round piece of unglazed stoneware used for baking breads and pizzas to produce well-browned crisp crusts. Appreciated for its efficient heat distribution, it is usually placed on the lowest rack or sometimes on the floor of the oven and preheated for at least 45 minutes before baking. The best ones are made of the same type of clay used to line kilns, as they are less apt to crack than ordinary clay baking stones.

Bell Peppers These sweet-fleshed, bell-shaped members of the pepper family are also known as capsicums. Most are sold in their unripe green form; ripened red and yellow varieties are also available.

TO PREPARE A RAW BELL PEPPER Cut it in half lengthwise with a sharp knife. Pull out the stem section from each half, along with the cluster of seeds attached to it. Remove any remaining seeds, along with any white membranes, or ribs, to which they are attached, then cut the peppers as directed.

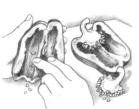

TO ROAST A BELL PEPPER Preheat a broiler (grill). Cut the bell pepper lengthwise into quarters, then remove the stems, seeds, and ribs as directed above. Place the pepper quarters, skin side up, on a broiler pan and broil (grill) until the skins blister and turn black. Remove from the broiler, cover with aluminum foil, and let stand until the pepper softens and is cool enough to handle, about 10 minutes. Peel off the blackened skins, then cut the pepper as directed.

Bulgur Wheat berries that have been steamed, dried, partially debranned, and cracked into coarse or fine particles with a chewy texture and nutlike taste. Also know as burghul.

Butter For the recipes in this book, unsalted butter is preferred, unless otherwise specified. Its light, delicate flavor is better suited for use in sweet preparations than the salted variety, and the absence of salt allows the cook greater leeway in seasoning all recipes using salt to taste.

Capers The small buds of a bush common to the Mediterranean, capers are much too bitter to eat raw. They are available packed in vinegar brine and sometimes salt to be used as a savory flavoring or garnish

Chocolate Purchase the best-quality chocolate you can find. Many cooks prefer the high-quality chocolate made in Switzerland, Belgium, or France.

Bittersweet Chocolate Eating or cooking chocolate enriched with cocoa butter and sweetened with sugar, which accounts for about 40 percent of its weight (the percentage may vary).

Milk Chocolate Primarily an eating chocolate, enriched with milk powder —there is the equivalent of up to 1 cup (8 fl oz/250 ml) whole milk in an average-sized candy bar.

Semisweet Chocolate Eating or cooking chocolate that is usually—but not always—slightly sweeter than bitter-sweet chocolate. Bittersweet chocolate can usually be substituted.

Unsweetened Chocolate Pure chocolate liquor ground from roasted cacao beans and solidified in block-shaped molds. Combined with sugar and butter, milk, or cream in recipes, it provides intense chocolate flavor, but it is unpalatable when eaten on its own. Also known as bitter chocolate.

White Chocolate A chocolatelike product for eating or baking, made by combining pure cocoa butter with sugar, powdered milk, and sometimes vanilla. Check labels to make sure that the white chocolate you buy is made exclusively with cocoa butter, without the addition of coconut oil or vegetable shortening.

Cocoa Richly flavored, fine-textured powder ground from the solids left after much of the cocoa butter has been extracted from chocolate liquor. Cocoa specially treated to reduce its natural acidity, resulting in a darker color and more mellow flavor, is known as Dutch-process cocoa. Available sweetened or unsweetened.

Coconut For baking, shredded or flaked coconut is sold ready to use in cans or plastic packages in the baking section of most food stores. The label on

Cheese

Because of their moisture content, soft and fresh cheese do not keep as long as firm and semifirm cheeses. Wrap cheese first in waxed paper to hold in the moisture, and then wrap it with plastic wrap or aluminum foil, and refrigerate.

Cheddar Firm, smooth-textured, whole-milk cheese, pale yellow-white to deep yellow-orange. Ranges in taste from mild and sweet when young to rich and sharply tangy when aged.

Cream Cheese Smooth, white, mild-tasting cheese made from cream and milk, used on its own as a spread or as an ingredient that adds rich flavor and texture to baked goods and desserts. If possible, purchase cream cheese at a good-quality delicatessen for better taste and a creamier texture.

Bringing cream cheese to room temperature eases its blending with other ingredients. Achieve the correct temperature quickly by cutting the cheese into $^1/_2$-inch (12-mm) pieces and processing briefly in a food processor. Alternatively, if the cheese is in an airtight commercial wrapper, leave it wrapped and immerse it in a bowl of hot water until the desired consistency is reached, 2–3 minutes.

Gouda Firm, rich, yellowish Dutch cheese, with a flavor ranging from mild to strong. It is available at most well-stocked markets and is often sold encased in red wax. Similar to Edam, Smoked Gouda develops a rich, slightly sweet, nutlike taste.

Monterey Jack Semisoft mild white cheese with a buttery texture, either with tiny "eyes" or smooth. It is often sold infused with hot red chiles, but can be found plain as well.

Mozzarella Rindless, white, mild Italian cheese traditionally made from water buffalo's milk and sold fresh. Commercially produced kinds are widely available but have less flavor. Look for fresh mozzarella sold immersed in water.

Parmesan Hard, thick-crusted Italian cow's milk cheese with a sharp, salty, full flavor that is the result of at least two years of aging. Buy in block form, to grate fresh as needed rather than buying it already grated. Parmigiano-Reggiano is the finest variety.

Swiss Firm whole-milk cheese, pale creamy yellow in color, with distinct holes that grow larger and more numerous with ripening. Popular on its own or in recipes for its mild, slightly sweet, nutlike flavor.

the package will say whether the product is sweetened or unsweetened. Be sure to purchase the coconut from a store with a rapid turnover, to ensure freshness. Canned sweetened cream of coconut, a rich and thick concentrate of the fruit's liquid and fat, is available in the baking or liquor section.

TO TOAST COCONUT Some recipes call for toasting shredded or flaked coconut to develop its flavor: Spread the coconut evenly on a baking sheet and bake in a 350°F (180°C) oven, stirring occasionally, until pale gold, for about 8 minutes.

Cognac Dry spirit distilled from wine and, strictly speaking, produced in the Cognac region of France. Other good-quality dry wine-based brandies may be substituted.

Cornmeal Granular flour, ground from the dried kernels of yellow or white corn, with a sweet, robust flavor, sometimes known by the Italian name polenta. Most commercial cornmeal sold in food stores lacks the kernel's husk and germ and is available in fine or coarser grinds. Stone-ground cornmeal, made from whole corn kernels, produces a richer flour.

Cornstarch Fine, powdery flour ground from the endosperm of corn—the white heart of the kernel. Also known as cornflour, it is used as a thickening agent in some desserts.

Corn Syrup Neutral-tasting syrup extracted from corn. Sold either as light corn syrup or dark corn syrup, which has added color and flavor.

Cream, Heavy Cream with a butter-fat content of at least 36 percent. For the best flavor and cooking properties, purchase fresh cream, avoiding long-lasting varieties that have been processed by ultraheat methods. Also called double cream.

Cream, Sour Commercial dairy product made from pasteurized sweet cream, with a tangy flavor and thick, smooth consistency.

Cream of Tartar Acidic powder extracted during wine-making that is used as an additive to stabilize egg whites and to increase their heat tolerance. Also used as a leavening agent, most commonly combined with baking soda to make commercial baking powder, and as an ingredient in sugar syrups to prevent crystallization.

Eggs Although eggs are sold in the United States in a range of standard sizes, large grade A eggs should be used for most of the recipes in this book, unless another size is specified.

TO SEPARATE AN EGG Crack the shell in half by tapping it against the side of a bowl and break the shell apart with your fingers. Holding the shell halves over the bowl, gently transfer the whole yellow yolk back and forth between them, letting the clear white drop away into the bowl. Take care not to break the yellow yolk. Transfer the yolk to another bowl.

Alternatively, gently pour the egg from the shell onto the slightly cupped fingers of your clean hand, held over a bowl. Let the whites fall between your fingers into the bowl; and the whole yolk will remain in your hand.

The same basic function is performed by an egg separator placed over a bowl. The separator holds the yolk intact in its cuplike center and allows the white to drip out through slots in its side.

Espresso Powder The strong, full flavor of espresso-roast coffee beans provides a distinctive source of flavor for baking recipes. For an easy-to-blend source of this intense flavor, use instant espresso powder or granules, found in the coffee section of food stores, in Italian delis, or in specialty coffee stores.

Extracts Flavorings that are derived by dissolving essential oils of richly flavored foods—such as almond, peppermint, vanilla, lemon, or orange—in an alcohol base. Use only products labeled "pure" or "natural."

Figs Late-summer and early-autumn fruits characterized by their many tiny edible seeds, sweet, yet astringent flavor, and succulent, soft texture. It is best to buy fresh figs ripe and use them immediately.

Flour Buy flour in amounts that you can use in 4–6 months. It will keep longer but is best used fresh. Transfer flour to an airtight container and keep it in a cool, dry place away from light.

All-purpose Flour The common flour for baking, this bleached and blended variety is available in all food markets. Also called plain flour.

Bread Flour An unbleached, hard-wheat flour. Its high protein content creates an elastic dough for higher rise and more structure in breads and pizza crusts. Bread flours sometimes include malted barley flour to feed the yeast.

Cake Flour Very fine-textured bleached flour for use in cakes and other baked goods. Also called soft-wheat flour. Do not substitute with all-purpose flour.

Chestnut Flour A very fine, flavorful flour ground from dried chestnuts, often used in desserts.

Potato Flour Ground from steamed and dried potatoes and used in baked goods; also called potato starch

Rye Flour Fine flour ground from grains of rye grass, a close relative of wheat, with a sweet-sour flavor.

Whole-wheat Flour Pale brown flour derived from whole, unbleached wheat berries, from which neither the bran nor the germ has been removed. Also known as wholemeal flour, it should be wrapped tightly and refrigerated for up to 6 months or kept in the freezer for up to 1 year.

Garlic Pungent bulb, with a flavor that is popular worldwide, used both raw and cooked. For the best results, purchase whole and separate cloves from the head as needed.

TO PEEL A GARLIC CLOVE Place one clove on a work surface and cover with the side of a large chef's knife. Press firmly on the side of the knife to gently crush the clove; the dry skin can be easily slipped off and discarded.

Gelatin, Unflavored Unflavored commercial gelatin gives delicate body to some frozen desserts. One envelope holds about 1 tablespoon ($^1/_4$ oz/7 g), and is sufficient to jell about 2 cups (16 fl oz/500 ml) of liquid

Ginger The rhizome of the tropical ginger plant, which yields a sweet, strong-flavored spice. Fresh ginger is found in the produce section of well-

Herbs

Choose herbs that look bright and healthy, and are very fragrant. Avoid any that have wilted, yellowed, or blackened stems.

Bay Leaf Pungent and spicy dried whole leaves of the bay laurel tree. French bay leaves are milder and sweeter than California varieties. Discard before serving.

Cilantro Green, leafy herb resembling flat-leaf (Italian) parsley, with a sharp, aromatic, somewhat astringent flavor. Also known as fresh coriander or Chinese parsley.

Oregano Aromatic, pungent, and spicy Mediterranean herb—also known as wild marjoram—used fresh or dried as a seasoning for all kinds of savory dishes.

Rosemary Mediterranean herb with such a strong aromatic flavor that it is generally used sparingly.

Sage A soft, gray-green herb with a sweet, aromatic, yet somewhat pungent flavor. Sage is used either fresh or dried.

Thyme Fragrant, clean-tasting, small-leafed herb popular in savory recipes, used either fresh or dried.

Nuts

Look for nuts that are free of cracks, holes, and discoloration. Also, shake the shells to make sure the nutmeat is not old and dried out inside.

Almonds The meat found inside a dry fruit related to peaches, the almonds are mellow, sweet-flavored nuts with an oval shape. They are available sliced (flaked) or slivered.

Hazelnuts Also known as filberts these small, spherical nuts have a slightly sweet flavor. To peel hazelnuts, toast them, then wrap the warm nuts in a kitchen towel, and rub them with the palms of your hands.

Macadamia Spherical nuts grown in Hawaii that are about twice the size of hazelnuts (filberts), with a very rich, buttery flavor and crisp texture.

Peanuts Not true nuts, these legumes are produced on a low-branching plant. When roasted, they have a rich, full flavor and satisfying crunch.

Pecans Brown-skinned, crinkly-textured nuts that come in easy-to-break shells. Pecans have a distinctive sweet, rich flavor and crisp, slightly crumbly, texture.

Pine nuts Actually small, ivory seeds from the cones of a species of pine tree, with a rich, slightly resinous flavor. Usually used whole as an ingredient or as a garnish.

Pistachios Slightly sweet nuts with green, crunchy meat, these are usually sold in their thin but hard shells, which split when the nut is ripe and ready to use as directed.

Walnuts Rich, crisp-textured nuts with distinctively crinkled surfaces. English walnuts, the most familiar variety, are grown worldwide, although the largest crops are in California.

TO BLANCH NUTS Some nuts, such as almonds, require blanching to loosen their papery skin. To blanch nuts, put them in a pan of boiling water for about 2 minutes; then drain and, when they are cool enough to handle, squeeze each nut between your fingers to slip it from its skin.

TO TOAST NUTS Toasting brings out the full flavor and aroma of nuts. Preheat the oven to 350°F (180°C). Spread the nuts in a single layer on an ungreased baking sheet and toast for 5–10 minutes, until they just begin to change color, (about 3 minutes for pine nuts). Remove from the oven and let cool.

stocked stores. Ground dried ginger is available in the spice section of food stores. Candied or crystallized ginger is made by first preserving pieces of ginger in sugar syrup and then coating them with granulated sugar; it can be found in the baking or Asian food sections of well-stocked stores.

Grits Also known as hominy grits, grits are a fine-, medium-, or coarse-ground meal derived from hominy (hulled and dried corn kernels).

Half-and-Half A commercial dairy product consisting of half milk and half light cream. Also known as half cream in Britain.

Honey The natural, sweet, syruplike substance produced by bees from flower nectar, honey will subtly reflect the color, taste, and aroma of the blossoms from which it was made. Mild  kinds, such as clover and orange blossom, are lighter in color and better suited to general cooking purposes to add a mellow sweetness.

Mahaleb Small, pale brown seed—slightly smaller than a coriander seed—that is the kernel of a black cherry stone. Look for the whole spice in Middle Eastern markets. Pulverize

Seeds

A variety of tiny seeds offer flavor and rustic texture to baked goods. They can be used either as a topping or as an ingredient in bread doughs.

Aniseeds Sweet licorice-flavored spice of Mediterranean origin, the small crescent-shaped seeds of a plant related to parsley. Generally sold whole, then crushed with a mortar and pestle or in a spice grinder.

Caraway Seeds Small, crescent-shaped dried seeds used whole or ground as a savory seasoning. Caraway seeds are often added to rye bread for their distinctive flavor.

Fennel Seeds Small, crescent-shaped seeds of a plant related to the bulb vegetable of the same name, prized for their mild anise flavor. Can be used both whole or ground.

Poppy Seeds Small, round, blue-black seeds from a type of poppy; traditionally used by European cooks, they add a rich, nutty flavor to many baked goods.

Sesame Seeds Tiny, pale ivory-colored seeds with a mild, nutty flavor. They are often sprinkled over bread doughs as a topping. Because of their high oil content, sesame seeds can go rancid quickly and should be stored in the refrigerator.

mahaleb in a mortar with a pestle or grind in a spice grinder before using.

Milk, Sweetened Condensed A canned product made by evaporating 60 percent of the water from whole milk, then sweetening it with sugar, for use as an ingredient in baked recipes and dessert sauces. Available in the baking section of food stores.

Molasses Thick, robust-tasting, syrupy sugarcane by-product of sugar refining, a procedure that may or may not include the use of sulfur. Light molasses results from the first boiling of the syrup; dark molasses from the second boiling. Either type of molasses can be used in most bread recipes with darker varieties of molasses yielding a more intense flavor than lighter ones.

Mortar and Pestle A bowl-shaped mortar holds ingredients while the club-shaped pestle grinds them. Mortars vary in size and material. Pestles are usually made of the same material as the mortar, but they can also be carved from hard wood. Either the mortar or the pestle must have an abrasive surface to work effectively.

Oats Coarse-, medium-, or fine textured cereal ground from hulled oats, prized for its nutlike taste and texture when added to baked goods. If baking, be sure to use old-fashioned rolled oats—not quick-cooking or instant—unless otherwise specified.

Oils Oils may be used in bread doughs to enrich them or to serve as a shortening agent. When the term "vegetable oil" is used, it refers to any of several refined pure or blended oils pressed or otherwise extracted from any of a number of sources—corn, peanuts, safflower seeds, soybeans, or sunflower seeds, which are prized for their pale color and neutral flavor. A wide variety of olive oils are available in most markets. Each brand varies both in color (from golden to deep green) and in flavor (from fruity to herbaceous); choose one that suits your taste. The higher-priced extra-virgin olive oils, made from the first pressing of the olives, are usually of better quality; products labeled pure olive oil are less aromatic and flavorful. Walnut oil conveys the rich taste of the nuts from which it is pressed; seek out oil made from lightly toasted nuts. Store all oils in an airtight container away from heat and light.

Polenta Italian term for specially ground coarse cornmeal and for the mush that results from its cooking. The latter may be enriched with butter, cream, cheese, or eggs. When cold, it has a consistency firm enough for it to be shaped and grilled or fried.

Puff Pastry Form of pastry in which pastry dough and butter or some other solid fat are repeatedly layered to form thin leaves that puff up to a flaky lightness when baked. Commercially

Spices

Ideally, spices should be bought whole and ground just before use. Keep spices tightly covered in a cool, dark place. Stored properly, whole spices will keep for up to 1 year; ground spices should be replaced after 6 months.

Allspice Spice of Caribbean origin with a sweet flavor suggesting a blend of cinnamon, cloves, and nutmeg.

Cardamom Sweet, exotic-tasting spice mainly available in Middle Eastern markets. Its small, round seeds grow enclosed inside a husklike pod and may be purchased whole or already ground. Crush whole seeds with a mortar and pestle.

Chili Powder Commercial blend of spices featuring ground dried chile peppers along with such other seasonings as cumin, oregano, cloves, coriander, pepper, and salt. It is best purchased in small quantities, as the flavor diminishes rapidly.

Cinnamon Popular sweet spice for flavoring desserts. The aromatic bark of a type of evergreen tree, it is sold ground or as whole dried strips known as cinnamon sticks.

Cloves Rich and aromatic East African spice. Used whole or ground in both sweet and savory dishes.

Nutmeg Popular sweet spice that is the hard pit of the fruit of the nutmeg tree. May be bought already ground or, for fresh flavor, whole. Whole nutmegs should be kept inside nutmeg graters, which have hinged flaps that conceal a specially-designed storage compartment.

Pepper Pepper, the most common of all savory spices, is best purchased as whole peppercorns, to be ground in a pepper mill as needed, or coarsely crushed. Pungent black peppercorns derive from slightly underripe pepper berries, whose hulls oxidize as they dry. Milder white peppercorns come from fully ripened berries, with the husks removed before drying.

Saffron Intensely aromatic, golden orange spice made from the dried stigmas of a species of crocus. Sold either as threads—the dried stigmas—or in powdered form. Look for products labeled "pure" because powdered saffron may be mixed with other ingredients and is thus less flavorful.

manufactured frozen puff pastry is available in well-stocked markets.

Rhubarb A perennial plant with long celery-like stalks that is actually a vegetable, but is usually treated like a fruit when used in baking. It is usually cooked with a good dose of sugar to balance out the tartness, and is also often combined with strawberries or raspberries. Note that rhubarb leaves and roots are mildly toxic and should always be discarded before using the stalks. Find frozen rhubarb in the freezer section of well-stocked stores.

Salt A little common table salt is added to most bread doughs to enhance their flavor. Larger grains may be used as a topping for loaves or rolls. Coarse salt, with grains about the size of tiny pebbles, is similar in composition and taste to table salt. Salt extracted by evaporation from sea water is known as sea salt. It has a more pronounced flavor than regular table salt and is available in both coarse and fine grinds.

Sherry Fortified, cask-aged wine, ranging from dry to sweet; enjoyed as an aperitif and used as a flavoring.

Sugar Sugar sweetens, helps foods to caramelize, encourages yeast to grow in bread dough, gives stability to egg whites, and preserves foods.
Brown Sugar A rich-tasting granulated sugar combined with molasses in

different quantities to yield golden, light, or dark brown sugar, with crystals that vary from coarse to fine. Available in the baking section.

Confectioners' Sugar Finely pulverized sugar, also known as powdered or icing sugar, which dissolves quickly and provides a thin, white, decorative coating. It is often used for dusting or decorating foods, as well as for icings. To prevent this sugar from absorbing moisture in the air, it is often mixed with a little cornstarch.

Granulated Sugar The standard, most widely used form of pure white sugar. Do not use superfine granulated sugar (also known as caster sugar) unless specified in the recipe. For baking purposes, be sure to buy only sugar that is specifically labeled cane sugar.

Superfine Sugar Also called caster sugar, granulated sugar that has been ground to form extra-fine granules that dissolve quickly in liquids. To make your own superfine sugar, simply whirl granulated sugar in a blender or in a food processor.

Sun-Dried Tomatoes When sliced crosswise or halved, then dried in the sun, tomatoes develop an intense, sweet-tart flavor and a pleasantly chewy texture that enhance savory recipes. Available either dry or packed in oil, with or without herbs and spices. Look for them in specialty stores and well-stocked food markets. Fresh tomatoes are not a substitute.

Vanilla One of the most popular flavorings in baked desserts, vanilla beans are the dried aromatic pods of a variety of orchid. Although vanilla is most commonly used in the form of an alcohol-based extract (essence), the bean and particularly the seeds inside it are a good source of pure vanilla flavor. Vanilla extract and beans from Madagascar are the best.

TO SCRAPE VANILLA BEANS Soak the bean and cut it in half lengthwise, if directed. Use a small, sharp knife to scrape the seeds from the pod and add both the seeds and pod as instructed. Remove the pod from the mixture before serving.

Wheat Germ Refers to the embryo within whole grains of wheat. Toasted wheat germ is available in jars. Roast unprocessed wheat germ in a dry frying pan over medium heat, stirring constantly, until lightly browned.

Xanthan Gum Powder A natural carbohydrate derivative of corn syrup, this powdery substance is used in breads made from gluten-free flours to add springiness to the dough

Yeast Yeast is the living substance that eats the sugars in bread dough and gives off carbon dioxide and ethyl alcohol to expand the gluten in the flour and raise the bread. Active, dry yeast, one of the most widely available forms of yeast for baking, is sold in individual packages containing about $2^{1}/_4$ teaspoons. Also popular is quick-rise yeast, which raises bread doughs in about half the time of regular active dry yeast. If using fresh cake yeast, substitute $^1/_2$ oz (15 g) for 1 package active dry yeast.

Zest The thin, brightly colored, outermost layer of a citrus fruit's peel, containing most of its aromatic essential oils—a lively source of flavor. When zesting fruit, try to buy organic or be sure to scrub the fruit well to remove any wax or chemicals. Zest may be removed using one of two methods:

1. Use a simple tool known as a zester, drawing its sharp-edged holes across the fruit's skin to remove the zest in thin strips. Alternatively, use the fine holes of a handheld grater.

2. Holding the edge of a small, sharp knife or a vegetable peeler away from you and almost parallel to the fruit's skin, carefully cut off the zest in thin strips, taking care not to remove any bitter white pith with it. Then thinly slice or chop on a cutting board.

Index

First published in the USA by Time-Life Custom Publishing.
Originally published as Williams-Sonoma Kitchen Library:
Pies & Tarts (© 1992 Weldon Owen Inc.)
Cookies & Biscotti; Chocolate; Muffins & Quick Breads; Pizza
(© 1993 Weldon Owen Inc.)
Fruit Desserts; Gifts from the Kitchen (© 1994 Weldon Owen Inc.)
Cakes, Cupcakes & Cheesecakes; Holiday Baking
(© 1995 Weldon Owen Inc.)
Cooking Basics; Breads (© 1996 Weldon Owen Inc.)
Healthy Cooking; Mediterranean Cooking; Thanksgiving;
Breakfasts & Brunches; Kids Cooking (© 1997 Weldon Owen Inc.)
Kids Cookies; Festive Entertaining; Casual Entertaining
(© 1998 Weldon Owen Inc.)

In collaboration with Williams-Sonoma Inc.
3250 Van Ness Avenue, San Francisco, CA 94109
OXMOOR HOUSE INC.

**Oxmoor
House.**

Oxmoor House books are distributed by Sunset Books
80 Willow Road, Menlo Park, CA 94025
Telephone: 650-321-3600 Fax 650-324-1532
Vice President/General Manager: Rich Smeby
National Accounts Manager/Special Sales: Brad Moses

Oxmoor House and Sunset Books are divisions of
Southern Progress Corporation

WILLIAMS-SONOMA
Founder and Vice-Chairman: Chuck Williams

WELDON OWEN INC.
Chief Executive Officer: John Owen
President and Chief Operating Officer: Terry Newell
Chief Financial Officer: Christine E. Munson
Creative Director: Gaye Allen
Publisher: Hannah Rahill
Art Director: Nicky Collings
Associate Editor: Donita Boles
Editorial Assistant: Juli Vendzules
Production Director: Chris Hemesath
Production and Reprint Coordinator: Todd Rechner
Color Manager: Teri Bell

Williams-Sonoma Baking was conceived and
produced by Weldon Owen Inc.
814 Montgomery Street, San Francisco, CA 94133
Copyright © 2005 Weldon Owen Inc.
and Williams-Sonoma Inc.

First printed in 2005
10 9 8 7 6 5 4 3 2 1

ISBN 0-8487-3074-7

Printed in China by Leefung-Asco Printers Ltd.

CREDITS
Authors: Lora Brody: Pages 74, 194, 205, 210, 232, 243, 247, 248, 267, 280, 284, 293, 300, 303, 307, 308, 315 (Raspberry Sauce), 317 (Chocolate Whipped Cream, Chocolate Ganache); Lorenza de' Medici: Pages 163, 312 (Basic Pizza Dough); John Phillip Carroll: Pages 14, 17, 18, 19, 20, 22, 25, 26, 28, 31, 32, 34, 35, 37, 38, 41, 42, 44, 45, 47, 48, 49, 50, 52, 53, 55, 58, 60, 64, 67, 68, 69, 70, 73, 77, 78, 80, 81, 82, 83, 85, 87, 88, 91, 164, 270, 272, 273, 275, 279, 283, 289, 290, 294, 297, 298, 313 (Savory Butters, Basic Pie Pastry, Basic Tart Pastry), 315 (Strawberry Jam Butter, Strawberry Jam, Pear-Ginger Jam), 316 (Whipped Cream), 317 (Basic Glaze); Joyce Goldstein: Pages 188, 220, 227, 260, 286, 287, 304, 311; Susan M. Katzman: Pages 167, 172, 173, 180, 181, 184, 193, 200, 201, 301; Jeanne Thiel Kelley: Page 124; Kristine Kidd: Pages 170, 175, 176, 177, 178, 183, 185, 186, 189, 191, 192, 196, 197, 199, 202, 206, 209, 211, 212, 276, 315 (Vanilla Sugar), 317 (Caramel Glaze); Norman Kolpas: Pages 23, 27, 92, 216, 219; Jacqueline Mallorca: Pages 61, 63, 86, 97, 98, 101, 102, 105, 106, 109, 110, 111, 112, 115, 116, 118, 119, 120, 123, 125, 126, 128, 129, 131, 132, 134, 135, 137, 138, 141, 142, 143, 144, 145, 148, 150, 151, 153, 154, 157, 158, 159, 160, 166, 312 (Sourdough Starter), 313 (Tapenade), 314 (Candied Citrus Peel); Sarah Tenaglia: Pages 223, 224, 228, 229, 230, 233, 235, 236, 239, 240, 244, 250, 251, 253, 257, 258, 261, 263, 264, 266, 316 (Vanilla Buttercream, Confectioners' Sugar Icing, Cream Cheese Frosting), 317 (Bittersweet Chocolate Glaze)

Photographers: Paul Moore (front cover), Allan Rosenberg (recipe photography), Allan Rosenberg and Allen V. Lott (pages 220, 260, 286, 287, 304, 311), and Chris Shorten (pages 151, 166, 167, 172, 173, 180, 181, 184, 193, 200, 201, 301)

ACKNOWLEDGMENTS
Weldon Owen would like to thank Carrie Bradley, Ken DellaPenta, Elizabeth DerNederlanden, George Dolese, Arin Hailey, Emily Jahn, Karen Kemp, Norman Kolpas, Rachel Lopez, Renée Myers, Joan Olsen, Kam-Yin Stinnett, and Colin Wheatland for all of their expertise, assistance, and hard work.

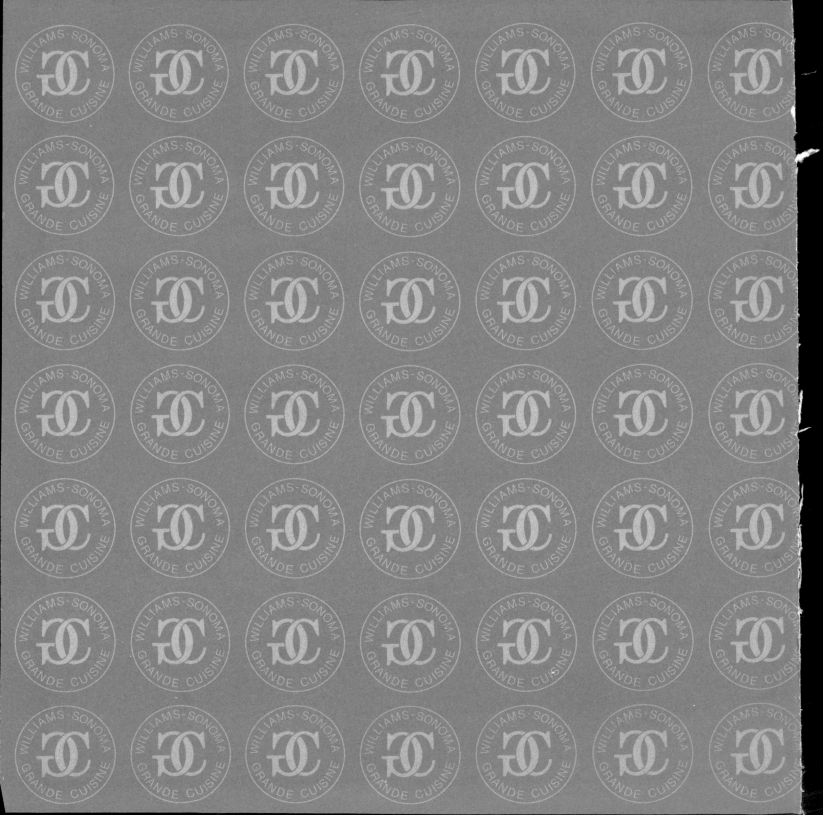